GET RICH
WITH OPTIONS

GET RICH WITH OPTIONS

Second Edition

Four Winning Strategies
Straight from
the Exchange Floor

LEE LOWELL

WILEY

John Wiley & Sons, Inc.

Published by John Wiley & Sons, Inc., Hoboken, New Jersey.
Published simultaneously in Canada.

For general information on our other products and services or for technical support, please contact our Customer Care Department within the United States at (800) 762-2974, outside the United States at (317) 572-3993 or fax (317) 572-4002.

Wiley also publishes its books in a variety of electronic formats. Some content that appears in print may not be available in electronic books. For more information about Wiley products, visit our web site at www.wiley.com.

Library of Congress Cataloging-in-Publication Data:

Lowell, Lee, 1967–
    Get rich with options: four winning strategies straight from the exchange floor/Lee Lowell.—2nd ed.
        p.   cm.
    Includes index.
    ISBN 978-0-470-44589-1 (cloth)
    1. Options (Finance)   I. Title.
    HG6024.A3L69 2009
    332.64'53—dc22

                                                                                    2009032181

Printed in the United States of America

10   9   8

To my wife, Amy, and my three children—
Sydney, Josie, and Griffin—all whom I
love more than anything in the world

CONTENTS

PREFACE TO THE
SECOND EDITION

When I was approached recently by the team at John Wiley & Sons about writing a revision for this book, I had already been thinking about how and what I would change if ever given the chance. Now that I have the opportunity, let me fill you in on what you can expect to see in this version.

Before I tell you what has changed, I just want to say thanks to my friends and colleagues for giving me their insight on what they'd like to see be different if I ever revised the book. But I must say, the biggest input on what I needed to revamp has come from the reviews from random readers who were nice enough to post their thoughts on Amazon.com. Yep, that's right. To date, there have been 44 reviews of my book at Amazon and all have been helpful to me.

The most common remarks from the few readers who didn't think my book was up to snuff were the problems they had with the title (of all things!). They felt duped by the title and that the book didn't show them the ways to *Get Rich with Options*.

I've put every bit of my knowledge and experience into this book to show ordinary people how to use options the way that has brought me success over the last 17 years. You can definitely get rich trading options, but you must do it correctly. I'm convinced, though, that these readers just didn't connect the title with how well the strategies really work to increase your wealth. As you will read in my book, the one fact that I keep advocating over and over again is that you need to be on the sell side of options trading.

I think some of the naysayer reviewers of my book didn't really understand the concept of selling options as a means of immediate income generation through safer speculation and hedging techniques, or they didn't really understand how to do it, or maybe they got burned in the past by selling options incorrectly.

My goal was to show you how to trade options the proper way with the four strategies (and a bonus fifth one at the end of the book) that I've used continuously over the years. All the money that you can bring into your account by selling options can add up to incredible sums over time. Just think about what you'd be leaving on the table if you never sold options in the first place—you'd be leaving lots of money for someone else to pick up.

So, on that note, I'm going to stress a bit more directly in this edition about how you can get rich with options. None of the strategies that I discuss are different from the first edition of this book. They're still as sound as the day that I first wrote about them. I'll just be a little more detailed on how options trading can fatten your wallet.

You'll also be seeing more examples of two of my favorite strategies—option credit spreads and put-option selling. Since I now run two option advisory services that focus specifically on these two strategies, I am including real-life, archived recommendations that show my members what trades to take and when to take profits.

I've also been asked to discuss in more detail the ways in which I find the stocks or commodities that I trade the options, on as well as exit strategies during profitable and not profitable trades. Since the intention of this book was solely to teach the reader how to trade options profitably once they've already picked their stock or commodity market, the discussion of how to find the stocks or commodities was kept at a minimum. I will tell you this: Most of my decisions on which stock or commodity to pick is based primarily on chart patterns and, to a lesser degree, the fundamentals of the underlying.

There are parts already within the book in which I briefly discuss how I came to choose the underlying that I did, but I make the effort to expand on it a bit more in this revised edition. There are many great books out there now that can teach you about technical and fundamental analysis to help you get started on being able to pick the underlying, but those lessons are beyond the scope of this book. And as far as discussing exit strategies, I also go over this as much as I can as we discuss each strategy individually.

The last thing I want to say about some the reviews that I received is that you cannot please everyone. Someone will always find fault in whatever you do—and this applies to life in general, not just my book.

I tried to make this book as complete as possible to get you on your way to surviving and profiting in the options market. But by no means is this book the end-all and be-all of options books. No one could provide that to you no matter what the adviser's background or experience has been. I encourage you to use this book as a great starting point and reference it well into the future.

I hope you decide to stick around and read (or reread) my book because I really tried to make it as fun and enjoyable as I could for you to learn about options trading and how you can get your hands on some of the wealth that is there for the taking in this arena.

—LEE LOWELL
January 2009

ACKNOWLEDGMENTS

I would like to thank the fine folks at Agora and John Wiley & Sons for giving me the opportunity to have this book published.

PART ONE

THE OPTION BASICS

CHAPTER 1

IT'S ALL ABOUT
THE CALLS
AND PUTS

Let's start at the beginning. There are only two types of options—calls and puts. It's really very simple, and it doesn't have to be any more complicated than that. Call and put options are a direct form of investment and should be seen as such. You can achieve everything you want on an investment basis with options, just as you would with any stock, bond, or mutual fund. That fact is very important to remember.

Every position that is built using options is composed of either all calls, all puts, or a combination of the two. One thing that smart option traders know is that you can sell options as easily as you buy them. That is going to be one of the main themes of this book as you will soon see that a majority of my trades entail the selling of options. Don't fret if you've heard that selling options is risky. The way that I do it has limited risk. One of the great aspects about the financial markets is that you can sell something first that you don't own yet. Instead of the usual "buy low, sell high," we can reverse it and "sell high, buy low." In this case, the sale transaction comes first.

What are call and put options? In short, options are another form of investment that can be bought and sold just like a stock, a bond, or a commodity. They are referred to as "derivative" investments because an option's value is derived from other sources, which we will talk about later on in the book. If you've read some of the mainstream literature that is published about options, you will see the examples given from the buyer's view of the market. I want to let you know that I'm going to teach you to trade from the short side (selling) as well as the long side (buying) of an options contract. Why limit yourself to one strategy?

The main purpose of buying options is to gain leverage on your investment and to cut down on your initial capital outlay. This is a smart way to use your money. Options allow you to take a directional position in an underlying security using a small down payment. The reward is the potential for a big gain. It's just like buying a house with your 10 percent down payment. You only have to put up a fraction of the price, yet you get to control the whole house. In simple terms, you're using options as a substitute for the stock or commodity. But you have to know how to choose your options correctly to maximize your potential gains. And since I've found that most option buyers do not do this correctly, that's why I'm here to help.

OPTION BUYERS HAVE RIGHTS; OPTION SELLERS HAVE OBLIGATIONS

How do options work? In short, a buyer of a call option has the expectation that the underlying security is going to move up. And when I say "underlying security," I'm referring to the stock or commodity in which you are trading options on. A call buyer has the right to control a bullish directional position of long 100 shares of stock (in the case of stock options) for a specified period of time (until option expiration day) at a certain strike price level (the price at which you will buy the stock). The buyer pays a fee to the option seller for this right, which is called the "premium." In the case of commodity options, the call buyer has the right to control one long futures contract for a specified period of time at a certain strike price level. The buyer has no obligation to exercise the option contract and turn it into a bullish position in the underlying security if it is not profitable to do so.

The option buyer has a limited loss potential equal to the price paid for the option, but also has an unlimited upside gain potential.

The put option buyer has the expectation that the underlying security is going to move lower in price. A put buyer has the right to control a bearish directional position of short 100 shares of stock (in the case of stock options) for a specified period of time at a certain strike price level. In the case of commodity options, the put buyer has the right to control one short futures contract position for a specified period of time at a certain strike price level. The put buyer has no obligation to exercise the option contract and turn it into a bearish position in the underlying security if it is not profitable to do so. The put option buyer has a limited loss potential equal to the price paid for the option, but also has an unlimited upside gain potential.

Sometimes it's difficult to understand the put-buying side of options. Most people understand call option buying because we're all so used to going long the market. I think people get caught up in the terminology of buying something to sell it. It sounds confusing. When you buy a put option, you're giving yourself the opportunity to sell something at a certain price for a specified period of time, no matter where the price of the underlying security may be. As I have already mentioned, the financial markets allow you to sell something that you don't own first. That's a hard concept to grasp. If you own a stock and are willing to sell it, either you can just sell your shares or you can buy a put option contract, which allows you to pick the price level at which you may want to sell the stock and the expiration date of when to do it.

On the flip side, sellers of calls and puts have different views and obligations. The seller of a call option has a neutral to bearish view of the underlying security and has an obligation to fulfill the terms of the contract if the option buyer decides to exercise the option contract. The seller of a put option has a neutral to bullish view of the underlying security and has an obligation to fulfill the terms of the contract if the option buyer decides to exercise the option contract. In short, the option seller is at the mercy of the option buyer with regard to exercising the option contract. The option seller has a limited gain potential equal to the price paid for the option by the buyer, but also has an unlimited downside loss potential.

PROBABILITY IS THE KEY

Why would anyone want to sell options if the loss potential is unlimited? That's a great question and one that's asked just about every time I discuss options trading. The reason that option selling is such a useful strategy if used correctly is because of the probabilities involved. Option trading is all based on probability and statistics. Many investors or option buyers tend to see options as a lottery type of trade where they know it will cost them only a few dollars to play. If the stock or commodity makes the big move, then they're headed for Easy Street. But how often does that happen? As often as you win the lottery—which is practically never.

Those are low-probability trades and most of them are the "close-to-expiration, far out-of-the-money (OTM)" options. But people are still drawn to the gambler mentality, which of course is fun from time to time; but if you continually lose, you won't last in the game very long. As smart option sellers, we want to be the ones who take the other side of those low-probability losers and turn them into high-probability winners for us. To reiterate, selling options can be profitable because of the high probability of success if used correctly. Three out of the four strategies I will show you in the book are of the selling type, and I will give many examples later on down the road.

Buying OTM options is the speculation game pure and simple (don't worry, I'll tell you more about what OTM means very soon). We all like to speculate because the payoff can be great, especially with options where leverage plays a big part. Where else can you plunk down $100 to control a few hundred shares of stock for a limited time? This is the options market. You get to control something very large for a small amount of money. Unfortunately, this is where I believe the option market advertising went off track. A majority of people only see options as a lottery type of investment and continue to focus on buying the low-probability trades.

You need to remember that options are not an investment unto themselves. An option's value is derived from other sources; hence, options are considered derivative investments. The most important of these other sources is the prediction of the direction you think the underlying security is going to move in the time allotted before option expiration. For one reason or another, many investors believe they can predict where a stock or commodity is headed in a very short time frame. They are lured into playing that hunch by buying the cheap options that have little chance of success. So once again, we're going to focus on how we can take advantage of those probabilities and turn those opportunities into our gains.

Even though I like to focus on selling options to take advantage of the buyer's low probability of profit, I also know how to buy options correctly as a form of investment. There's a certain way to buy options correctly as a substitute for a stock or commodity, and when I'm interested in purchasing options, there's only one way I do it. That way is to buy **deep-in-the-money (DITM)** options, which I'll explain later.

AN OPTION EXAMPLE

Let's walk through an example of what to do when you have a stock idea and you want to give options a try. We're bullish on Intel stock (INTC) and we want to use options to leverage our money. That's a great idea. But we have to decide what strike price and expiration month to pick. INTC is trading for $21 and we opt to buy a five-month option with a $25 strike price (as of February 2006). This option trades for a premium of $.40 per option contract (see option chain in Figure 1.1). Option prices have a $100 multiplier so our fictional call costs $40 ($.40 × $100). Since each option contract is the equivalent of 100 shares of stock, this means that we get to control 100 shares of INTC for the next five months at a cost to us of only $40. In order to find our cost-basis or breakeven price, we add our cost (option premium) to the strike price: $.40 + $25 = $25.40. If the option is held to expiration, we won't make money on the position unless INTC rises above $25.40. If you plan to trade out of the position before expiration, then you may see a profit, depending on how fast and how far INTC moves higher during the course of the trade. But I want to focus on the trade as most investors would—keeping the option until expiration.

Figure 1.1 is a screenshot of a typical option chain from one of my options brokers, optionsXpress (www.optionsXpress.com). The strike prices are listed down the "Strike" column and the bid/ask market

Calls									
Symbol	Last	Chg	Bid	Ask	Vol	OpInt		Strike	Symbol
Jul 06 Calls			(162 days to expiration)					INTC @ 21.00	
NQGC	6.40	+0.40	6.20	6.30	54	983	trade	15.00	NQSC
NQGW	4.10	+0.30	4.00	4.10	517	7,496	trade	17.50	NQSW
NQGD	2.25	+0.30	2.10	2.15	2,254	26,828	trade	20.00	NQSD
NQGX	0.90	+0.09	0.90	0.95	2,733	21,875	trade	22.50	NQSX
INQGE	0.35	+0.05	0.35	0.40	313	31,605	trade	25.00	INQSE
INQGY	0.15	0	0.10	0.15	360	25,552	trade	27.50	INQSY
INQGF	0.05	-0.05	0.05	0.10	16	13,728	trade	30.00	INQSF
INQGZ	0.05	0	0	0.05	0	2,826	trade	32.50	INQSZ
INQGG	0.05	0	0	0.05	0	299	trade	35.00	INQSG

Figure 1.1   INTC Option Chain, July 2006 Expiration
Source: optionsXpress.

for the call options is in the middle of the graphic. Our five-month option would take us to the July 2006 options, where the $25 call can be bought for $.40.

The advantage of buying options instead of the stock is the leverage you get. You only have to spend a little money up front to control the 100 shares. Instead of paying $2,100 to buy 100 shares of INTC outright, we only have to pay $40 today by using options. That's the key.

Eventually, if INTC gets above our breakeven price of $25.40, we will be faced with a decision: We can either sell the option back to the marketplace and pocket our gain, or "exercise" the option and turn it into actual stock shares.

If we decide to exercise, then we must pay the full stock purchase price. It's like making a balloon payment at the end of a loan. In this case, we'd have to come up with the extra $2,500 to pay for the 100 shares of stock we just exercised. I will go into this in more detail when I discuss buying deep-in-the-money (DITM) options.

You have to understand, though, that you're buying something that has no "real" value right off the bat. You're entering into a contract to buy INTC at $25 per share. Why would you want to buy INTC at $25 per share when you could buy it today for $21 per share? Good question. The answer, I believe, comes down to "hope and cheapness." Many people don't want to plunk down the $2,100 today to buy INTC but they feel okay spending only $40 for the chance that INTC will get above the breakeven price of $25.40 within five months. Some people would rather spend a little money today hoping that the stock will go up and become profitable, rather than buying the stock at current market prices.

THE PROFIT/LOSS SCENARIO

Regardless of which strike price you choose, let's see what the profit/ loss (P/L) scenario looks like graphically for a typical "long call" strategy. It helps to visualize your position with the use of P/L charts as seen in Figure 1.2.

Our P/L chart plots our position with the stock price on the bottom and our potential dollar gain/loss on the left side. The vertical line

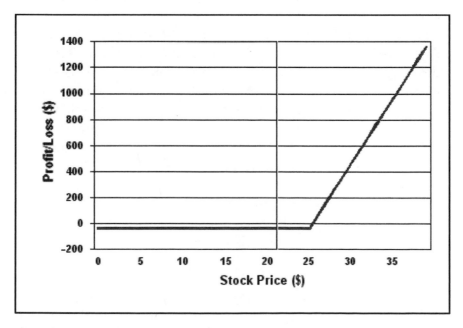

Figure 1.2   Call Option Profit/Loss Chart

represents the price of the stock today ($21) and the thick line represents our long call position. Since the call cost us $40, that is the maximum we can ever lose as indicated by the thick horizontal line that stretches from $0 to $25. As mentioned earlier, when you buy options you have limited risk, $40 in this case, and unlimited profit potential. The thick line starts to bend upward at our strike price of $25 and crosses the $0 P/L line at $25.40—which is our breakeven price. Once INTC gets above $25.40, we're making money for as long as INTC heads higher. As the price of the stock increases, our profit goes up indefinitely.

The question is, will INTC get above $25.40 in the next five months? Nobody knows, but that's what you're hoping. Remember that word "hope." Are you in an investment based on hope? When you buy the INTC $25 call option, you're really holding something that has no value right off the bat. It becomes valuable only when INTC goes above the breakeven price of $25.40 (if held until expiration). That's over $4 higher than where INTC is trading in the marketplace today. So, do you want to pay $2,100 to own 100 shares outright of INTC stock, or do you want to shell out a measly $40 and hope INTC goes up another $4 in the next five months? Only you can make that decision. Sure, it costs you only $40, but what's the probability of INTC getting to your breakeven price? Luckily for us, we have tools that can help figure out that probability. Using my probability calculator shown in Figure 1.3, our fictional INTC $25 call has a 21.9 percent chance of hitting breakeven by option expiration. Is that a high enough probability for you to take this trade?

When looking at the probability calculator in Figure 1.3, you want to focus on the box that reads, "Finishing above highest target." This is the box that tells us our chances of INTC being above our breakeven price of $25.40 at the time of option expiration based on the price of INTC, days to expiration, and the level of volatility that exists at the time of the trade. (As we get into Chapter 5, I will tell you why it's important to focus on the box that says, "Ever touching highest target.")

When you see it graphically in front of you that your investment has a 21.9 percent chance of being profitable, you might think twice about it. I know it's only $40, but it could be larger than that in some cases depending on how many option contracts you buy. Do this

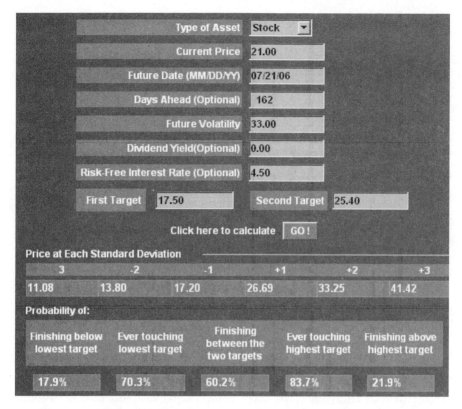

Figure 1.3 Probability Calculator
Source: © Copyright Optionvue Systems International, Inc.

enough times with those small chances and you'll end up walking away in disgust from the options market.

The problem here is that many investors tend to pick strike prices too far away from the current price of the stock and/or an expiration period that's too close in time. These investors think that they can predict the very short-term moves with pinpoint accuracy in the short time allotted. Nobody is that good. Later on when I discuss DITM options you'll see how we use them in lieu of buying the stock and how you will get all the same movement of the stock, plus the leverage and at least a 50 percent risk reduction to boot.

Let's see what a P/L chart looks like for a "long put" strategy. (See Figure 1.4.) When you buy a put option, you're betting on the price of the stock or commodity to go down. As with the long call strategy, your risk is limited to what you pay for the option and your

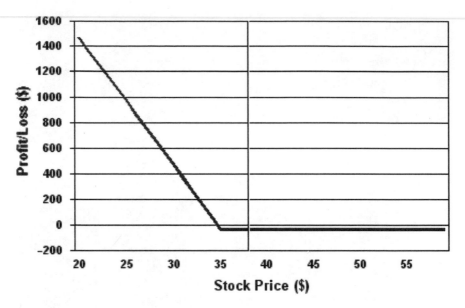

Figure 1.4   Put Option Profit/Loss Chart

reward is unlimited up to the point of the stock or commodity falling to zero. But like the long call, investors tend to concentrate on buying the low-probability, OTM, close-to-expiration options.

In this case, the chart looks reversed. This is because your profit goes up when the stock goes down. In this example of a put option purchase, the stock was at $38 and we bought a $35 put option for $.35 ($35 in actual dollars). The horizontal part of the thick line represents the maximum we can ever lose, which is $35. No matter how high this stock may trade, we can never lose more than $35. On the upside, our profit is unlimited as you can see in the thick line extending upward to the left. We can make as much money as possible to the point of the stock falling to $0 per share.

STOCK PRICE AND STRIKE PRICE RELATIONSHIP

The next thing we need to understand about the basic principles of options trading is the relationship between the strike price you choose and the current price of the underlying security. There are three terms you need to know. They are: in-the-money (ITM), at-the-money (ATM), and out-of-the-money (OTM). Unfortunately, the options game does come with its own language so you need to know some of these terms to get a grasp of how to effectively navigate the battlefield. I've touched on some of these terms already, but I want to give the textbook definitions of each. We're just going to scratch the surface here with these terms and later on we'll dig deeper to see how they can affect your trading profitability.

For call options, if the strike price is higher than the current price of the stock or commodity, it is called OTM. For example, if INTC is at $20 then all strikes above $20 are OTM. Any strike that is priced near the current price of the stock is called ATM. The INTC $20 strike would be considered ATM. Lastly, all call strike prices that are below the current price of the security are ITM. If INTC is at $20, all strikes below that would be ITM.

Put options are the opposite. Any option whose strike price is lower than the current price of the stock or commodity is considered OTM. For example, if INTC is at $20, then all strikes below $20 are OTM. Any strike that is priced near the current price of the stock is considered ATM. The INTC $20 strike would be considered ATM. Lastly, any put option strike price that is above the current price of the security is considered an ITM put option. If INTC is at $20, all strikes above that would be ITM.

It's important to know these terms because each one will act differently due to the degree of the option being in-, at-, or out-of-the-money. We will talk extensively about how each of these types of options can affect the profitability of your position. It also helps to know the terms because you might be working with a full-service broker who can help you tailor your investment ideas to the types of options available.

SUMMARY

We learned the basics of options in this chapter—specifically what call options and put options are. They can be used as a substitute for taking a position in an outright stock or commodity trade.

The relationship between the price of the stock and the strike price is the key to determining whether the option is out of the money (OTM), at the money (ATM), or in the money (ITM). Picking the option's correct strike price will ultimately help decide the probability of profit for your trade—something we dive in to more deeply in subsequent chapters.

CHAPTER 2

HOW OPTIONS
ARE PRICED

Options are not independent investments, so to speak. Yes, you can buy them individually, but their values are based on and derived from other variables, the most important of which is the movement of the underlying security. Hence, options are classified as "derivative" products.

When you look to buy or sell an option and you see its price, do you ever wonder how that price was calculated or where it came from? If you don't, then you may be either overpaying for it when you buy or underselling it at too cheap a price. There's a certain formula that's used to calculate an option's premium, and if you want to be a smart option trader, then you need to familiarize yourself with how it's done. The option's price doesn't just magically appear out of thin air. The market makers on the options exchanges use very precise software to price each and every option according to all the conditions that exist at that very moment in time.

The price, or "premium," of an option is dependent on several variables. They are:

- Intrinsic value.
  - Current price of the underlying security.
  - Strike price of the option.

- Extrinsic value.
  - Days left to option expiration.
  - Volatility (historical or implied).
  - Interest rates.
  - Dividends (stock options only).

You then take these numbers and enter them into an option pricing calculator. Most option pricing calculators and software will use a formula like the standard Black-Scholes option pricing model, which is named after the gentlemen who created it, Fischer Black and Myron Scholes. The software will then produce a result that tells you what your option should theoretically cost. I say "theoretically" because what you get from your option calculator might be quite different from what the option is trading for on the exchange. I will explain that discrepancy when we talk about the volatility component.

Finding and inputting these numbers is quite simple, with the exception of the volatility component, which can get a little tricky. I say this because it is the only input that is not readily agreed upon by all market participants or set by the exchanges. When using an option calculator, it's easy to find all the other input numbers. We can always get a current quote for the stock or commodity, the exchanges set the strike prices and days to expiration, and interest rates and dividends are all widely disseminated; you can find them online or in any financial newspaper. And just to cut through some of the bull, I'm here to tell you that the first two intrinsic and the first two extrinsic items on the list are the only ones that really matter when it comes to pricing out options. Dividends and interest rates play such a minor role that we never need to be overly concerned with them.

I need to explain the two option-jargon concepts above that relate to the option pricing inputs: **intrinsic value** and **extrinsic value**.

Intrinsic value explains the relationship between the price of the underlying security and the strike price of the option. We went over these earlier and referred to them as out-of-the-money (OTM), at-the-money (ATM), and in-the-money (ITM). Intrinsic value tells us whether an option has any "real" or "true" value to it. Only ITM options, whether they are ITM calls or ITM puts, can have intrinsic value. An example will help:

Microsoft (MSFT) is at $27 per share. The ITM $25 call is trading for a premium of $3, but has only $2 of intrinsic value. How's that? Simple. All you need to do is to subtract the call strike from the current price of the stock ($27 − $25 = $2). The $25 call is made up of $2 of intrinsic value and $1 of extrinsic value. You do the same thing for a $30 ITM put option that trades for $4 with MSFT at $27. There is $3 of intrinsic value ($30 − $27 = $3) and $1 of extrinsic value. Intrinsic value lets you know whether an option is truly worth something at that moment in time.

What's extrinsic value? Extrinsic value is what's left over after you subtract the intrinsic value. The last four items on the list make up the extrinsic part of an option (days to expiration, volatility, interest rates, and dividends).

Another way to tell if an option has intrinsic value is by seeing if it would have any *real* value if it was exercised. Exercising an option means that you turn it into actual shares (futures contracts) of the stock or commodity.

Let's say that INTC is still at $27 per share. The $25 call option (which has its strike price below the current price of INTC) can be exercised right now, which means we can buy shares of INTC for $25 per share ($2 below its current price). If we immediately turned around and sold the shares in the open market, we could get a minimum of $2 per share extra for our trade. That option then has $2 of intrinsic, or *real,* value.

All ATM and OTM options have no intrinsic value. They are composed entirely of extrinsic value. How do we know that? Because it we tried to exercise an ATM or OTM option, we'd lose money. Again, suppose MSFT is at $27. The closest ATM call would be the $27.50 call option and the closest OTM call would be the $30 call option. If we exercised either one of those, we'd have to purchase 100 shares of MSFT at either $27.50/share or $30/share. Why would you want to do that when MSFT is trading for $27 in the open market? You wouldn't. So, all ATM and OTM options have no intrinsic, or real value.

Jeez, enough of the vocabulary already. Okay, sorry. I just needed to get that out of the way because later on when I explain the strategies, I will be referring to these principles.

ANATOMY OF A PREMIUM

Let's move on to see how the six inputs create an option's price. See Figure 2.1 for a typical option calculator that I like to use, courtesy of one of my favorite web sites, www.ivolatility.com.

We've priced out the Intel (INTC) $25 strike calls and puts as of the close on February 24, 2006. The left-hand side of the calculator is the "input" section and the right-hand side is the "output" section. The current price of INTC is $20.36, the strike price is $25, there are 203 days to option expiration (September 2006), and the interest rate and dividends are automatically plugged in for us at 4.99 percent and $.10 respectively. The volatility component of 24.87 percent is defaulted for us as well, but that is a number calculated by the people at IVolatility. We'll get into the subject of volatility a little later on, but for right now I want to explain the calculator.

With our inputs set, we see the calculated theoretical values (on the right-hand side) for the Intel September 2006 $25 call and $25 put options are at $.33 and $4.71 respectively. This gives us a rough estimate of what these option contracts "should" be trading for on the exchanges at that moment in time. As I mentioned earlier, your theoretical value doesn't always match up to what the pit is giving as a market price, and that is usually due to volatility reasons.

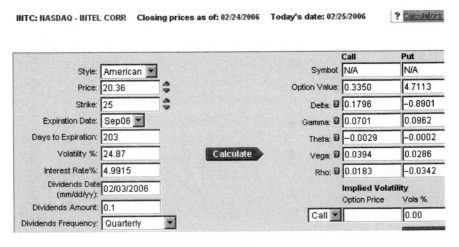

Figure 2.1 Option Calculator, INTC Options
Source: Courtesy of www.ivolatility.com.

An option calculator is also a great tool for computing "what-if" scenarios. You can change any input item on the left-hand side and see how it affects the option prices on the right-hand side. If you're looking to buy or sell an option at a certain price, you can switch the underlying price, days to expiration, strike price, or volatility component until you find the right combination to give you your desired result.

GOT MOVEMENT?

The other items listed below "Option Value" are what we call the "Greeks." These are by-product outputs from the option pricing formula. Gamma, vega, and rho are useful features, but mostly for floor traders or very active professional options traders. But two of the Greeks—delta and theta—are extremely important for all of us to know. They are key indicators that play a huge role in a majority of option trades and in the strategies that I'm going to show you later. But in short, the delta figure tells us how much the option price will move in relation to a $1 move in the underlying security, and theta tells us how much an option's premium will decay on a daily basis. Don't be alarmed if these concepts are confusing right now. I will spend considerable time in subsequent chapters discussing these items.

Let me just touch on a few features of delta, though, for a minute. Delta values range from 0 to 1.00, with 1.00 being the highest correlation with the underlying security. It's actually quoted in percentage terms, so deltas range from 0 percent to 100 percent, but you will see them quoted in decimals. An option contract that has a delta of .60, for example, will see its price change 60 percent of the price change of the stock or commodity. This is assuming all other factors are unchanged. If an IBM call option has a price of $4.50 with a delta of .60, and IBM stock moves from $82 to $83, theoretically, that option should see its price move up $.60 to $5.10.

What you need to ask yourself before you buy any option is, "Am I looking to get good movement from my option choice in relation to the move that the stock makes?" Most people don't understand that property about options. They think they can buy any call or put

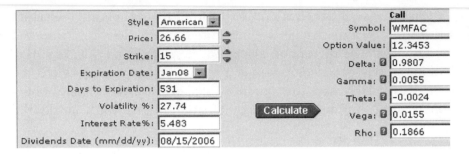

Figure 2.2   Option Calculator with MSFT at $26.66

Source: Courtesy of www.ivolatility.com.

option on the board and that it's going to move as long as the stock moves. This is not always the case. I'm sure many of you have experienced this scenario: You buy a call option that expires in a few weeks and the stock starts moving up nicely, yet your option contract isn't gaining any value. What gives? Well, it's most likely because you didn't buy an option that has a large enough delta. This occurs in the out-of-the-money (OTM) options and ones that are too close to expiration. People like to concentrate on these options because they're cheap on a dollar basis. You will soon find out that even though they're cheap, they are not giving you the expected outcome. You want to focus on options that have a high correlation with the movement of the stock.

My DITM strategy (the subject of Chapter 6) will explain how to use delta to its fullest, but just to give you a brief glimpse, take a look at the three successive snapshots of the option calculators. In Figure 2.2 I have priced a DITM $15 call option on Microsoft (MSFT) that expires in January 2008 with Microsoft at a current price of $26.66 and the option valued at roughly $12.35. The $15 call is $11.66 in-the-money, giving it $11.66 of intrinsic value. We see the delta at a very high level of .9807 (right side of graphic). This tells us that the option value should move practically in lockstep with any move that MSFT makes.

In the next snapshot (Figure 2.3), we've taken MSFT up to $27.66. See what the $15 call is worth now?

The $15 call has moved up roughly $1 as well, to a new price of $13.33. The delta is working as it should. Its movement also works to the downside. See the next graphic in Figure 2.4.

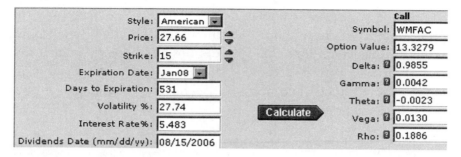

Figure 2.3   Option Calculator with MSFT at $27.66
Source: Courtesy of www.ivolatility.com.

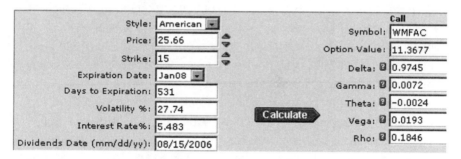

Figure 2.4   Option Calculator with MSFT at $25.66
Source: Courtesy of www.ivolatility.com.

Again, with all else constant, we took MSFT down to $25.66 and we see that the $15 call option lost roughly $1 in value with a new premium of $11.37. Delta works, and you should pay special attention to it because it's a great gauge for telling you how your option will perform.

If you're a stock investor and you want to use options as a way to gain more leverage and use less capital, sticking with options that have higher deltas will give you the most bang for your buck. You want your option price to move, and the only way to assure you of that is to have an option with a high delta. Where investors go wrong with options is that they tend to buy cheap, low delta, OTM options that have a very low probability of profit. You can't just buy any old option and think it's going to move point for point with the stock. Options are more complex than that.

Now, if you're the gambler type and you're looking for a fun speculation play from time to time, then there's nothing wrong with taking the chance on those cheapie options and hope they hit it big. This is fine as long as you know ahead of time that your chances are slim to have a winner, and that you might lose 100 percent of your option investment.

THE MARKET MAKER'S DELTA

Just as a side anecdote here, I want to tell you how we used delta in our portfolio management while working as option market makers on the floor of the exchange. Delta not only told us how much the option price should move in relation to the price change of the underlying futures contract, but it also told us how many futures contracts were needed to offset any directional risk we had from our options trades.

Option market makers are not there to pick a direction and hope that the stock or commodity moves in their favor. Market makers are there to provide continuous bid/ask quotes for all options associated with a specific stock or commodity. What the market maker wants to do is to buy very close to their bid price and sell at their ask price and lock in those gains as fast as possible. If we bought a specific option at our bid price and couldn't sell it immediately to someone else at our higher ask price, then what we needed to do was to offset the option's directional risk with an opposing trade in the futures market. The delta would tell us exactly how many futures contracts we needed to buy or sell to offset our option trade. Market makers always want to be delta-neutral, which meant that we had no directional bias. We were trying to capture the edge between what the option was worth and how much we could buy it below or sell it above that value. In order to do that, we used trading sheets similar to the one shown in Figure 2.5.

The graphic is a very simplified version of what an option market maker's "fair value sheets" look like. This one contains the fair value and delta calculations for various futures and option prices for crude oil options as of 10/03/2005 with a fictional expiration date of 10/21/2005. Here's how it works. Along the left-hand side are prices for the front-month crude oil futures market in five-cent increments. In this example we're seeing prices for the futures at $65.45, $65.50, and $65.55. A typical trader's sheets would

Crude										EXERCISE PRICES						
10/21/2005			62	62	63	63	64	64	65	65	66	66	67	67		
Futures	VOL	P/C	Fair	Delta	Fair	Delta	Fair	Delta	Fair	Delta	Fair	Delta	Fair	Delta
65.45	36.0%	P	0.828	-0.25	1.143	-0.32	1.532	-0.40	1.998	-0.47	2.539	-0.55	3.155	-0.62
65.45	36.0%	C	3.973	0.74	3.290	0.68	2.681	0.60	2.147	0.53	1.691	0.45	1.308	0.38
65.45	37.0%	P	0.875	-0.26	1.195	-0.33	1.588	-0.40	2.055	-0.47	2.596	-0.55	3.210	-0.62
65.45	37.0%	C	4.019	0.74	3.342	0.67	2.736	0.60	2.205	0.53	1.748	0.45	1.363	0.38
65.45	38.0%	P	0.922	-0.26	1.248	-0.33	1.644	-0.40	2.113	-0.47	2.654	-0.54	3.265	-0.61
65.45	38.0%	C	4.067	0.73	3.394	0.67	2.792	0.60	2.262	0.53	1.805	0.45	1.418	0.39
65.45	39.0%	P	0.969	-0.27	1.300	-0.33	1.700	-0.40	2.170	-0.47	2.711	-0.54	3.320	-0.61
65.45	39.0%	C	4.114	0.73	3.447	0.67	2.848	0.60	2.320	0.53	1.862	0.46	1.473	0.39
65.50	35.0%	P	0.769	-0.25	1.076	-0.31	1.457	-0.39	1.917	-0.47	2.455	-0.55	3.069	-0.62
65.50	35.0%	C	3.964	0.75	3.272	0.68	2.655	0.61	2.116	0.53	1.656	0.45	1.274	0.38
65.50	36.0%	P	0.815	-0.25	1.127	-0.32	1.513	-0.40	1.974	-0.47	2.512	-0.54	3.124	-0.62
65.50	36.0%	C	4.010	0.75	3.324	0.68	2.711	0.61	2.174	0.53	1.713	0.45	1.327	0.38
65.50	37.0%	P	0.862	-0.26	1.179	-0.32	1.568	-0.39	2.032	-0.47	2.569	-0.54	3.179	-0.61
65.50	37.0%	C	4.057	0.74	3.376	0.68	2.766	0.60	2.231	0.53	1.771	0.46	1.382	0.39
65.50	38.0%	P	0.908	-0.26	1.231	-0.33	1.624	-0.40	2.089	-0.47	2.627	-0.54	3.234	-0.61
65.50	38.0%	C	4.103	0.74	3.428	0.67	2.822	0.60	2.289	0.53	1.828	0.46	1.437	0.39
65.50	39.0%	P	0.956	-0.27	1.284	-0.33	1.680	-0.40	2.147	-0.47	2.684	-0.54	3.290	-0.61
65.50	39.0%	C	4.151	0.73	3.480	0.67	2.878	0.60	2.346	0.53	1.885	0.46	1.493	0.39
65.55	35.0%	P	0.757	-0.24	1.060	-0.31	1.438	-0.39	1.893	-0.46	2.427	-0.54	3.038	-0.62
65.55	35.0%	C	4.002	0.76	3.307	0.69	2.686	0.61	2.143	0.53	1.679	0.46	1.290	0.38
65.55	36.0%	P	0.803	-0.25	1.112	-0.32	1.493	-0.39	1.951	-0.46	2.485	-0.54	3.093	-0.61
65.55	36.0%	C	4.048	0.75	3.358	0.68	2.741	0.61	2.200	0.53	1.736	0.46	1.346	0.38
65.55	37.0%	P	0.849	-0.25	1.163	-0.32	1.549	-0.39	2.008	-0.46	2.542	-0.54	3.148	-0.61
65.55	37.0%	C	4.094	0.75	3.410	0.68	2.797	0.61	2.258	0.53	1.793	0.46	1.401	0.39

Figure 2.5 Option Pricing Sheet

contain many dollars' worth of prices, so you would see market makers come into the pit with thick booklets of trading sheets, sometimes for more than one commodity. You should see what the floor of the exchange looks like at the end of the day. Actually, you wouldn't be able to see the floor because every inch would be covered with obsolete trading sheets.

The "P/C" column indicates whether you are looking at a put or a call, and the "VOL" column represents the volatility level you are using to help price the options. Along the top row of the sheet are the strike prices that are available to trade in that particular commodity. Here we see strike prices for crude oil options ranging from $62 to $67. The last pieces of the puzzle are the "Fair" and "Delta" columns. The first represents the fair market value for each put or call at the corresponding futures price along the left-hand side, and the "Delta" column lets the trader know how many futures contracts are needed to offset any option trade to balance out the directional risk.

(Continues)

THE MARKET MAKER'S DELTA *(Continued)*

A pit broker asks for a market on the $66 calls and we find out that the futures are trading at $65.50 at that moment in time. We check our sheet on the left-hand side for the calls at the $65.50 mark with a volatility of 38 percent, and then we move along the top until we intersect with the $66 strike of the "Fair" column. We see that the fair market value of the $66 calls at a corresponding futures price of $65.50 comes out to be $1.828.

Any attentive market maker in the options pit would yell to the broker, "$1.80 bid at $1.85." This means that the market makers are willing to buy that option at a price of $1.80 or sell it at $1.85. At this point, we don't know if the broker is a buyer or seller, so we always have to give both sides of the market (we don't care if we buy it or sell it). Now, if the broker decides to buy the option from us at our price of $1.85, we have to tell him how many option contracts we want to do. To make it simple, the delta sheets are based on a trade of 100 contracts. If we are lucky enough to sell 100 contracts to the broker, we look at our sheets again and see that the delta is .46. In order to offset our initial directional risk, we would hand signal to our "point man" to buy us 46 futures contracts. Since we are selling call options to the broker, our initial delta is bearish short 46 potential futures contracts; therefore we need to buy 46 long futures contracts to keep our delta at zero.

As I mentioned earlier, the option market maker is looking for an edge, not a directional trade. If that $66 call is valued at approximately $1.83 and we get to sell it at $1.85, then that's what we call getting an edge. Our best-case scenario is that someone wants to sell that option now and maybe we would be able to buy it back for $1.80. That's how market makers try to make their money. They continuously try to buy for less than what their sheets are telling them and to sell for more than what their sheets are telling them. Unfortunately, it's not as easy as that, but that's the main thrust of the market maker's job.

SUMMARY

That sums up the pricing of options. What I wanted to do in this chapter was to familiarize you with the inputs that make up the price of an option. The market makers on the options exchanges use high-end software to constantly give quotes all day long and to update as necessary as market conditions change. Altering any input into the option pricing formula will cause the option price to change, but the most important ones are the price of the underlying security, time to expiration, and volatility. Since volatility is such a confusing and esoteric type of input, I devote the next chapter entirely to that topic. It will be well worth your trading dollars' while to understand how volatility plays a key role in the pricing of options.

CHAPTER 3

OPTION
VOLATILITY

As we mentioned in the preceding chapter, which focused on the pricing of options, there are several determinants that give an option its price. Of those determinants, "volatility" plays a tremendous role, and it's the one that is the most elusive, confusing, and difficult for market participants to understand. Many people just don't seem to grasp the idea of what volatility is, and how it relates to options trading. As a former NYMEX floor trader, volatility was the basis for all of our trading and our profitability depended on our understanding and being able to use volatility to its fullest. As an off-floor retail trader, volatility can still play a large role in your success, so that is why I'd like to devote some time to explain this concept. By the end of this chapter you will see the importance of being able to understand and identify how to use volatility in your own trading.

WHAT IS VOLATILITY?

In simplest terms, volatility is a statistical measure of how erratic a stock or commodity has been in the past, and how erratic it's expected to be in the future. Getting a handle on the past price movements of a stock or commodity and its expected price range for the future will help you be a smarter player in the options world because you will know the effects that volatility is likely to have on the price of an option. These volatility levels get inputted into the option pricing model along with the other variables to help give an option its price.

There are two types of volatility as it applies to options trading:

1. *Historical Volatility (HV)* measures how volatile or erratic the stock or commodity has been in the past.
2. *Implied Volatility (IV)* measures how volatile or erratic the stock or commodity is expected to be in the future.

Historical Volatility (HV) is the easier concept to grasp and measure. It is based on actual past price movements of the security, so all we have to do is collect the data of past price movements and calculate the historical volatility. The issue now comes down to how much data we want to use and what intervals we want to concentrate on. Most measurements of historical volatility as used in the trading world will default to a 21-day look-back period, which corresponds to the number of trading days in a month. Since a majority of traders seem to be of the short-term type, defaulting to a 21-day volatility level is a good place to start. What this means is that we will collect the closing prices of the specific security from the past 21 days of trading and convert them into a volatility number to use in the option pricing model.

Some players like to calculate HV in other ways, preferring to use 10-day, 30-day, or 50-day look-back periods for calculating HV. Not only that, but instead of using closing prices, they might opt to incorporate the high, low, and closing price in their calculation. If you're unsure about what we mean by look-back period, just think of it in the same way as you would with a moving average technical indicator on a typical price chart. A 50-day moving average plots a single line on the chart using the last 50 days' worth of closing prices to configure the line. HV works in the same way.

Implied Volatility (IV) is a little more confusing. It is a forward-looking calculation in which the market makers will make an assessment of how they feel the stock or commodity will fluctuate in the future, or until option expiration, and they will use that calculation in the option pricing formula. IV is considered an up-to-the-minute gauge of the mood of the markets and it gets priced into the option's premium. It not only takes into consideration the security's past price performance (HV) but it also factors in any other external forces that might move the stock or commodity in the near future. External forces can consist of things like earnings reports, Food and Drug Administration (FDA) announcements, Federal Reserve meetings, Organization of Petroleum Exporting Countries (OPEC) meetings, crop reports, unemployment reports, and weather reports. These are items that can affect the price of the security; hence, the option prices will be affected as well. If the option market makers know that there is a big meeting coming up, they will start to reprice the options to reflect the uncertainty of the outcome of the meeting or news event. Once the news event is known or resolved, the IV will be readjusted to reflect normal trading conditions.

USING VOLATILITY TO YOUR ADVANTAGE

This is all well and good, but how does that affect us in our own option trading to help us make more money? I'm glad you asked. I'm going to show you a few tips about volatility that will help you pinpoint times when volatility is cheap and when it is expensive, which will allow you to buy and sell options at the most opportune times. Believe it or not, volatility will fluctuate just like the price of a stock or commodity. It will go through periods of high points and low points. You just need to know how to spot those levels. The reason why you need to understand that volatility is such an important part of trading is because it has a direct effect on the price of every option. If volatility is high, option prices will be more expensive than normal, and if volatility is low, option prices will be cheaper than normal. You want to concentrate on trying to buy and sell during the most opportune times.

If a stock or commodity has been very erratic, that in turn increases the volatility component of the pricing model, thus bumping up the price of the option. If the stock or commodity is a slow mover, you can guess that the volatility component will be low; thus you will get cheaper option prices.

So how do you tell when volatility is high or low? It's simple—look at a volatility chart! If you follow stock options, www.ivolatility.com is one of your best sources for volatility data and charts.

Figure 3.1 is a typical one-year stock volatility chart for IBM. Don't confuse this with a price chart for IBM. The volatility chart plots both HV (lighter line) and IV (darker line). The HV line is based on a 30-day look-back period, and the IV line is a proprietary model put together by the people at IVolatility.com. Most IV data is taken on a daily basis and is priced off of the front-month at-the-money (ATM) options. These are usually the most liquid and highly traded options, which will give us our best indicator of current IV. On the chart you will see the months of the year along the bottom and the volatility levels on the right-hand side. Volatility is always measured in percent, and that's how it's entered into the option pricing formula.

You can see that the lines almost always move in tandem, but there are times when they certainly diverge. This usually happens when news events are expected and the options market will reflect that volatility. This can be seen with the IV line spiking at certain times. The key here is to always compare present volatility levels to past volatility levels. That's how you define whether volatility is cheap or expensive. Let me show you what I mean.

We're going to price some IBM options using information from the volatility chart in Figure 3.1.

Using our options calculator again (Figure 3.2), we've priced out the April 2006 $85 call options on IBM as of March 27, 2006, with IBM stock at a closing price of $83.08. We've input a volatility value of 15 percent on the left-hand side, which corresponds to the lowest IV value for the IBM options (at the end of February 2006 on the

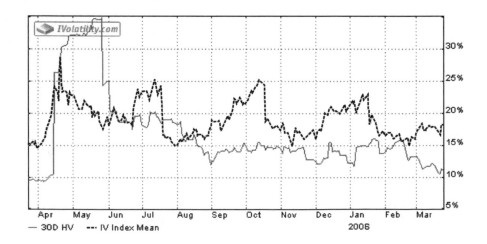

Figure 3.1 IBM Volatility Chart

Source: Courtesy of www.ivolatility.com.

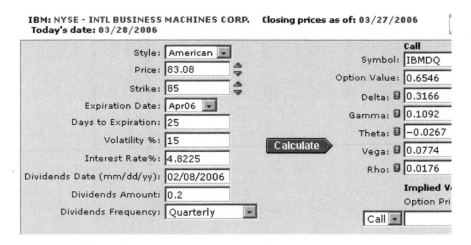

Figure 3.2 Option Calculator with 15 Percent Volatility
Source: Courtesy of www.ivolatility.com.

volatility chart in Figure 3.1). We see that the $85 call option had a theoretical value of $.65 with those inputs. Let's see what happens when we set a new volatility value of 27 percent, which corresponds to the highest level seen on the chart (during April 2005). (See Figure 3.3.)

With our new volatility estimate of 27 percent, we see the $85 call option is now worth $1.63, roughly $1 higher than before. So, there's

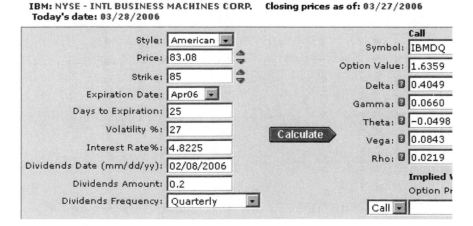

Figure 3.3 Option Calculator with 27 Percent Volatility
Source: Courtesy of www.ivolatility.com.

the proof that volatility does affect the option prices. The reason why I show you this is to get you accustomed to checking volatility levels before executing an options trade. You'll have an idea ahead of time whether you'll be buying or selling options during cheap or expensive times based on the volatility data. Of course, as a smart options trader, you'll want to focus on trying to buy options during lower periods of the security's volatility and concentrate on selling options during high volatility levels. We know that we can't always predict that our timing of options trading will correspond to high or low volatility levels, but you can always tailor your options strategies to take advantage of whatever volatility level exists at the time.

In order not to discriminate, I wanted to include a commodity volatility chart (Figure 3.4). This one plots the two-year IV range for natural gas. We can see from the chart that natural gas has traded in a range of roughly 35 percent on the low side to a recent high of 70 percent implied volatility. This is a reflection of how erratic the natural gas market tends to be.

TWO STOCKS, DIFFERENT VOLATILITY

I've just shown you one way in which volatility affects an option's price; now I want to show you how it can affect your other trading decisions as well. Take a situation where you're deciding between

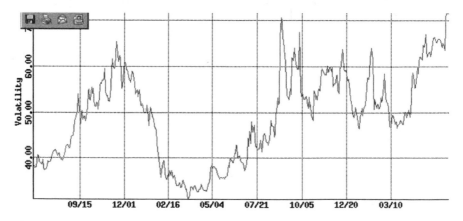

Figure 3.4   Natural Gas Volatility Chart
Source: Chart provided by Optionetics, Inc.

two different stocks to buy that are trading for roughly the same price. You know that you want to buy call options on either one, but you're not sure which one could be more profitable. Of course, nobody knows how the trade will work out in the end, but let me show you how volatility can play a huge role.

As you look at both stocks, you find to your surprise that the same call option on each stock is trading at a very different price level from the other. How can that be? Both stocks are at the same price, you're looking at the same strike price, and both expire on the same day. So why are the option prices so different? I'll tell you why—volatility!

To drive home the fact that volatility plays a huge role in the pricing of options, let's look at these two stocks with virtually the same price and their corresponding option chains. We have Anheuser-Busch (BUD) and the International Securities Exchange (ISE) as our two potential buy candidates, which are both trading for $42.82 on March 29, 2006. We are bullish and interested in purchasing call options. Let's choose the $45 calls for the month of May 2006, compare option prices, and see what our money would get us. See Figures 3.5 and 3.6.

The last price for each stock at the time of comparison ($42.82/$42.83) is listed in the top right-hand corner of each chain. We're looking at the $45 strike price, which you can see in the black column on the right-hand side. We scan left over to the "Ask" column to see the price at which we could potentially buy each option. Here's where we see the huge difference in option prices. The ISE

	INTERNATIONAL SECS. EXCH. INC.									
		Bid: 42.82			High: 43.47			Last: 42.82		
		–	Ask: 42.87		Low: 42.7596			Change: -0.07		
Bid	Ask	Last	Change	Prev	Imp Vol(B)	Imp Vol(A)	High	Low	Delta	Symbol
13.00	13.50	0.00	0.00	0.00	30.68	75.87	0.00	0.00	98	MAY06 30.00
8.50	8.90	0.00	0.00	0.00	49.22	60.66	0.00	0.00	89	MAY06 35.00
5.10	5.20	5.00	-1.00	6.00	54.07	55.79	6.00	4.90	69	MAY06 40.00
2.55	2.75	2.55	-0.05	2.60	52.04	55.16	2.55	2.55	44	MAY06 45.00
1.15	1.40	1.15	-0.10	1.25	51.74	56.46	1.15	1.15	24	MAY06 50.00
0.50	0.65	0.65	+0.05	0.60	52.51	56.69	0.75	0.65	11	MAY06 55.00
0.20	0.35	0.35	-0.45	0.80	52.78	59.52	0.35	0.35	4	MAY06 60.00
0.05	0.20	0.00	0.00	0.00	49.86	62.37	0.00	0.00	1	MAY06 65.00
	0.10	0.00	0.00	0.00		63.22	0.00	0.00	0	MAY06 70.00

Figure 3.5 ISE Option Chain, May 2006 Expiration
Source: eSignal.com.

Bid	Ask	Last	Change	Prev	Imp Vol(B)	Imp Vol(A)	High	Low	Delta	Symbol
7.90	8.10	0.00	0.00	0.00	0.00	31.51	0.00	0.00	99	MAY06 35.00
3.10	3.20	3.20	0.00	3.20	0.00	16.68	3.20	3.20	82	MAY06 40.00
0.20	0.30	0.30	−0.05	0.35	12.59	14.78	0.35	0.25	32	MAY06 45.00
	0.05	0.00	0.00	0.00		21.76	0.00	0.00	4	MAY06 50.00
	0.05	0.00	0.00	0.00		32.50	0.00	0.00	0	MAY06 55.00

(Table header: ANHEUSER BUSCH COS INC. + | Bid: 42.83 Ask: 42.85 | High: 43.00 Low: 42.70 | Last: 42.83 Change: +0.12)

Figure 3.6 BUD Option Chain, May 2006 Expiration
Source: eSignal.com.

$45 call is offered at $2.75 ask price while the BUD $45 call is offered at $.30 ask price. ISE's $45 call is nine times more expensive than BUD's $45 call. Nine times! Why is that?

Well, we know that there are six determinants to a stock option's price:

1. Price of the underlying stock.
2. Strike price of the option.
3. Time to expiration.
4. Volatility.
5. Interest rates.
6. Dividends.

Both stocks are trading for virtually the same price ($42.82/ $42.83), the strike prices are identical ($45 call), and the options all expire at the same time (May 2006). Interest rates and dividends play such a small role that they cannot be the reason. So that leaves us with only one culprit—volatility.

As I mentioned previously, volatility is a statistical number that measures the range of movements of a security over some period in the past as well as its expected movement in the future. When a stock has had big movements in the past and/or is expected to keep moving big, that inflates the volatility figure; this has the effect of increasing the option price. When a stock has been very quiet and/or is expected to stay quiet, the volatility figure will be smaller, thus decreasing the effect on the option price.

Okay. Let's see how the volatility is playing a role with these two stocks. If you look at the two columns in the option chains labeled "Imp Vol(B)" and "Imp Vol(A)," you will see that the numbers for

ISE are about four times those of BUD. Those numbers represent, in percentage terms, how the actual bid and ask prices of the options measure up in volatility terms. For instance, the $45 call for ISE has a bid/ask market of $2.55/$2.75. In volatility terms, that bid/ask market is equivalent to 52.04 percent/55.16 percent, whereas the BUD $45 call has a volatility market of 12.59 percent/14.78 percent.

As you're seeing on a comparison basis, the higher the volatility figure, the higher the option price will be. ISE's options have higher volatility numbers than BUD's; thus, the options are more expensive. **This is not to say that ISE's options are overpriced compared to BUD's.** We're just saying that ISE, for whatever reason, has experienced greater volatility in the past, and is also expected to have more volatility going forward. The option market makers are predicting that ISE will be more volatile than BUD down the road. The way to factor in that higher expected volatility is by raising the option prices. Each stock's options are priced according to the future expected movement of the stock. So both stocks in this case may have very fairly priced options according to how volatile each stock has been and is expected to be, even though ISE's options happen to cost more.

Remember, if you want to track an individual stock's volatility over some period in the past, just go to www.ivolatility.com and you can get a picture of how volatile it has been. See the one-year volatility charts for BUD (Figure 3.7) and ISE (Figure 3.8).

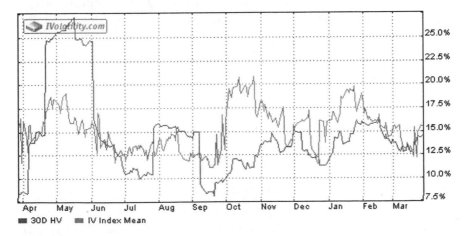

Figure 3.7 BUD Volatility Chart

Source: Courtesy of www.ivolatility.com.

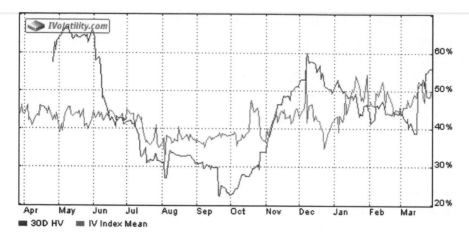

Figure 3.8   ISE Volatility Chart
Source: Courtesy of www.ivolatility.com.

The current numbers in the charts should roughly match the numbers in the volatility columns of the option chains. We see that BUD's current volatility numbers both on the chart and in the option chain are roughly in the 14 percent range and ISE's are in the 50 percent range. What's the point of showing you this information? It's really for your own knowledge of how volatility plays a huge role in the pricing of options. Even though ISE's options cost much more than BUD's, it doesn't mean ISE options are a bad deal. The probability of greater stock movement is reflected in the higher option prices. If you want to buy BUD options because they're cheaper in dollar terms, then you may be waiting longer for the option to gain in value because the stock is less volatile. If you want some potential manic action, then you could choose the ISE options. The greater movement in that stock should justify the higher option prices.

THE SKEW FACTOR

Another way you can use volatility to your advantage is when you are trading option spreads. An option spread is a strategy in which you are trading two options at the same time on the same order ticket, one being bought and one being sold. The options can be of the same month or different months, but the trade consists of one total price for the two options. Instead of buying one outright at one price and then selling the other at a different price, both options are done simultaneously as a single trade for one total spread price.

There's a characteristic of implied volatility called the "volatility skew." Each option on a stock or futures contract has its own implied volatility component, whether it's within the same expiration month or a different expiration month. The pattern of whether each option's implied volatility is higher or lower than its neighbor's makes up the skew curve. Take a look at the option chain in Figure 3.9.

On the right-hand side of the option chain are the put options on Google (GOOG) stock for May 2006 option expiration. Look at the columns labeled "Imp Vol(B)" and "Imp Vol(A)." As stated earlier, the numbers in those columns are the implied volatility percentages based on each option's actual bid and ask prices. For example, the GOOG $390 put option has a bid/ask market of $21.50/$21.90 and a corresponding bid implied/ask implied of 41.32 percent/42.00 percent.

GOOGLE INC.		c		Bid: 393.67 Ask: 394.00		High: 399.00 Low: 379.51		Last: 394.98 Change: +17.78		52WH 52WL

)| High	Low	Delta	Symbol	Bid	Ask	Last	Change	Prev	Imp Vol(B)	Imp Vol(A)
79.20	79.10	92	MAY06 310.00	2.45	2.65	3.00	-0.10	3.10	47.38	48.33
83.80	70.30	89	MAY06 320.00	3.40	3.60	3.60	-0.80	4.40	46.52	47.30
75.20	61.50	86	MAY06 330.00	4.60	4.80	5.00	-0.80	5.80	45.57	46.21
66.70	50.00	82	MAY06 340.00	6.10	6.40	6.50	-1.40	7.90	44.55	45.36
58.60	43.00	78	MAY06 350.00	8.10	8.40	8.10	-2.30	10.40	43.82	44.53
51.60	35.50	73	MAY06 360.00	10.50	10.80	10.60	-2.90	13.50	42.96	43.59
44.20	29.50	68	MAY06 370.00	13.70	13.90	13.80	-3.90	17.70	42.65	43.04
38.20	23.00	62	MAY06 380.00	17.20	17.60	17.20	-5.00	22.20	41.81	42.53
32.20	18.80	57	MAY06 390.00	21.50	21.90	21.80	-5.90	27.70	41.32	42.00
27.10	14.40	52	MAY06 400.00	26.40	26.70	26.60	-7.40	34.00	40.76	41.27
22.20	11.40	46	MAY06 410.00	31.90	32.30	31.50	-10.00	41.50	40.15	40.83
18.20	8.60	41	MAY06 420.00	38.00	38.60	38.10	-10.20	48.30	39.49	40.55
14.70	6.50	36	MAY06 430.00	44.90	45.50	44.90	-13.50	58.40	39.19	40.33
11.90	4.60	32	MAY06 440.00	52.30	53.00	52.30	-13.10	65.40	38.83	40.27
9.60	3.70	27	MAY06 450.00	60.30	60.90	60.20	-15.60	75.80	38.74	40.12
7.20	2.70	24	MAY06 460.00	68.60	69.30	77.10	-8.20	85.30	38.39	40.23
5.90	2.00	20	MAY06 470.00	77.30	78.00	86.90	-6.80	93.70	38.18	40.30
4.50	1.60	17	MAY06 480.00	86.30	87.10	105.60	-0.20	105.80	38.01	40.85
3.20	1.40	14	MAY06 490.00	95.50	96.40	98.70	0.00	98.70	37.70	41.49

Figure 3.9 GOOG Option Chain, May 2006 Expiration

Source: eSignal.com.

If you look at the rest of the numbers in the Imp Vol columns, you'll see the numbers getting higher as you move lower in strikes. This is what's referred to as a "reverse skew." If some of you are familiar with options, you know that when the market sells off in general, the volatility of options goes up because of the fear factor of downside moves. People start paying higher prices for downside protection, which in turn inflates option prices, which in turn heats up the implied volatility numbers.

That's all well and good. But how does the skew help us with our positions? The skew helps when you are executing these option spreads. At least 90 percent of my own option trades are in the form of spreads. The reason for this is twofold. First, I always like to hedge my initial option trade with an opposing option position. This will keep my initial cost down and let me participate in more trades. Second, doing spreads allows you to potentially offset an option purchase with a sale of an option at a higher implied volatility level. These spreads can be straight debit, straight credit, or ratio spreads (all of which will be explained later). Buying one option at a lower volatility level and selling another option that has a higher volatility level is what's called getting the "volatility edge" on your trades. Even though buying the spread will still cost you money, your total outlay is less than what it could be.

Let's say you are bearish on GOOG and think that by May 2006 option expiration it could trade back down to $330 per share. You could outright just sell short the shares and see what happens. But this is an extremely risky venture because, as we've seen with GOOG, the shares could pop on you and put you in a horrible short squeeze. That's why you are an astute investor and opt to go for the limited-risk appeal of options trading. But what strikes should you pick? Looking at the option chain, you can base your decision on the implied volatility of the options.

When I buy an option spread, I try to buy at-the-money options and sell out-of-the-money options. In our GOOG example, where our forecast is for the stock to trade down to $330 by expiration, we could buy the $390 put and sell the $330 put for a debit of $17.00 per spread (splitting bids/asks). This is an attractive spread based on implied volatility figures. We know this because we have the information right in front of us in the option chain. We are buying the $390 put at an IV of 41.66 percent (splitting Imp Vol(B) and Imp Vol(A) columns), and we are selling the $330 put at an IV of 45.90 percent.

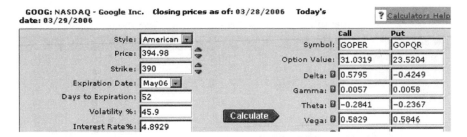

Figure 3.10   GOOG Option Calculator

Source: Courtesy of www.ivolatility.com.

That's putting the volatility edge in our favor. We're buying an option at a lower IV than the option we're selling. Whether or not GOOG meets our expected target of $330 by expiration, we know that we put on an attractive option spread based on the volatility figures.

What would happen if GOOG didn't have the reverse skew? Some stocks can exhibit a "flat skew" where the IV levels are similar to each other. For argument's sake, let's see what the spread would cost us if the $390 puts were trading the same as the $330 put's IV level of 45.90 percent. Plugging these numbers into our simple option calculator in Figure 3.10, we see the $390 put now costs us $23.50 instead of $21.70, which means the spread would cost $18.80 instead of $17.00.

That's a $180 difference in the cost of the spread with the flat skew compared to the reverse skew. So when you look to execute an option spread, it pays to check the volatility skew to see if you'll be able to gain the volatility edge in your trade. This is why I execute most of my trades with option spreads. I may not always be right with my directional bias, so it's good to have a sold option to offset my long option, especially if the sold option has a higher IV attached to it.

Just for fun, when I revised this chapter in January 2009, I thought I'd post another option chain for Google to see how the option premiums and volatility levels compared to the original option chain. The new option chain was for the March 2009 options expiration while the original option chain was for the May 2006 options. Both screen shots were taken roughly two months before expiration. (See Figure 3.11.)

In the original, GOOG was trading for roughly $395 per share and now it's at $299 per share. I've included put options again with a

Last: 299.67   Prev: 298.99   High: 308.25   Date: Jan16
Change: + 0.68   TSize: 100   Low: 295.70   Time: 20:00

Symbol	BSize	Bid	Ask	ASize	Last	Change	Prev	Imp Vol(B)	Imp Vol(A)
MAR09 210.00	33	3.80	4.00	46	3.90	-0.60	4.50	69.96	70.99
MAR09 220.00	33	4.90	5.20	134	5.70	-1.40	7.10	67.94	69.23
MAR09 230.00	33	6.30	6.60	124	6.40	-1.06	7.46	66.16	67.27
MAR09 240.00	33	8.00	8.30	131	8.30	-0.90	9.20	64.41	65.38
MAR09 250.00	44	10.00	10.30	34	10.20	-0.50	10.70	62.58	63.44
MAR09 260.00	61	12.40	12.80	48	13.47	-1.23	14.70	60.85	61.87
MAR09 270.00	57	15.30	15.70	39	15.50	-1.55	17.05	59.32	60.26
MAR09 280.00	56	18.70	19.10	13	19.04	-1.96	21.00	57.88	58.75
MAR09 290.00	46	22.60	23.00	13	23.07	-1.33	24.40	56.42	57.26
MAR09 300.00	10	27.20	27.60	34	26.95	-1.55	28.50	55.32	56.13
MAR09 310.00	34	32.20	32.70	34	32.30	-0.74	33.04	53.90	54.91
MAR09 320.00	34	37.90	38.40	23	39.60	+ 1.30	38.30	52.77	53.79
MAR09 330.00	10	44.20	44.60	13	46.50	+ 0.20	46.30	51.74	52.59
MAR09 340.00	54	50.90	51.50	24	49.60	-2.60	52.20	50.42	51.77
MAR09 350.00	54	58.20	58.90	34	58.50	-2.80	61.30	49.28	51.00
MAR09 360.00	54	66.10	66.70	13	63.60	0.00	63.60	48.50	50.14
MAR09 360.00	10	0.70	0.95	10	0.00	0.00	0.00	0.00	0.00
MAR09 370.00	33	74.40	75.10	24	77.70	+ 3.80	73.90	47.72	49.89
MAR09 370.00	10	0.70	0.95	10	0.00	0.00	0.00	0.00	0.00
MAR09 380.00	54	83.00	83.90	13	83.00	-3.50	86.50	46.76	49.97
MAR09 380.00	10	0.75	1.00	10	0.00	0.00	0.00	0.00	0.00
MAR09 390.00	23	92.10	92.90	23	96.50	-0.50	97.00	46.63	49.95

Figure 3.11   GOOG Option Chain, March 2009 Expiration
Source: eSignal.com.

$180 range between strike prices, with the lowest strike being about $90 OTM—we can compare strike prices this way that are the same distance from the current price of the stock that existed at the time.

What we can decipher about the differences, besides the obvious of GOOG being about $100 cheaper now, is that the implied volatility levels are higher now than in 2006. Has that affected the actual dollar cost of the options? Let's take a look.

If you look at the lowest strikes in Figures 3.9 and 3.11 ($310 versus $210) in the chains and the corresponding Implied Volatility (B) and Implied Volatility (A) columns, you'll notice that the March 2009 options are about 18 percent higher than the May 2006 options. This has made the actual bid and ask prices for the March 2009 $210 put options $1.35 higher than the actual bid and ask prices for the May 2006 $310 put options. Since both options are roughly $90 OTM and have the same amount of time before expiration, this is a fair way to compare how volatility is affecting them.

Let's look at the ATM options for each. The March 2009 $300 put options have about 14 percent to 15 percent higher implied volatility (IV) levels built in to them compared to the May 2006 $395 put options (take an average of the $390 and $400 put options). This difference in volatility has made the March 2009 $300 put options about $3 more expensive than the May 2006 $395 put options (averaging out the $390 and $400 put options). So once again, we see that different volatility levels have a direct effect on option prices.

If the skew concept is confusing you, take a look at the next chart. Sometimes it's easier to understand when seen graphically as in Figure 3.12.

Figure 3.12 is an IV skew chart of a random security. The strike prices are along the bottom and the volatility levels are on the sides. This is a typical "smiling skew," which incorporates both a reverse skew (which we talked about earlier) and a "forward skew." A forward skew develops when the higher-strike options have an increasingly larger IV. This particular security is trading for about $28.50, and its at-the-money (ATM) options are the cheapest on an IV basis. As you move higher and lower with its strike prices, the IV gets larger in

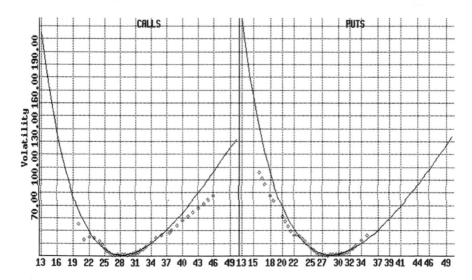

Figure 3.12   Volatility Smiling Skew Chart

Source: Chart provided by Optionetics, Inc.

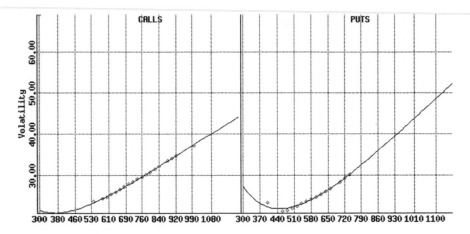

Figure 3.13 Forward Skew Pattern
Source: Chart provided by Optionetics, Inc.

both directions. The little squares are the actual IV of each strike. The solid line is basically a connect-the-dots line to show you the pattern.

Figure 3.13 is a graph of a forward skew pattern. This is very typical for the soybean market, especially during the summer growing months. Soybeans trade with IV levels getting higher as you move up in the strike prices. This is mostly due to the weather factor. Since there are chances that dry summers can produce potential droughts and a reduced supply of soybeans, investors tend to favor buying upside protection, which causes more interest in the upside strikes. Soybean prices can go as high as conditions allow, so the option market makers protect themselves by bumping up the IV on the upside strikes, which enables them to collect more money for those options.

Figure 3.14 depicts the typical reverse skew, which is commonplace in the stock indexes. We all know that when the stock market sells off in general, the downside put options begin to attract a lot of attention and volume. The lower you go in strike prices, the higher the IV becomes. The chart in Figure 3.14 sums it up.

I feel it is imperative that you check the option's skew pattern before initiating any kind of option spread to see what kind of potential volatility edge you may be able to capture. This doesn't mean that you can't put on the play even if the skew is unfavorable. Just know

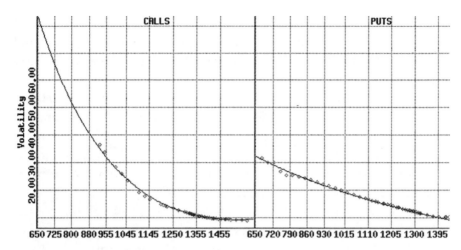

Figure 3.14 Reverse Skew Pattern

Source: Chart provided by Optionetics, Inc.

that you will be starting at a volatility disadvantage if you do. Even though this concept may seem confusing, it is a good subject to learn. Implied volatility is alive and well in the options market, and it is the primary basis for my own trading decisions.

EARNINGS DUD?

One last concept about volatility that many of you may have encountered. Have you ever bought call or put options right before a stock was about to have its earnings announced? I'm sure many of you thought that buying options as a form of leverage and speculation would be a good strategy, because the uncertainty of the earnings could cause a large move in the price of the stock.

What ended up happening to your options? I'll bet in most cases the options lost value (or didn't go up in value) even though the stock moved in the direction that you predicted.

What happens in this case? It's all due to volatility movement. The option market makers are very smart and sneaky. In the days leading up to the earnings announcement, the market makers are aware that speculators will enter the options market and start buying up options.

So the market makers will start bumping up the implied volatility of the options, which in turn starts making the options cost more and more each day, until they are finally priced extremely high on the day of the announcement.

Once the announcement has been made, you will experience what's called a *volatility implosion*—when the volatility of the options gets almost immediately repriced to the lower levels of preannouncement days. This large reduction in volatility brings down the price of all options, making it almost impossible to make a profit on the overpriced options you just bought the day before.

The option market makers are no dummies. They will reprice the options based on the level of uncertainty of the earnings announcement. They need to protect themselves and the only way to do that is to keep bumping up the price of the options.

So you may have bought call options in anticipation of the stock going up after the announcement. And even if the stock did go up, the options you bought may have been so overpriced to begin with that you had no chance to make a profit. You probably even saw your option go down in price even though the stock went up. This is volatility implosion at its most pronounced and another reason why you need to understand volatility.

SUMMARY

Let's sum up here what we've discussed about volatility as it applies to options trading. Volatility is a concept that describes a stock or commodity's propensity to move around in price, either on a historical basis or on a forward-looking basis. This movement is quantified into a percentage number that gets added into the option pricing formula as one of the determinants that make up an option's price.

We've seen that lowering or raising the volatility component has a direct effect on the price of an option. We've also seen that two different stocks that trade for the same price can have dramatically different option prices due to the volatility component. And lastly, we learned about volatility skew. This is a phenomenon where each individual option within an option chain will have its own volatility value, which may or may not be different from its neighboring option.

Volatility skews can take the shape of a reverse, flat, smiling, or forward pattern, and can be used to your advantage when initiating option spreads.

I hope this chapter has clarified some issues for you. I truly believe that understanding and applying volatility concepts to your own option trading will pay off handsomely in the future.

CHAPTER 4

STOCKS VERSUS OPTIONS

Before embarking on explaining the strategies that have helped me over the years, I need to emphasize the fact that options are different than stocks. Just because you think the stock is going to go up doesn't mean you can buy any old call option in the group. Options are sensitive not only to direction, but also to time left before expiration and how volatile the stock is. Stock trading is one-dimensional. Price is the only factor, and its direction is either up or down. Options are three-dimensional, and we need to take into consideration the three factors just mentioned—price, time, and volatility.

When you buy a stock, you have a cost-basis point. That point is whatever you paid for the stock plus commission. And you wait it out over the years to see how far the stock gets above (hopefully) your cost basis or breakeven price. You have the luxury of time. You can wait years if you like, or pass the stock down to your heirs if you wish. Stock options and commodity options are not like that. They all have a finite date of existence. If the stock or commodity price does not get above your breakeven by option expiration, you will lose money. So, the object of winning in the options market is to choose the best strike price that maximizes your probability of profit. That's what I'm going to show you how to do.

Before we can get into learning how to maximize our chances of winning, I want to reiterate what I said in a previous chapter about the relationship between the strike price of the option and the current price of the stock or commodity. This forms the basis of achieving the highest probability of profit with our options strategies. The next few paragraphs sum up the definitions of out-of-the-money (OTM), at-the-money (ATM), and in-the-money (ITM) options.

For call options, any option whose strike price is higher than the current price of the stock or commodity is considered out-of-the-money (OTM). For example, if INTC is at $20, then all strikes above $20 are OTM. Any strike that is priced near the current price of the stock is considered at-the-money (ATM). The INTC $20 strike would be considered ATM. Lastly, any call option strike price that is below the current price of the security is considered an in-the-money (ITM) call option. If INTC is at $20, all strikes below that would be ITM.

Put options are the opposite. Any option whose strike price is lower than the current price of the stock or commodity is considered OTM. For example, if INTC is at $20, then all strikes below $20 are OTM. Any strike that is priced near the current price of the stock is considered ATM. The INTC $20 strike would be considered ATM. Lastly, any put option strike price that is above the current price of the security is considered an ITM put option. If INTC is at $20, all strikes above that would be ITM. It's important to know these terms because each one will act differently due to the degree of the option being in-, at-, or out-of-the-money.

The whole idea and advantage of buying call options instead of paying for the stock is because of the amount of leverage you can get. With options, you only need to pay a fraction of what the stock would cost, yet you get to control the same amount of shares. Since one option contract is the equivalent of 100 shares of stock, you can theoretically control hundreds or thousands of shares of stock for just a few hundred dollars. But, even though you are now armed with this great leverage, you still need to know which strike prices will take the best advantage of that leverage.

Let's say you are interested in purchasing shares of Microsoft (MSFT). The current price is $27.50 per share. You can buy any amount of shares you like, but to compare how options can benefit you, let's concentrate on 100-share increments. Now, you can go out and buy 100 shares for your account and pay $2,750 up front, or if you trade on 50 percent margin, they would cost you $1,375. With the current price and your cost basis being $27.50, the maximum you could lose is your investment of $2,750, and your potential gain is unlimited to the upside.

If you want to try your hand at call options, you need to decide which strike price and which expiration month to choose. Many stocks have expiration months spanning from days, weeks, months, and years to option expiration. You just need to know how long you're willing to hold the investment. If you are willing to hold onto the stock for a long time, then you should tailor your option investment to the same time frame. LEAPS options are long-dated options that can expire up to three years into the future. You would want to concentrate on buying LEAPS call options if your investment horizon is that long. Later on in Chapter 6 when I talk about the deep-in-the-money (DITM) strategy, I'll show you how to incorporate LEAPS call options as well.

But for now, I want to show you a few scenarios in which you can purchase different strike prices for our MSFT position. We'll compare ITM and OTM options in this example. You'll see how the short-term OTM options are truly worthy of the "speculation" stigma. Not forgetting about our friend delta, I'm going to show you how it can become your best ally in terms of picking the type of trade with the highest probability of profit.

WHAT DO WE DO?

So, MSFT is at $27.50. What are we going to do? The first course of action is to check the option prices. If you're like many investors, you'd probably start looking at the option month that is closest to expiration because those contain the cheapest options based on actual dollar cost. Look at the option chain in Figure 4.1.

As this chapter was being written, the May 2006 options were the nearest to expiration. For some reason, when people turn to the options market, they lose all sense of prudence and want to try to hit the short-term lottery.

Since we are discussing options terminology, I want to revisit two of the most important of the Greeks concepts that will play a big role in the potential profitability of any option strategy that you choose.

Calls								
Symbol	Last	Chg	Bid	Ask	Imp. Vol	Delta	Strike	Syn
May 06 Calls			(31 days to expiration)				MSFT @ 27.22	
MQFEU	20.00	0	19.70	19.80		1.00	7.50	MQI
MQFEB	17.70	0	17.20	17.30		1.00	10.00	MQI
MQFEV	15.20	0	14.70	14.80		1.00	12.50	MQI
MQFEC	12.70	0	12.20	12.30		1.00	15.00	MQI
MQFEW	10.00	0	9.70	9.80		1.00	17.50	MQF
MQFED	7.50	0	7.20	7.40		1.00	20.00	MQI
MSQEX	4.40	-0.10	4.70	4.90		1.00	22.50	MS(
MSQEJ	2.40	+0.35	2.30	2.40	18.5	.95	25.00	MS!
MSQEY	0.40	+0.10	0.40	0.45	15.9	.46	27.50	MS(
MSQEK	0.05	0	0	0.05	18.3	.04	30.00	MS(
MSQEZ	0.05	0	0	0.05	30.4	.03	32.50	MS(

Figure 4.1   MSFT Option Chain, May 2006 Expiration
Source: optionsXpress.

The Greeks, as they apply to options trading, are five of the by-products of the option pricing model. They are delta, gamma, vega, theta, and rho. Each one is an indicator that lets you know your risk exposure to the market before, during, and after you have an option position in place. The two that I deem most important for everyday traders, and the ones we are going to concentrate on exclusively, are the delta and theta. I want to focus on delta first, as it plays a large role in the strategies I will discuss with you, and then I'll touch on theta in a later chapter.

THE DELTA FACTOR

There are a few definitions for delta, but the most commonly used is the one that describes the relationship between the option price's movement and the price movement of the stock or commodity. We all know that if we buy call or put options on Microsoft (MSFT), the option price should move as well. But do you know *how much* the option price will move? I think many traders mistakenly believe that the option price is going to move just as much as the stock moves. Not so. Many times the option price will not move at all, and sometimes it will move in the opposite direction even though the stock or commodity moved in the way you thought it would.

Delta is our best weapon in alerting us to how much the option price should theoretically move in conjunction with a move in the stock or commodity. The reason you buy a stock in the first place is to get some movement out of it, hopefully in the right direction. Don't you want that same movement from your option? Here's a little tip, and a preview of one of the upcoming chapters: **Buy options that have a 90 percent or greater delta.** That is a secret not many people know and one you will hardly ever hear from the mainstream option community.

When looking at the option chain in Figure 4.1, concentrate on the "Delta" column, as it will give you an idea of how responsive the option will be to any move in the stock. Make sure you always check the delta before buying an option. The whole point of investing or trading is to get movement in the right direction of your selected security. If you can buy the security more cheaply with less risk, then you should do so. That's where options come in to play. Buying options entails less up-front cost and less downside risk, but you also need to make sure that you're going to get movement from your option. Picking an option with a high delta assures you of that movement.

Let's look at a couple of scenarios and see what happens when we choose options with varying degrees of delta. We'll start with a cheap OTM option as that's what most people are drawn to. Using our MSFT option chain in Figure 4.1, we'll buy a $30 call for the least amount an option can trade for—a nickel; $5 is all that option will cost us. Remember, you must multiply the option price by the $100 multiplier to get your actual dollar cost ($.05 × $100 = $5). So, one $30 call option contract will cost us $5. We get to control 100 shares of MSFT until May 2006 for $5 while everyone else needs to shell out $2,722 to own 100 shares.

The only problem is that we won't start to make any money on the option until MSFT gets above our breakeven price of $30.05 ($30 strike price + $.05 option price = $30.05 breakeven) if held to option expiration. MSFT has to travel almost $3 higher in the next 31 days (at time

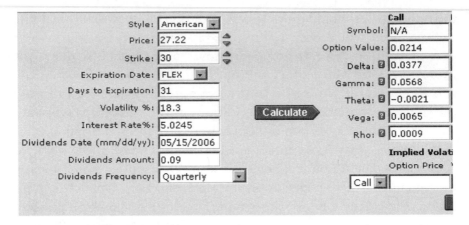

Figure 4.2 MSFT $30 Call Option Calculator
Source: Courtesy of www.ivolatility.com.

of this writing) before we see any significant results. Look at the delta of that $30 call in the option chain. It's a 4 percent delta. Now that's low. That's telling us that if MSFT were to move up $1 to $28.22, then the option would move only 4 percent, or roughly $.04 on our option. It would be worth about a dime and we'd make $5 on our option position while the stockholders would make $100 on their 100 shares. You don't believe me? Look at the two option calculators in Figures 4.2 and 4.3.

Here we've priced the $30 call with 31 days to option expiration with MSFT trading at $27.22. The calculator has given this option a

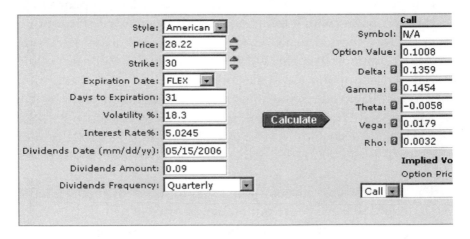

Figure 4.3 MSFT $30 Call
Source: Courtesy of www.ivolatility.com.

value of $.02, but since the minimum option price is $.05, then that's what we'll pay for it. It also has given it a delta value of .0377, which is roughly 4 percent as we saw in the optionsXpress chain (see Figure 4.1). Now, let's take MSFT up a dollar to $28.22. (See Figure 4.3.)

What do you know? With MSFT gaining a dollar in value to $28.22, our measly little $30 call is now worth only a dime, just like I said. See the option value of $.10? While all the stockholders made $100 on their shares, we made only $5 on our option. Not what you were expecting, was it? I know I would be a little disappointed if I saw MSFT spike up $1 per share and my option didn't gain any value to speak of.

Here's our trusty probability calculator again (Figure 4.4). It's going to show us our chances of MSFT getting above our breakeven price of $30.05 by option expiration.

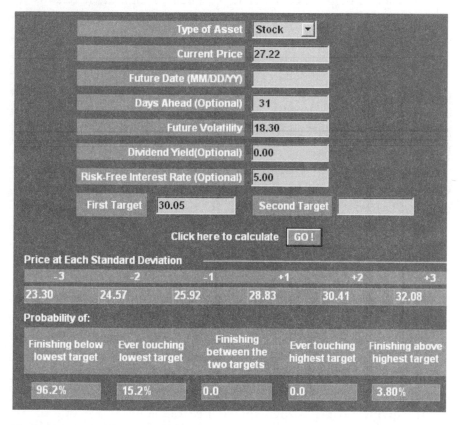

Figure 4.4 Probability Calculator
Source: © Copyright Optionvue Systems International, Inc.

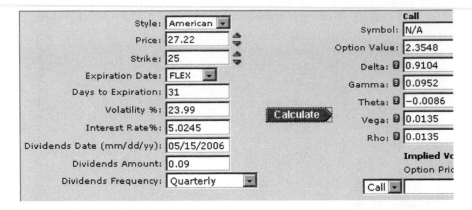

Figure 4.5 MSFT $25 Call
Source: Courtesy of www.ivolatility.com.

The bottom-right box is what we need to look at. It tells us we have a 3.8 percent chance of getting above our breakeven at expiration—not much chance (too low for my taste).

So how can we remedy that situation? Well, for starters, take my advice and buy higher-delta ITM options. Here's how. How about we purchase the $25 call for $2.35 (splitting bid/ask), which has a delta of 95 percent. Our new breakeven price would be $27.35, which is just barely higher than where MSFT is trading now. That's much better. Let's see what it's worth now and what it would be worth if MSFT went up a dollar again to $28.22. The 95 percent delta tells us that the option price should move about 95 percent of the move of the stock, or roughly $.95. (See Figure 4.5.)

The calculator agrees with the option chain that the $25 call is worth $2.35 with MSFT at $27.22 and with 31 days to option expiration. Now let's bump MSFT up to $28.22. (See Figure 4.6.)

There you go. The $25 call is now worth approximately $3.30, which is exactly $.95 higher than our starting point of $2.35. Delta really works. We got almost point for point movement with the stock, yet we only had to spend $235 for the option while all the stockholders had to spend $2,722—a great deal for us. That's a 40 percent return on the option versus a 3.7 percent return on the stock. What's the probability calculator saying? (See Figure 4.7.)

It's giving us a 49.6 percent chance of being above our breakeven at expiration—much higher than the $30 call. If you think about

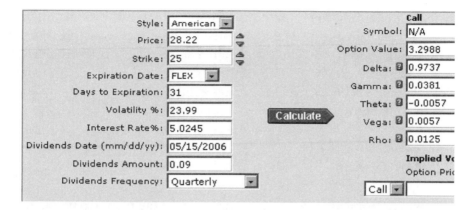

Figure 4.6   MSFT $25 Call

Source: Courtesy of www.ivolatility.com.

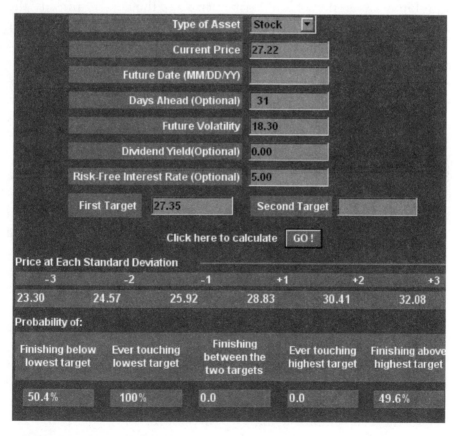

Figure 4.7   Probability Calculator

Source: © Copyright Optionvue Systems International, Inc.

it, that's practically the same odds as if you owned the stock, right? There's a 50 percent chance that you will be above your breakeven price on any given day when you own a stock. Our option purchase of the $25 call is giving us almost the same probability of profit as if we owned the stock, yet it cost us almost $2,500 less to buy the option. I like those qualities.

SUMMARY

The whole point of this chapter was to get you to understand that stocks and options are completely different investments. Options are much more complex than stocks and are very dependent on the relationship between the option's strike price and the current price of the stock. You need to concentrate on getting good movement from your option in order to obtain profitability. The best way to do that is to concentrate on picking options with higher deltas. There's no point in spending money on options if they're never going to move, even if they do cost you only a few bucks to buy them.

And I just want to make a point here in reference to the reviews I received about the title of this book not doing justice to the readers (remember I mentioned this in the Preface?).

This chapter shows you the first step to getting rich with options. Look at the money you will save by buying high-delta, deep-in-the-money (DITM) call options. In the example I just presented, you only had to spend $235 per option for the $25 call, versus spending $2,722 to buy 100 shares of stock.

Now with many people buying 1,000 shares of stock in a typical trade, the numbers get larger and you can see a real difference in your wallet. If you bought 1,000 shares of MSFT in this example, it would cost you $27,220, but the 10 options that you needed to make the equivalent position would cost you only $2,350—almost $25,000 less!

Look at the amount of money you're saving while getting all of the same benefits from the option position. You can take that $25,000 of savings and put it in the bank and have it earn interest. When we get to the chapter on buying DITM options, I will drive this fact home a bit more.

That's how you get rich with options.

CHAPTER 5

OPTION SELLING IS YOUR KEY TO SUCCESS

This might be my favorite chapter to write in the whole book as it's a precursor to the option-selling strategies that I will lay out for you in the following pages. I'm going to let you in on a closely guarded secret of many successful option traders. Selling options, when done correctly, can give you an overwhelming advantage in the marketplace. Don't confuse the strategy of "selling options" with taking a bearish directional position. They are totally unrelated. We're talking about selling options instead of buying options. This is the secret that I learned many years ago, and I will teach you the correct and safe way to do it. It is by far one of the best ways to put the probability of profit on your side. I sell options in 90 percent of my trades because of that high probability to win.

As you'll see in the subsequent chapters, a huge advantage for selling options rather than buying them is that picking the correct direction of the stock or commodity isn't the main driving force to being profitable. Sure, it's helpful to be able to get the direction right, but the trade can still produce a winner even if you're wrong on the direction.

The biggest downfall for most option buyers is that they just can't pick the correct direction in the time allotted for their option trade, or they get the direction completely wrong from the outset. Selling options gives you a huge margin for error in your directional assessment. I can't impress this fact upon you enough. So many option traders rely on their directional guess as the only way to give them a profitable trade in the time allotted. As I've shown, that is an extremely hard task to accomplish with options. I'm here to tell you that selling options gives you the most fabulous way to get around that obstacle. You can't get that outcome when buying options.

Another major enemy of the option buyer, and one that works in favor of the seller, is the concept of "time decay." As an option buyer, whether it's a stock option or a commodity option, time decay is one obstacle that you have to face every day. Time decay is a characteristic of options that describes the erosion of its price, causing it to lose a little bit of its value day after day after day, regardless of whether the underlying stock or commodity moves at all. This is especially evident in the at-the-money (ATM) and out-of-the-money (OTM) options. When you buy an ATM or OTM option, you are paying for something that has no real, or intrinsic, value to it. You are buying something that is entirely priced on the value of volatility and the amount of time left before expiration. As each day passes and the option is still not in-the-money, its premium will be repriced to a lower amount (all else being constant). The less time to be profitable, the smaller that option's price will be. This is time decay in action. If you're a longtime option trader you may be aware of this issue, but many novice traders don't understand this concept.

Earlier, I had mentioned the Greek concept called theta. Theta gives us the dollar amount of the daily time decay for each option. When we get into the strategies on option selling, you'll see how time decay is a major part of their success, and the cause of failure for many option buyers. An option will lose just a little bit of its value every day. If it's worth $2.75 today, then it probably will be worth $2.70 tomorrow (all else being constant). There's no way around that fact.

To see how time decay works, let's run through an example. Suppose currently IBM is at $77 per share and you're bullish, so you opt to buy an $85 call that expires in roughly four months. What you're doing is paying a little bit of money today in the form of the option premium in exchange for the chance that IBM will go above $85 per share before expiration. Since that option has no real value to it yet (no intrinsic value), the option premium is made up entirely of volatility and time. A typical price for that $85 OTM call might be $.75.

So let's say your option price starts at $.75 and you have four months before expiration. IBM starts waffling around in a price range between $75 and $80, with a dip down to $72 and a rise up to $82. Is that option worth anything yet? Yes and no. It still has a price to it but it's still OTM with no real value to it.

Two months go by and IBM is still at $77 per share. That option might be worth $.25 now. You've lost $.50 in option value just because of the passage of time. IBM hasn't really gone anywhere, so your option is losing its value. There's less of a chance now that IBM will get past $85 per share. Even if IBM goes up to $84 per share by expiration, your option will still expire worthless because IBM didn't get above $85. Actually, you need IBM to go above $85.75, as that is what your cost basis would be ($85 strike price + $.75 option price = $85.75 cost basis).

Let's plug those numbers into a real option calculator and see how close we were to those figures. (See Figure 5.1.)

In the calculator, we have our inputs on the left-hand side. We've priced out the IBM October 2006 $85 call option, which has 114 days left until expiration. The outputs on the right-hand side give us an initial value of $.70 for the $85 call with a theta of −.01. The theta number tells us that from this moment in time, the $85 call option is

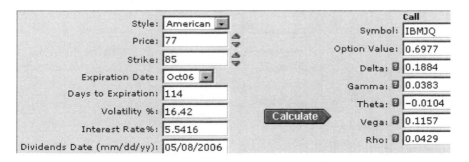

Figure 5.1 IBM Option Calculator, 114 Days to Expiration
Source: Courtesy of www.ivolatility.com.

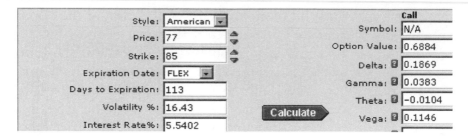

Figure 5.2   IBM Option Calculator, 113 Days to Expiration
Source: Courtesy of www.ivolatility.com.

going to lose about $1 a day (–.01 × $100 multiplier). If the option costs us $.70 ($70 in actual dollars) today, then tomorrow it will be worth roughly $.69 ($69). (See Figure 5.2.)

And after two months, in Figure 5.3 we see that our $85 call option has lost more than 75 percent of its value, just as we predicted (all else being constant).

Can you see how time decay works? It's like an ice cube melting away while it's sitting on the counter. If something doesn't happen fast (like putting it back in the freezer, or IBM moving higher in price quickly), the ice cube and the IBM option will slowly melt away until they've expired worthless. The option will truly be worth something only if it gets above the breakeven level (if held to expiration). The forces of time are stripping away a little bit of its value every day.

Figure 5.4 is an industry standard chart—the Time Decay Curve. This can explain what happens to option prices (more pronounced with OTM options) as they get closer to expiration. In this nine-month

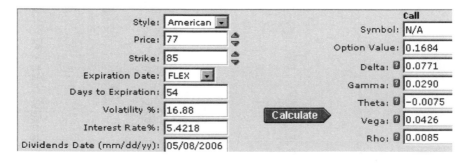

Figure 5.3   IBM Option Calculator, 54 Days to Expiration
Source: Courtesy of www.ivolatility.com.

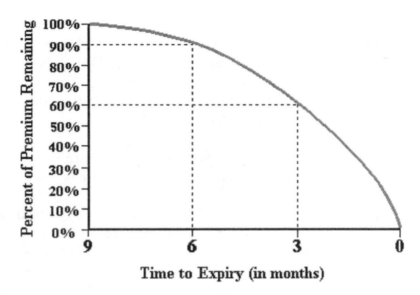

Figure 5.4 Time Decay Curve
Source: Courtesy of www.deltainterval.com.

chart, we see that in the first three months, from nine months to six months, time decay erodes only 10 percent of the option's price; it will then erode 30 percent from month six to month three, and then the last three months takes up the majority of the erosion— 60 percent! It is also known in the options industry that the last 30 days of an option's life are the most time decay intensive. You will see an option lose the rest of its time value during this period. This is a definite occurrence, whether the stock price moves or not. Time marches on, and it will **always** strip away the time value portion (extrinsic value) of the option. If you are an option buyer, the time decay works against your position. Option sellers have time decay on their side.

HOW TO BATTLE TIME DECAY

So is there a way to get around time decay when buying options? Absolutely. In short, my advice is to always buy in-the-money (ITM) options, and I devote Chapter 6 to a strategy that deals with that specific topic. ITM options have intrinsic (real) value already built into them and are the ones with the lowest amount of daily time decay, so they will suffer the smallest loss due to the passage of time. ITM options will always cost more in total dollars, but you'll still be paying less for them than you would if you bought the stock outright.

Even though time decay is a major reason why many option traders lose money, I still believe the investing public gravitates toward buying options instead of selling them. Here are my thoughts on why:

- Option selling can entail unlimited risk. That is true, but certain option selling strategies don't entail unlimited risk, especially the ones I will teach you.
- A good portion of brokerage firms don't really understand the true risks of options, and if they're confronted with someone who wants to sell them, the brokerages shy away and tell the customer it's too risky.
- The mainstream media mostly understands the buying side of options. The unlimited reward, limited risk appeal of buying options is highly touted as the only way to play the game.

These reasons apply to the general investing retail public—the everyday joes out there. These are the people I'm aiming to reach with this book. I want to show that trading options doesn't need to be highly skewed to the buy side.

Example: What made you buy that OTM stock option in the first place? Was it because your friend gave you a hot tip? Was it because you knew that buying options costs only a few dollars? Or was it because you were looking to try to "hit the big one"? Regardless of the reasons, you probably have found by now that most of the options you've bought have ended up expiring worthless. Why is that? Here's my guess:

- You bought the option too far out-of-the money.
- You didn't give yourself a long enough option expiration period.
- You picked the wrong direction.
- You might have bought overpriced options based on implied volatility.

These are a lot of obstacles to overcome. I believe that being successful with option buying is one of the hardest games in town.

Option trading isn't easy. You have to juggle all these components to work in your favor at the same time. Most people are not that adept at picking the right direction, time, strike price, and volatility all in one trade. You may have seen in the past that you were right on your directional call, but the option expired before the stock made that move. Or the stock moved in the right direction in the time allotted, but your strike price was too far out-of-the-money to become profitable. These are some of the things that can go wrong when buying options.

When you buy a stock, you have an indefinite period of time to be right on your prediction. You don't have to worry about the stock expiring on you. You also have one price point to worry about—the price at which you bought the stock. You don't need the stock to move a certain distance (to your option breakeven price) just to be profitable as you would when buying out-of-the-money options.

My objective for this chapter is to compare option buying versus option selling and explain why I believe option selling, when done correctly, is a far superior way to profit in the option market. Don't get me wrong—option buying certainly has its place. I buy option contracts from time to time, but in my book there's only one way to do it: **with DITM options**.

PROBABILITIES

One thing that many option buyers tend to forget is that option trading is a game of probabilities. Option pricing is based on mathematical and statistical models. You can figure out ahead of time the exact level of probability that your option has of being profitable. I bet many of you didn't know that. Once you're able to see how low your chances are of being profitable when buying options, you might never buy those cheap out-of-the-money options again.

And talking about probabilities of winning, did you know that an option buyer has only one way to win with an options trade? That's right. The stock or commodity has to move in the right direction in the time allotted for you to see a profit. There's no other way. But for the option seller, there are actually three scenarios for you to be profitable. As I'll show you in the option-selling strategies, you can be profitable if the market moves higher, moves lower, or stays flat.

That's three scenarios in which you can be profitable. Compare that to the buyer who has only one situation to be right and you'll soon see why option selling can be one of your main keys to success.

In addition to knowing that option sellers have three profitable scenarios, we can actually see the overall probability of profit from the outset of the trade. How do we do that? With a probability calculator, of course. After looking at the snapshot of the probability calculator in Figure 5.5, you might think twice in the future before purchasing that option.

In this example, you're buying a $35 call option for $.50 that expires in 60 days. As of today, the stock is trading at $31. The call option is OTM by $4. What are your chances of having a successful trade if you hold the option to expiration? Look at the bottom

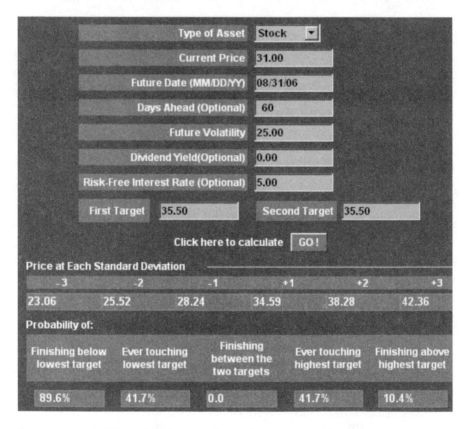

Figure 5.5 Probability Calculator

Source: © Copyright Optionvue Systems International, Inc.

right-hand box. Your chance of at least breaking even on the trade is 10.4 percent. Breakeven is $35.50 (strike price + option premium). That doesn't even give you a profit. If you want to show a profit, you need the stock to be *higher* than $35.50, which would reduce your chances of profitability even more.

At this moment in time, you have only a 10.4 percent chance of breaking even. Are those high enough odds for you? Who wants to risk money on a trade that has only a 10.4 percent chance of winning? Not me. You might be thinking, "But it's only $50 wasted if it expires worthless." Right, but if that's how you approach every trade, you're more likely to lose that $50 every time. That can add up to a 100 percent loss of your investment.

Now, if you didn't plan on holding the trade to expiration and thought that you might unwind the trade early, then you might be interested in the box that reads, "Ever touching highest target." You'll see that the probability of the stock hitting the breakeven of $35.50 at any point during the next 60 days is 41.7 percent. That's actually not too bad, to tell you the truth. But in my experience, too many people opt to hold an option trade to expiration so they can hopefully see a maximum gain. People like to hold onto that last bit of hope that their investment will not let them down.

We're going to be the ones who take the other side of those low-probability trades. Our chance of winning if the option is held to expiration is 89.6 percent. It's exactly the opposite of the buyer's chance of winning. That's sweet. And getting back to the three possible scenarios for the option seller to win, all we need is for the market to **NOT** go above $35.50 and we win. So, the market can move lower from where it is now, it can stay at the same level, and it can actually go up, too, but not past $35.50. There are your three scenarios right there. The option buyer has only one way to be right—for the market to go up past $35.50 by expiration. It looks like 3:1 odds in favor of the seller. This is the basic theme of the option-selling strategies that I'm about to present to you.

But let me also say something to you: I don't want to make you think that option selling is the end-all, be-all of option strategies— because it's definitely not. Option-selling strategies just happen to be the right strategies for me based on years of experience and observing losses of other less-informed option traders. I want you to learn these strategies to give yourselves a better opportunity to succeed in the options markets. Feel free to use any tactic you want in addition to what I show you.

My one piece of advice for any option buyer, specifically OTM option buyers, is: **DON'T HOLD THE OPTION TO EXPIRATION. SELL THE OPTION WHEN YOU HAVE A PROFIT!** This is sage advice coming from years' worth of option trading experience. Don't be complacent and don't be lazy or greedy. Take the profit when you can. Too many people opt to hold the position to expiration only to see all their gains wiped out due to time decay. Don't be one of those people. As I mentioned back in Chapter 1, when looking at the probability calculator, concentrate on the box that says, "Ever touching highest target." This is one of your best keys to profiting when buying options. Take the profit when you get it.

OPTION SELLING PREREQUISITE

One thing that you must know ahead of time before you implement option-selling techniques: You **DO** need to have an initial directional call. If you don't have a plan, or some kind of trading methodology to give you a directional call, you might as well throw darts at the board. The main advantage of the option-selling techniques that I show you entails using out-of-the-money options. That's the key. Selling OTM options gives you the ultimate directional cushion. But like I said, you need to have somewhat of a directional bias first to get you going on the trade.

I've gone on and on about the benefits of option selling, but some of you might be wondering exactly how an option seller makes money. Good question. The option seller is the person who collects the money straight from the option buyer. We take that money and it gets deposited right into our trading accounts. The goal of the option seller is to be able to keep all that money. The way that we do this is by having all the options expire worthless. The only profit an option seller can generate is the amount of money received up front from the buyer. Remember, the option seller's maximum gain is what he or she receives from the buyer. The option seller can't make any more than that. So, the ultimate goal of the seller is to have time pass so the option's time value will melt away. If the OTM option expires worthless, the option seller gets to keep the cash. Or, the option seller can always buy the option back, hopefully at a cheaper price.

If the option expires worthless, the seller doesn't need to spend an extra commission to offset the trade. Brokers do not charge you another commission if your option expires worthless (if they do, it might be time to find another broker). Note: Some of you may be silent victims of your broker charging you up front for both a buy and a sale of an option contract even though it may expire worthless. When I get to Chapter 13 about brokers, I'll let you in on this secret. It's a big one.

We're ready to move on to Part Two of the book. The rest of the chapters will go over in great detail the option strategies that will put you well on your way to achieving greater financial security and freedom. Enjoy.

PART TWO

THE STRATEGIES

CHAPTER 6

BUY ALL
THE STOCK YOU
WANT FOR HALF
THE PRICE

Before we dive into my three favorite option-selling techniques, I want to show you the one and only option-buying strategy that I wholeheartedly recommend for acting as a substitution for buying stock. I would play the market no other way when wanting to have full-blown exposure to the stock of my choice. So sit back and listen, as this is strategy #1. It falls into the "speculation" category, because let's face it, anytime you buy a stock, you're doing exactly that.

If you're a stock buyer, you're going to love reading this chapter. I'm going to show you a fantastic way to buy into any stock you want for as much as 50 percent off the going price while taking on half as much risk. It's an options strategy, but probably one that you've never considered before. Building on my 17 years of experience as a professional options trader, I can still find no better way to buy into the stock market than the strategy I'm about to show you, whether it's the purchase of an individual stock or a play on the market as a whole.

This strategy will allow you to spend less cash up front, give you less downside risk, and still allow you to participate in all the same movement as you would if you owned the stock outright. Out of all the option-buying strategies in existence, this is the only one that I will allocate a majority of my funds to when appropriate. We are going to substitute long call options in place of long stock. Let's get to it!

As I've stated many times, most investors who try their hand at options will opt to purchase the cheap, out-of-the-money (OTM) options that have short life expectancies. These investors are buying options that have a very small probability of payoff and a short time frame to reap those potential benefits. They want to take their chance at a lottery type of trade and hope for the big payoff. OTM options are the ones that have their strike prices well away from the current price of the stock. For OTM call options, the strike prices are much higher than where the stock happens to be right now.

As an example, here's the type of trade I'm referring to. You're bullish on Microsoft stock (MSFT). It's currently trading at $25 per share. You think it might go up to $30 over the next three months and you want to buy some call options on it. What do you do? Many investors would choose a $30 call, which is $5 out-of-the-money. This three-month option can typically cost roughly $.10 per option contract (that's $10 in real dollars with the option multiplier). "Wow," you think, "that's great—only $10 to control 100 shares of MSFT for three months." Sure, it's great. Any investment that costs $10 to potentially yield you unlimited profits is terrific. But you have to remember to consider the probability of reaping that reward. That $30 call option typically has less than a 10 percent chance of ever reaching your breakeven point by expiration.

You did consider what it will take to reach your breakeven point, didn't you? Do you even know what your breakeven point is for this option trade? Once again, in order to find your breakeven point with an option trade, you must add the option premium to the strike price of the option. You're buying the $30 call, which costs $.10, so your breakeven price is $30.10.

Let's see what our trusty probability calculator has to say about the true odds of reaching that level. (See Figure 6.1.)

A typical probability calculator like the one in Figure 6.1 takes into consideration all the parameters that exist at the time of the trade

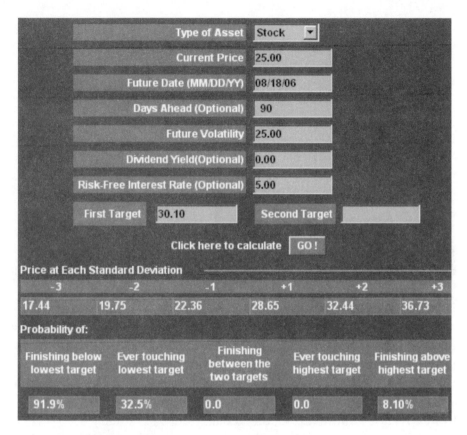

Figure 6.1 Probability Calculator

Source: © Copyright Optionvue Systems International, Inc.

and gives us a glimpse of how high (or low) our chances are of reaching a desired level. This is a great little tool for estimating ahead of time the likelihood of having a successful trade. We've inserted our MSFT parameters into the input section at the top. We want to see what our chances are of our 90-day, $30 call reaching our breakeven price of $30.10.

Our chances are not too high, according to the calculator. Our target price is $30.10. If we look at the bottom right box that says "Finishing above highest target," we see that we have only an 8.10 percent chance of getting there by option expiration in 90 days. That doesn't always mean that we won't be successful, but it does mean that our chances are low at that very moment in time based on the input criteria. Just know that 8.10 percent probability just gets us to our breakeven; no profits occur at that level. We need to get *above* the breakeven level to see extra money in our pocket. Anything above $30.10 will give us an even lower probability.

So while every stock buyer has been able to purchase MSFT for $25 per share, we're essentially waiting to purchase MSFT at $30.10 per share. We're buying something today that has no real value yet. We're contracting to buy MSFT at $5 higher than everyone else. Sure, it's costing us only $10 today per option contract to do the trade, but if MSFT moves from $25 to $30, we won't be fully participating in that big move (if it happens). Here's why:

Since we bought a very cheap OTM option, its price will not move in lockstep with the stock. It's going to move just a tiny fraction. This is when investors get very upset with options trading because they think that the option they bought should be exploding. It doesn't happen with those cheapie options.

Delta, which we talked about earlier (and will be explained in more detail in this chapter), tells us how much the option price should move in relation to how much the stock moves. A 90-day option like the $30 call will have an initial delta of maybe 10 percent. That means the option will only gain roughly 10 cents (10 percent) for every dollar that MSFT moves. If MSFT moves up $5, theoretically our call should gain 50 cents, depending on how fast or slow the move occurs. This is not the kind of payout we were hoping for, especially when all the stockholders got to participate in that full move. And to top it off, that $5 move higher **must** happen rather quickly if we want to see any appreciation at all to our option contract. We have only three months to be right.

What was our reasoning for buying the option instead of buying the stock? Were we looking to just take a long shot, or did we really want to own MSFT? If so, why didn't we just buy the shares instead? I'll tell you why. When it comes to investing, most people try to get things cheap. They don't want to pay full price. Maybe we didn't have $2,500 free cash to buy 100 shares of MSFT. There's nothing wrong with buying call options as long as you know ahead of time your risk, reward, and probability of profit.

The mentality of many investors is that options are used for speculation and gambling purposes only. Sure, you can play it that way, but that's certainly not the only way to use options. It's not the way that I use options. Yes, every once in a while I'll take the highflier, but generally I use options to generate income and to reduce my risk. So, if you really want to own MSFT stock, then listen up. Here's the best way to do it.

WHY PAY $2,289 FOR SOMETHING WHEN YOU CAN BUY IT FOR $1,120?

That's a great question, and for the life of me I still can't figure out why people are doing it. Because I've been in the option trading business for 17 years, I get asked which stock people should buy, or what I think of a stock they recently purchased. I usually decline when asked to comment on a stock for someone, but I know I can get more bang for my buck by purchasing a stock's call options instead of buying the stock outright, *if done correctly*. That's why I immediately go into my speech about how buying call options is superior to buying a stock outright, not only because it will cost less, but also because there is less downside risk as well.

My modus operandi has always been about how I can save money on everything I do. It's just a smarter way to use my cash, and if there is a way to buy exactly what I want for a cheaper price, then for sure I'm going to do it. That includes comparison shopping, clipping coupons, using employee discounts, buying on eBay, and, sure enough, buying stock call options instead of actual stock.

How do we pay $1,120 for something that's worth $2,289 and end up with the same product with less risk? In the financial world, that problem is solved by using stock options instead of actual stock. But you have to use a certain strategy. And that strategy is **buying deep-in-the-money (DITM) call options**. That's your golden ticket for substituting call options versus buying the stock.

The benefits of the DITM strategy are amazing. Not only are we going to get all the same movement as if we had bought the stock, but our downside risk is slashed in half. How great is that? The reason for buying a stock in the first place is to gain price appreciation. Why not invest half as much money in the play to reap the same reward? Not only will you save 50 percent or more on the investment, but that just leaves you with more money to spread around on other opportunities.

Let's look at the mechanics of the DITM strategy in Figure 6.2.

Calls								
Symbol	Last	Chg	Bid	Ask	Imp. Vol	Delta	Strike	Syn
Jan 07 Calls			(246 days to expiration)				MSFT @ 22.89	
MQFAM	11.10	0	11.10	11.20		1.00	12.00	MQI
MQFAC	8.20	0	8.20	8.40		1.00	15.00	MQI
MQFAO	6.40	0	6.40	6.60	22.0	.97	17.00	MQI
MQFAP	4.40	+0.20	4.20	4.40	21.9	.88	19.50	MQ
MQFAD	3.80	0	3.80	4.00	21.8	.85	20.00	MQI
MQFAQ	2.40	+0.05	2.40	2.50	20.8	.70	22.00	MQI
MSQAX	2.10	−0.02	2.15	2.20	21.1	.65	22.50	MS(
MSQAR	1.13	+0.03	1.10	1.20	19.9	.45	24.50	MS(
MSQAJ	0.95	+0.10	0.90	1.00	19.6	.40	25.00	MS(
MSQAS	0.40	−0.02	0.40	0.45	19.0	.22	27.00	MS(
MSQAY	0.35	0	0.30	0.40	19.1	.19	27.50	MS(
MSQAT	0.10	0	0.10	0.15	18.4	.08	29.50	MS(
MSQAK	0.15	0	0.10	0.15	19.4	.08	30.00	MS(
MSQAA	0.05	−0.05	0.05	0.10	21.0	.05	32.00	MS(

Figure 6.2   Option Chain for MSFT, January 2007 Expiration
Source: www.OptionsXpress.com.

During the trading day of May 18, 2006, MSFT was trading at $22.89, as seen at the top of the option chain. Anyone who wanted to buy 100 shares of MSFT would pay a total of $2,289. The total risk in this trade will be $2,289. Our breakeven price is $22.89. Anything above $22.89 is profit; anything below $22.89 is a loss (excluding commissions).

MOVEMENT IS THE KEY

When you buy a stock, you want movement in an upward direction. We're going to use the DITM strategy to give us that movement but with less of an up-front cost. In essence, we're using the call options as a proxy for the stock. The option chain in Figure 6.2 lists some of the available call options for MSFT with an expiration date of January 2007, about eight months away. Looking at the "Bid" and "Ask" columns, you could buy the $12 call for $11.20. In dollar terms, that's an investment of $1,120 if you buy this option. That's more than 50 percent cheaper than buying MSFT shares outright. Our total downside risk in this case is $1,120, which is what it cost us to buy the option. Our breakeven, or cost basis, on this trade is $23.20. Remember, in order to find the breakeven price, we must add the option premium of $11.20 to the strike price of $12, which equals $23.20. Our breakeven price with the option is $.31 higher than if we actually bought the shares outright. Not a big deal. We need to look at the advantages to buying the option:

- It cost us less in actual dollars to buy it—$1,169 less to be exact, more than 50 percent cheaper than buying the stock.
- Our total downside risk is only $1,120.

One of our biggest advantages is that we'll get to participate in the same amount of movement that MSFT makes—a high delta.

Some of you might be thinking, "Well, I still have to pay $1,120 to buy those call options. That's a lot of money. If I bought the $27 strike calls, I'd only have to pay $45. I thought the whole point of buying options was to get a great bargain." Okay, let's step back for a minute. Assuming you really want to buy MSFT, what are your choices?

- Buy 100 shares of MSFT for an investment outlay of $2,289.
- Buy one DITM call option for an investment outlay of $1,120.

How much more of a bargain are you looking for? If 50 percent off the retail price isn't good enough, then I don't know what is. If you bought the $27 call options for $45, what are your delta, probability, and movement going to be? You're going to get only a fraction of the movement that MSFT makes. But with the DITM $12 call, you're going to get all the same movement. Here's how.

DELTA IS YOUR WEAPON

The beauty of buying options is the leverage you get. Leverage is just a fancy word that describes a way of buying something large for very little money. That's how options work. You pay less money up front in the form of the option premium and then you get to control 100 percent of the stock. Since one stock option contract represents 100 shares of stock, you get to control all those shares for a fraction of the cost. But you must know how to use that leverage. Your biggest leverage play is with buying OTM options. They cost only a few dollars. But we've seen that your probability of profit is very low with those and can prevent us from regularly pulling gains from the market. The DITM strategy uses leverage as well. But, we're also going to get all the movement that the stock makes. How do we know that? Delta, baby!

Look back to the option chain at the column labeled "Delta." That number tells us percentage-wise how much the option price will move in conjunction with a move in the underlying stock. The $12 call is giving us a delta of 100 percent. That means the option will move practically penny for penny with the stock. If MSFT moves up $.50, the $12 call should increase in value by $.50 as well (give or take a few pennies). The OTM $27 call has a delta of only 22 percent, not high enough for us smart options traders.

DELTA IN ACTION

Take a look at the next few snapshots in Figures 6.3 through 6.5.

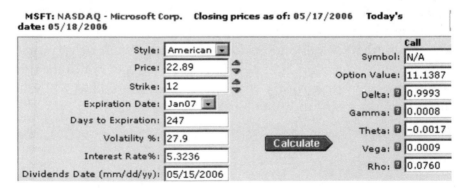

Figure 6.3 Option Calculator
Source: Courtesy of www.ivolatility.com.

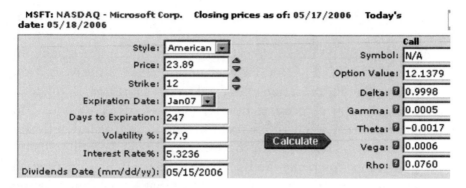

Figure 6.4   Option Calculator

Source: Courtesy of www.ivolatility.com.

These images are typical option calculators that can be found at one of my favorite options-related web sites: www.ivolatility.com. They have a wealth of information with regard to stock options. I highly recommend using them for the free data they provide.

In the first calculator we have priced out the MSFT January 2007 $12 call option based on the data we used earlier. Along the left-hand side of the calculator is the input section. We've manually inserted the price of $22.89 with a strike price of $12 and an expiration period of January 2007. The rest of the inputs are default settings used by IVolatility.com.

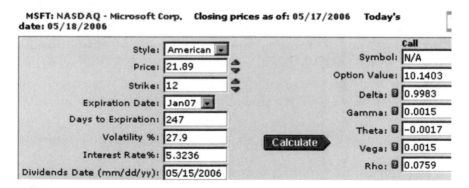

Figure 6.5   Option Calculator

Source: Courtesy of www.ivolatility.com.

On the right-hand side of the calculator is the output section. We're getting a value of $11.13 for the $12 strike call option, which matches what the market priced it at within the option chain. In our example, we paid $11.20 for that option. Here's the key: Look at the delta value in the option chain and in the calculator. Both are at approximately 100 percent. It doesn't get any better than that in terms of movement. The 100 percent delta tells us that the option is going to move in lockstep with the stock in terms of pricing. That's what you want. You want the option that you purchase to have all the same movement that the stock has. And that's what you're going to get.

Look at the second option calculator (Figure 6.4). I've taken the price of MSFT up one dollar to $23.89 per share in the input section. Now look at the output section. Our $12 call is priced at $12.13. It has gone up in value by a dollar as well. Sweet! That's delta working for you. In case you're wondering what can happen on a down move, look at the third graphic (Figure 6.5). We've taken MSFT down a dollar to $21.89. Our option has moved down a dollar as well to $10.14. It works both ways. But you have to remember the four benefits of buying the option instead of the stock:

1. Less money invested—$1,120 versus $2,289.
2. Less downside risk—$1,120 versus $2,289.
3. About 100 percent of the movement.
4. Higher return on investment (ROI)—more leverage.

You need to get over the fact that the DITM option will cost you more in total dollars than a cheapie, highflier OTM option. You're not here to do that. You're here because you want to invest in a stock. The best way to get all the same movement as you would with a stock is to buy a DITM call option. Period. Just remember, the option *will* always cost you less money than if you had bought the stock outright. So don't think that you're not getting a bargain. That's key.

Figure 6.6 is a visual breakdown of the profit/loss (P/L) scenario of the DITM strategy versus buying the stock outright. Sometimes it helps to see the benefits presented visually in front of you. We're comparing

Stock Price	Stock P/L	Stock Return	$12 Call P/L	$12 Call Return
$0.00	($2,289.00)	-100.00%	($1,120.00)	-100.00%
$5.00	($1,789.00)	-78.16%	($1,120.00)	-100.00%
$10.00	($1,289.00)	-56.31%	($1,120.00)	-100.00%
$15.00	($789.00)	-34.47%	($820.00)	-73.21%
$20.00	($289.00)	-12.63%	($320.00)	-28.57%
$25.00	$211.00	9.28%	$180.00	16.07%
$30.00	$711.00	31.06%	$680.00	60.71%
$35.00	$1,211.00	52.91%	$1,180.00	105.36%
$40.00	$1,711.00	74.75%	$1,680.00	150.00%
$45.00	$2,211.00	96.60%	$2,180.00	194.64%
$50.00	$2,711.00	118.44%	$2,680.00	239.26%

Figure 6.6   Profit/Loss Breakdown

the P/L of buying 100 shares of MSFT at $22.89 versus buying the $12 call for $11.20.

We see in our worst-case scenario that the loss to the stock buyer is double that of the call buyer (as noted throughout this chapter). Once we hit positive numbers, the call buyer's actual dollar profits are lagging behind by only a few dollars and the percentage gains are always more than double. You're getting the best of all worlds—less

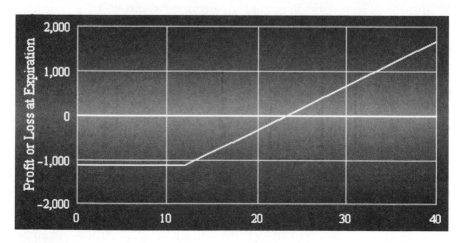

Figure 6.7 $12 Call Profit/Loss Chart
Source: Option-chart.com.

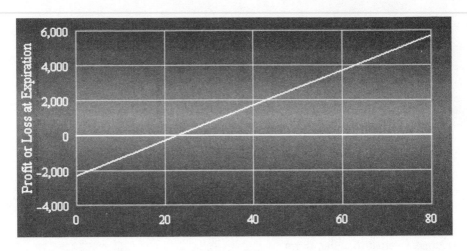

Figure 6.8   MSFT Stock Profit/Loss Chart
Source: Option-chart.com.

money invested, less downside risk, and greater percentage returns. **The DITM is King!**

A picture is worth a thousand words (or should I say $1,120?). (See Figures 6.7 and 6.8.)

It also helps to see the P/L charts graphically to get an idea of how much you can potentially make or lose when investing in stocks or options. These P/L charts are an industry standard in the options trading world and are looked at without hesitation by any smart option trader.

The first chart shows us the P/L profile of our long $12 call purchase. On the left-hand vertical side is the dollar profit/loss scale, and the stock prices are listed along the bottom. With our call purchase, the line showing our potential P/L flatlines horizontally at (−$1,120), which is the maximum we can ever lose. It starts to bend upward once we hit our strike price level of $12, and it goes positive once we surpass our breakeven price of $23.20. Everything above $23.20 is pure profit and is unlimited, depending on how far MSFT may go.

The second chart is the P/L profile of the long stock purchase. There's not much to tell. Profit is unlimited to the upside, just like with the call option, but the downside is unlimited to MSFT going to $0 per share, in which case the stock buyer would lose the entire investment of $2,289. The potential P/L line for the stock crosses over into positive territory at the breakeven price of $22.89. All these numbers correspond to the P/L figures noted in Figure 6.6.

CHOOSING THE STRIKE PRICE

Which strike price should you choose for the DITM strategy, and why did we choose the $12 strike for this example? If your funds allow it, you should always choose the deepest in-the-money call option that has a delta of at least 90 percent. Or you can just choose the lowest strike price listed by the exchange. In the case of our MSFT example, we did choose the deepest option—the $12 call. The reason for doing this is because that particular option will have the highest delta and the closest breakeven price to that of the stock.

You may have noticed from the option chain that we have three strikes to choose from that have deltas of 90 percent or greater. Which one is best? We need to weigh the cost, breakeven price, and delta factor. (See Table 6.1.)

In this case, any of these options would be suitable. I like to choose the option that will have the closest breakeven price to that of the stock. Since MSFT is at $22.89 currently, the $12 call is the closest to that. But this is a personal decision. If you truly do not have enough cash to spend $2,289 to buy MSFT outright, then you need to decide, based on what your wallet can afford, how high a delta to choose, and what breakeven you'd like. In Table 6.1, the $17 strike

TABLE 6.1 Breaking Down the Numbers

Strike Price	Delta	Cost	Breakeven
$12	100%	$11.20	$23.20
$15	100%	$ 8.40	$23.40
$17	97%	$ 6.60	$23.60

call costs only $660 but its breakeven is $.71 higher than the current price of MSFT. However, it does have a 97 percent delta. That's
pretty attractive. Once again, this is a personal decision. I want to give
you the strategy and educate you on your choices.

A REFRESHER

Let's back up for a minute and make sure that we're all on the same
page. Just in case you're wondering, what does buying the $12 call
actually do for us, anyway? It allows us to enter into a contract to buy
MSFT for $12 per share anytime until the option expires in January
2007. How are we going to buy MSFT for $12 when everyone else is
buying it for $22.89? You have to remember that you're also paying
the option premium of $11.20, which you'll add to the strike price of
$12. So in essence, you're actually entering into a contract to buy
MSFT for $23.20. See that?

And if that explanation doesn't help, then let me make one
more analogy. Compare buying a call option to getting a mortgage
on a house. What happens when you buy a house? Well, you have to
make a small down payment to the bank, which is usually just a
fraction of what the house costs. That down payment is equivalent to the option premium you pay when you first buy an option.
With a mortgage, you now get to control your whole house even
though you haven't paid for it in full yet. It's the same with the call
option—you now get to control all 100 shares of stock even though
you haven't paid for the stock in full yet. But the option purchase is
even one step better. Unlike a mortgage, once you buy an option,
you'll never have to make monthly payments. That's the beauty of
stock options.

THE PROBABILITIES

I want you to see how the probabilities stack up for the $12 call versus
buying the actual stock. When you first buy a stock at $22.89 (or any
price for that matter), you're always going to have an equal chance of

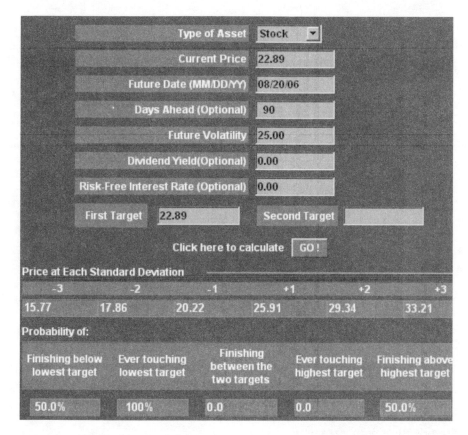

Figure 6.9 Probability Calculator
Source: © Copyright Optionvue Systems International, Inc.

being above or below your cost basis, or breakeven price, at that moment in time. You will never have better odds than 50 percent. (See Figure 6.9.)

Just like we thought, we have a 50 percent chance of being above or below our breakeven price of $22.89 in 90 days' time. How about our $12 call purchase? What are its odds? (See Figure 6.10.)

The $12 call has just a slightly lower chance of finishing above its breakeven price than the stock does, but its 45.7 percent chance is much higher than the 8.10 percent chance that the $30 call option had of finishing above its breakeven price, as we saw earlier in the chapter. Once again, we can see how the $12 call option closely mimics the outright stock purchase in all respects.

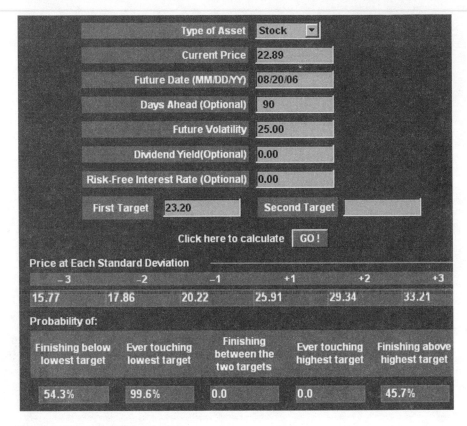

Type of Asset	Stock ▼
Current Price	22.89
Future Date (MM/DD/YY)	08/20/06
Days Ahead (Optional)	90
Future Volatility	25.00
Dividend Yield(Optional)	0.00
Risk-Free Interest Rate (Optional)	0.00
First Target	23.20	Second Target	

Click here to calculate GO !

Price at Each Standard Deviation

– 3	–2	–1	+1	+2	+3
15.77	17.86	20.22	25.91	29.34	33.21

Probability of:

Finishing below lowest target	Ever touching lowest target	Finishing between the two targets	Ever touching highest target	Finishing above highest target
54.3%	99.6%	0.0	0.0	45.7%

Figure 6.10   Probability Calculator

Source: © Copyright Optionvue Systems International, Inc.

BUYING THE WHOLE MARKET

Another beautiful thing about the DITM strategy is that it can also work with a position in the market as a whole, as in the case of an S&P 500 index fund. This way you can diversify your investment in addition to or in lieu of just one specific stock. One of the easiest ways to play the whole market is through the super-liquid S&P 500 exchange-traded fund (ETF)—the SPY. The SPY, or Spiders as the shares are called, is a tracking stock for the S&P 500 that trades just like a stock. You can trade it from your regular stock brokerage account. The SPY is better than your typical index mutual fund because you do not need to wait until the end of the trading day to purchase it at the closing net asset value (NAV). Here's how we do it.

The option chain in Figure 6.11 has priced out the December 2008 options on the SPY. If we go as deep as we can and choose the $60 call, our out-of-pocket expense will be $6,790 (splitting the bid/ask price). Compare that to buying 100 shares of the SPY, which would cost you $12,690, a full $5,900 extra or roughly 87 percent more. Our breakeven on the $60 call would put us at $127.90, a full dollar higher than where the SPY is currently. The reason for this is the large amount of time left before expiration. I still would choose the options in this case even though the breakeven is higher.

You can also see that there are many options that have a 90 percent or higher delta. If you're planning on holding the option to expiration, I would still choose the deepest in-the-money option due to the closest breakeven price to the stock. If you choose the $115 call, for example,

Bid	Ask	Last	Change	Prev	Symbol(short)	Delta	Symbol
67.70	68.10	67.60	0.00	67.60	CYY LH	100	DEC08 60.00
63.40	63.90	67.60	0.00	67.60	CYY LM	100	DEC08 65.00
59.10	59.60	63.20	0.00	63.20	CYY LR	100	DEC08 70.00
54.90	55.40	59.20	−0.30	59.50	CYY LW	100	DEC08 75.00
50.80	51.30	54.60	+ 0.30	54.30	CYY LB	100	DEC08 80.00
46.70	47.20	50.80	0.00	50.80	CYY LG	100	DEC08 85.00
42.80	43.20	0.00	0.00	0.00	CYY LL	100	DEC08 90.00
38.90	39.30	0.00	0.00	0.00	CYY LQ	100	DEC08 95.00
35.10	35.40	34.50	−1.04	35.54	CYY LV	99	DEC08 100.00
31.40	31.80	3.10	−30.60	33.70	CYY LA	97	DEC08 105.00
27.90	28.30	27.80	−0.10	27.90	CYY LF	94	DEC08 110.00
24.50	24.90	24.00	−0.60	24.60	CYY LK	90	DEC08 115.00
21.20	21.50	20.70	−1.10	21.80	CYY LP	86	DEC08 120.00
18.20	18.50	17.70	−1.10	18.80	CYY LU	81	DEC08 125.00
15.30	15.70	15.70	+ 0.50	15.20	CYY LZ	75	DEC08 130.00

SPY — DEC08 — SPDR TRUST   Last: 126.90   Bid: 126.90   Ask: 126.90   High: 127.63   Low: 126.90

Figure 6.11   Option Chain for SPY, December 2008 Expiration
Source: eSignal.com.

your cost is $2,470, but your breakeven at $139.70 is a full $13 higher than the current price of the SPY. The SPY has to move that much farther in order to break even. You might still be thinking that it's better to buy the $115 call because you'll still get 90 percent of the movement. That might be true at the outset of the trade, but as time passes, the delta will get smaller if the SPY doesn't start moving higher toward your breakeven. To get the full benefit of the DITM strategy, I still recommend going as deep as you can with the strike prices, but of course it is always a personal decision.

What would happen if in December 2008 the SPY moved up to $139.50? You wouldn't make any money on your investment if you chose the $115 call and held it to expiration. You'd be a measly $.20 shy of breaking even. But had you stuck with the $60 call, you'd be way in the black. Think about it.

AN ADDED BENEFIT

We've gone over in detail the four main benefits of the DITM strategy versus buying stock:

1. Lower up-front cost.
2. Less capital at risk.
3. Maximum movement—high delta.
4. Higher ROI.

But there's an added benefit to the strategy that you may not have expected. What can you do with the extra 50 percent cash that you've saved with the DITM strategy? Two things come to mind.

1. You can use the money to buy other DITM call options on other stocks you like.
2. Put the money in ultrasafe investments like Treasury bills or certificates of deposit (CDs), both of which can offer attractive rates of return.

Those two ideas are great side benefits. They actually offer you extra downside cushion in case the stock (and call options) happen to fall in value. If you lose value on the call options, the T-bills will still bring you guaranteed income to offset part of the loss. The outright stock buyer doesn't have that added benefit of extra cash to put into CDs or T-bills. This is how you use your money wisely.

EXPIRATION ACTION?

So what do we do when option expiration comes knocking at our door? No fear, as I will tell you exactly what you can do. You have four possibilities:

1. Your option will expire worthless, giving you a 100 percent loss on your investment. We hope it won't come to this, but you always know ahead of time what your maximum loss can be.
2. You can sell the option at any time before expiration. There are no rules governing how long you have to hold onto the option.
3. You can roll the option to a later date. This is a two-part trade in which you will have to sell your original option contract and then purchase another DITM option.
4. You can exercise the call option. If you choose this route, you will be required to pay for the balance of the stock at this time. Remember, you only made a down payment at the outset of the MSFT trade and now you have to pay the balance. In the case of our $12 call, we will have to pay the $1,200 balance, which is the strike price ($12) multiplied by the option multiplier of $100. Just think of it as making a balloon payment at the end of a loan.

A word of caution with the last choice: Make sure you have the available funds necessary to pay for the shares' worth of option contracts you bought. If you bought five option contracts, that's equivalent to buying 500 shares of stock. With our MSFT $12 call, you would need $6,000 ($1,200 × 5 contracts). If you don't want to get caught, or don't have the funds available, you should consider either selling the option outright or rolling to another expiration date.

RISK MANAGEMENT

Everyone should have a risk management plan in place regardless of the type of security you buy or sell and regardless of your expected holding period. If a security isn't performing the way you'd like it to, then get out. What's the point of holding it? Everyone's threshold is different so I can't give specific individual advice, but at least I can offer some ideas.

An option contract can be bought and sold at any time. If you feel uncomfortable in the position, then by all means unwind the trade. If you've taken a position with the DITM strategy and the stock is not moving the way you wanted, then you can always sell the call. You are not obligated to hold it until option expiration. With that said, it's up to you to decide what may be your stop-out point. Don't feel bad about selling a loser. Believe me, you'll feel much better selling it now than waiting to sell it later after it's fallen much farther.

There are many ways to decide on a stop-out point for the trade if it happens to move against you. You can set a dollar figure that is the maximum loss you can tolerate. You can base your sell decision on certain support levels for the stock. You can use a time stop, which forces you out of the trade when the option reaches a certain point in the expiration cycle. Or, you can use a percentage stop such as 25 percent below your cost-basis. Whatever works for you is best.

DRAWBACKS?

I couldn't end this chapter without giving you an idea of the potential drawbacks to the DITM strategy. Are there any drawbacks? In my opinion, not really, but I'll tell you what other people might think are drawbacks.

When buying options, you do not get to receive dividends that the company may pay. This applies to all option buyers, whether they're buying DITM or OTM options. Also, you do not receive any voting rights for that specific company. Are these reasons enough to not buy the options? Not for me. I'll gladly settle for an investment that costs me almost 50 percent less in total dollars, half as many total dollars at risk, and the opportunity to participate in all the same movement in exchange for a sometimes paltry dividend (if the stock pays dividends at all!). Remember, no dividend will fully cushion the fall of a stock in a downtrend.

The other drawback may be the limited life span of the options. Remember, options can be bought for many different expiration periods, some of which stretch out to three years in time. With the DITM strategy, you can choose one of these LEAPS options. LEAPS is the acronym that describes a long-term option. In fact, I recommend using the longest-dated LEAPS you can find for any stock you're considering holding in your portfolio. This way, you're giving your investment many years to mature. Still, some people may consider having any expiration date (even though it's three years away) a drawback. I don't know about you, but if a stock I own doesn't make the move I anticipated within three years' time, I think it's time to find another stock.

That's it. The drawbacks are small. It really is an ideal strategy.

SUMMARY

I've just outlined an excellent option trading strategy that allows you to make an investment in a stock or market sector with half as much money at risk, with half as many dollars invested, getting all the same movement as the stock itself, and allowing you to receive a much better return on your money.

This is a very smart way to invest. You've comparison-shopped and found the exact same item for less. This is what a DITM call option is all about. It gives you all the same benefits as a long stock strategy but for half the price and half the risk.

Two things to remember when initiating the DITM strategy:

1. Make sure you go as deep-in-the-money as possible when picking a strike price.
2. Make sure the delta is 90 percent or higher.

These are the two most important items to look for when buying a DITM call option. Of course, you have the final decision on which strike to purchase. You have to do what's right for your budget and time frame. Just remember, the probabilities are best when adhering to the two items just listed.

The money saved by buying a DITM call option can be used to purchase other DITM call options, or you can place the extra funds in guaranteed income investments such as government-issued T-bills or interest-paying money market funds.

This is one of the best ways to get rich with options. The money that is put into those interest-bearing investments or other diversified holdings can increase your wealth faster and faster because the interest will compound and the diversity of your holdings will provide a larger cushion during market declines.

One last item to note before we go. This chapter is designed to show you how to best buy into the stock market using options contracts. I specifically did not get into how to choose the stock that you will buy options on. Stockpicking can encompass a whole textbook in itself, or even many textbooks for that matter on technical and fundamental analysis. That's not the intention of this book. My job here is to focus on how to use options once you've chosen your designated stock.

The strategy has been laid out for you to use. Good luck.

CHAPTER 7

GETTING PAID TO BUY YOUR FAVORITE STOCK

Have you ever found yourself locked out of buying a quality stock because it's above your buy price? Are you waiting, waiting, waiting for the price to come down so you can buy it cheaper? Well, I'm going to show you a more productive way to use your time and money during those waiting periods. If someone offered you cold, hard cash today for the opportunity to buy your favorite stock at a lower price than where it is now, would you take it? I would, and I always do, and I'm betting you will too after reading this chapter.

Listen up, because I'm going to dish out strategy #2, which is one of my favorite option-selling strategies. It's a fabulous way to collect option premium, which generates income for you while you wait to potentially purchase your stock at a lower level. How great is that? Someone will actually give you cash today in exchange for the opportunity to buy a stock at a lower price. You can see it as a consolation prize given to you for your fine patience as you wait for your stock to get cheaper. As a result, this strategy falls into the "income-producing" category. Here's how to do it.

THE STRATEGY

The trading method is called **"naked put selling,"** and it is an incredible way to earn passive income while you sit on the sidelines of the stock market. It's a tactic that not many individual investors or traders take advantage of, or even know exists, yet it is used all the time by people in the know. Being an alternative way to take advantage of your bullish outlook in the stock market, it's one that is easy to understand, a great way to potentially acquire stocks, and get paid cash up front for your efforts. I love this method so much that I use it in both my wife's retirement account and my own. In my opinion, there is no better way to generate income while waiting for a stock to come down to your buy point.

Naked put selling is not some secret, arcane system that only a physics scholar will understand. No, naked put selling is a time-tested, legitimate, and popular strategy. Like I said, I use it all the time in my own trading. If you've ever looked through the educational material published by the U.S. options exchanges, you will see the naked put selling strategy listed right along with all the other strategies like the ultra-simple "long call" and the more advanced "iron butterfly." It's not a mystery, and it's not an illegal strategy, either. It's just one more form of investing that every person should know how to do.

HOW DOES IT WORK?

Before I get into the details, heed this warning:

DO NOT SELL NAKED PUT OPTIONS ON STOCKS THAT YOU DON'T WANT TO POTENTIALLY OWN!

In other words, execute this strategy only for quality stocks you want to keep in your portfolio. I can't emphasize this point enough, because once you see how the strategy works, you might be tempted to try it on low-grade stocks that pay you more money up front, but that tactic could be a big loser and get you into trouble down the road.

Okay, with that disclaimer out of the way, how do naked put options work? First and foremost, you pinpoint a stock that you would like to buy after you've done all your fundamental and technical research. Your stock screening process might tell you to look for a strong stock that meets your requirements for good earnings, high cash reserves, solid management, increasing dividend payouts, and the like. Plus, it could be making a low point on the charts and looking to move higher. That is how I do it whenever I'm researching an investment.

You've decided that you want to buy this stock and keep it in your portfolio for a long time, but at the moment it's a little more expensive than you'd like to spend. Plus, you'd rather wait for it to pull back to its 50-day moving average line, for example. What can you do in the meantime, then? If you're like most folks, you'd just sit and wait for the stock price to come back down. But not you, because you're smarter than that.

Since you know what level you'd be comfortable purchasing your stock, your second step is to start consulting put option prices of various expiration dates for that stock. This can be done either through your online data provider, your favorite Internet site, yesterday's newspaper (this will be old data), or your options broker. For me, since I run my own business, I always consult my data provider. You will look at the strike prices that correspond to your buy level and how much time you want to give the stock to reach that level (expiration date).

Let's run an example using our old friend Microsoft (MSFT). You know the stock, you know the product, and you know that the founder is one of the richest men in the world. You've never owned any of the stock before, but you think it's about time you did. It's a dominant player in its sector, and you know it will be a good long-term position to keep in your portfolio. It's at $22.63 today and you've estimated that $20 per share would be the ideal level for you to buy MSFT. How can you get someone to pay you cash today and allow you to potentially buy shares of Microsoft at $20? By selling naked put options, of course!

In contrast, most people would place an order to buy the shares of MSFT the old-fashioned way—they would call their brokers and have them buy the shares outright for them once (if) MSFT got down to $20 per share. Or, if you are connected to the Internet, you could put in a limit-buy order at $20/share yourself through your online stock account. At the time of writing (June 20, 2006), MSFT is trading for $22.63 per share—still above your buy point. So, if you were like most traders, you would wait patiently for MSFT to come down to $20. But you're not like most traders, and here's why . . .

Because you know how to potentially achieve the same trade with naked put selling and get paid cash up front for your time and effort. Now check the option prices. Here's how I do it using my options broker optionsXpress. Figure 7.1 is a snapshot of the option chain for MSFT with an expiration date of January 2007 (about seven months away).

The column on the left lists some of the put option strike prices for MSFT that expire on the third Friday of January 2007. We see there are strike prices that stretch from $27.50 all the way down to $12. At the time of this screen shot, MSFT was trading for $22.63 per share. For this trade, all we need to do is to look at the "Bid" column for each corresponding strike price. You will notice that the numbers in the Bid column get smaller as you go lower in strike prices.

		Puts						
Strike	Symbol	Last	Chg	Bid	Ask	Vol	OpInt	
MSFT @ 22.63							Jan 07 Puts	
12.00	MQFMM	0.05	0	0	0.05	0	1,528	trade
15.00	MQFMC	0.15	0	0.05	0.10	0	147	trade
17.00	MQFMO	0.15	0	0.15	0.20	0	11,134	trade
19.50	MQFMP	0.43	-0.02	0.40	0.50	557	61,284	trade
20.00	MQFMD	0.55	0	0.50	0.55	155	50,956	trade
22.00	MQFMQ	1.05	-0.10	1.05	1.10	124	191,891	trade
22.50	MSQMX	1.30	0	1.25	1.30	11,946	129,428	trade
24.50	MSQMR	2.32	-0.16	2.30	2.40	163	115,351	trade
25.00	MSQMJ	2.70	-0.05	2.65	2.75	254	77,488	trade
27.00	MSQMS	4.40	-0.30	4.30	4.50	53	99,917	trade
27.50	MSQMY	5.10	0	4.80	4.90	0	17,099	trade

Figure 7.1   MSFT Option Chain, January 2007
Source: optionsXpress.

These numbers tell you how much money you will get up front for selling each of those options. For instance, if you sell the $20 puts, you will receive $.50. This is called the option's "premium." Since each single option contract controls 100 shares of stock, you need to multiply the $.50 by $100. So if you sell one $20 strike put option contract for a premium of $.50, you will receive $50 in your brokerage account. If you sell five $20 put option contracts, you will receive $250 in your brokerage account, and if you sell 10 of them, you will receive $500! Understand how this works?

WHAT HAPPENS WHEN YOU SELL NAKED PUT OPTIONS?

When you sell a put option contract, you are entering into a binding agreement where you have an obligation to fulfill the terms of the deal. Being a put seller, you are entering into a "bullish" scenario for the stock on which you sell put options. In our MSFT example, you are entering into a bullish trade because you want to buy MSFT shares. The terms of a "put sell" contract require you to buy 100 shares of MSFT at the stated strike price ($20) at any time until option expiration (January 2007) under any condition if called upon by the option buyer.

When you sell one MSFT January 2007 $20 put option for $.50, you are guaranteeing someone that you will purchase 100 shares of MSFT for $20 per share at any time until that option expires on the third Friday of January 2007 under all circumstances (if directed by the option buyer). In return for your taking on the risk of buying MSFT for $20 per share, the buyer of that option (remember, you are the seller, so someone will be buying it from you) will pay you $50 today per option contract.

What **risk** are we talking about? And why would someone pay you money to buy MSFT cheaper than where it is today? Sounds like a no-brainer. MSFT is trading for $22.63 today. How will you ever be able to buy it for $20? And if you buy it for $20, how is that a risk? Let's say, for example, that the day after you sell that $20 put option, the courts decide that Microsoft has been in breach of every copyright law imaginable and that it will no longer be able to sell any of its products ever again—the company is sure to go bankrupt. Well, the next trading day, MSFT opens for trading at $1 per share. Guess what happens to that put option you sold? The buyer will force you to fulfill the terms of the contract and require you to buy 100 shares of MSFT for $20 each while everyone else can now buy it at $1 per share. You've just locked yourself into a $19 per share loss (minus the $.50 collected up front, so it's really an $18.50 per share loss). There's your risk.

The risk is that the stock can potentially go a lot lower than the price at which you are required to buy it. Actually, it's no different than the situation of anyone who happened to buy MSFT outright in their brokerage account before the hypothetical incident happened. Anyone who bought 100 shares of MSFT for $22.63 per share the same day you sold your put option has paid $2,263 up front and is now sitting with a $21.63 per share loss (−$2,163). At least with your trade, your loss is less at −$1,850.

Now, we all know that the preceding scenario is an extremely unlikely one, but I just wanted to show you the risk involved with naked put selling. Now remember, you're taking on that risk only until the third Friday of January 2007. After that date, if you are not required to buy the stock, the option will expire and you will no longer have any obligation. Remember, this is a stock that you **wanted** to own and you felt extremely lucky to have a chance to buy MSFT below where it was trading, and someone was willing to pay you up front to wait and see what would happen at expiration. So in your eyes, this was a fantastic opportunity to buy a quality stock and get paid to do it.

HOW DO WE GET OUR SHARES?

What happens if MSFT closes below the strike price at expiration? Let's say MSFT closes at $19.80 on expiration day. You're in luck! The buyer will "exercise" his side of the contract and you will get "assigned" 100 shares of MSFT stock for $20 per share. The words *exercise* and *assign* are terms that describe the process by which the buyer of your option executes (exercises) his end of the agreement and makes you buy (assigns) 100 shares of MSFT. The 100 shares will show up in your brokerage account on the following Monday morning and you must have at least $2,000 in your account to cover the cost of the shares that you were assigned. In reality, you are paying only $1,950 for the 100 shares because you received $50 up front at the beginning of the option transaction. Your true cost basis is $19.50 per share.

So there you have it. You got to buy 100 shares of MSFT below where it was trading the day you sold the put option, and someone gave you $50 per option contract for your effort. Even though in this hypothetical scenario MSFT is now trading at $19.80, you're still ahead of the game because your cost basis is $19.50.

WHY DON'T WE GET OUR SHARES?

We talked about what would happen if MSFT is trading below $20 at expiration day. What happens if MSFT is trading *above* $20 on that third Friday of January 2007? If MSFT is trading above $20 when the third Friday of January 2007 closes for trading, the option expires worthless and no transaction takes place after that. You get to keep your initial $50 free and clear but you do not get to buy 100 shares of MSFT. "What do you mean?" you ask. "I thought the whole idea of the strategy was to buy the stock below its current price and get paid to do it." The idea of the strategy is to **potentially** buy the stock below its current price. The only way that you will be able to buy the stock below its current price is if the stock actually closes for trading on the third Friday of the expiration month **below** your strike price. This is the one and only catch to the strategy. In order to absolutely be assigned and have shares show up in your account, the price of the stock **must** close on expiration day below your strike price level.

In the preceding scenario, you were able to buy 100 shares of MSFT at $20 per share because it closed for trading at $19.80 at expiration day, which is lower than the $20 strike price. As long as the stock is trading below your strike price, you will get assigned the stock. If the stock is trading above your strike price at expiration, then it is not beneficial for the buyer to execute that end of the contract so he or she will let the option expire. You will not get to buy any shares of stock, but like I said, you will get to keep the premium of $50. You can now repeat the process and sell another put option for a future expiration date.

About a year and a half into my days as an options market maker on the floor of the New York Mercantile Exchange (NYMEX), I discovered the strategy of selling short-term, out-of-the-money (OTM) options. OTM put options have their strike prices below the current price of the underlying futures contract and OTM call options have their strike prices higher than the current price of the underlying futures contract.

During my time on the floor from 1991 to 1998, the crude oil energy futures stayed mostly in a range of $15 to $25 per barrel. I noticed that many people would pay good money for options that were well above and well below the current price of the nearest futures contract. If oil was at $20 per barrel, people would buy options on the $15 puts and/or the $30 calls, hoping the price of oil would get to one of those two levels by the time of options expiration. What I noticed was that these options were expiring worthless most of the time because of the large distance that the futures contract had to move for the option to become profitable, plus the fact that the options had such a short life span. So I decided to start selling these options, which allowed me to pocket the money from the buyers. All I had to do was wait for expiration to see these options expire worthless.

Over time, I realized that due to the increasing potential unrest in the Middle East and the effect that the Organization of Petroleum Exporting Countries (OPEC) had on the price of oil, there could possibly be more violent movements to the upside than to the downside. At that time, I started restricting my OTM option selling tactics to just the put options. People were still paying high premiums for these options and I was willing to sell them. What I didn't realize at the time was that not only was I taking in monthly premium income, but I was also setting myself up to possibly buy crude oil at unheard-of cheap prices.

At the time, in the early 1990s, I was selling put options with strike prices from $15 all the way down to $9. If I was ever assigned on my short put options (meaning that the buyers execute their right to sell crude oil futures to me), I would be buying crude oil at very cheap levels, not such a bad thing to do with a worldwide commodity in such high demand. As it turned out, I was never assigned on any of my short options, and that was mostly due to the short life span and large distance of being OTM.

Over the years, I became the market maker that most of the brokers would come to when their clients needed to buy some OTM put options. Other traders would shy away from these selling tactics, claiming the "unlimited loss potential" of short options. They said I was crossing over to the "Dark Side." But for me, the strategy was sound. I was taking in good premium, I could possibly buy crude oil at unbelievably low levels, and I had risk money management plans in place. The NYMEX futures contracts would trade electronically during the night after the open-outcry session closed, so if I had to protect myself, I could buy or sell futures contracts if need be.

After I left the NYMEX, I started up a trading business from my own home office. I began trading stock options with the same methodology. I would sell put options below the market (OTM) on stocks that I really wanted to own. This would allow me to collect the premium up front, and potentially allow me to buy the stock at a great price. This is the benefit of selling put options on stocks you're looking to buy at a cheaper level.

When you are looking to buy a favorite stock at a cheaper level, selling put options is a viable strategy to potentially set a limit price while earning income in the meantime. The way I was using it on the NYMEX was mostly to collect the steady monthly premium income, but when applying it to the stock market, you are potentially letting yourself buy a great stock at a great price level that you decide on in advance. That's a winning strategy in my book.

PICKING A DIFFERENT STRIKE PRICE

What if you wanted to choose a lower or higher strike price? We can see in Figure 7.1 that the $17 strike put option is paying $15 for every put option contract you sell. In this case, you will be assigned the shares only if MSFT closes below $17 on the third Friday of January 2007. As you can see, the lower you go in strike price, the smaller the premium is. This is because there is not much chance that MSFT will fall that far by this expiration; thus, the buyer is not willing to pay you that much up front. If you still want to choose the $17 strike price but get paid more money, then you will have to sell put options on a farther-dated contract, something like the March 2007 or the July 2007 options. The reason you will get paid more for longer-dated options is because now you are giving the buyer more time for MSFT to move around (and possibly get much lower in price). Whenever you give someone more time for an event to occur, you must charge them more money. That's how it works with options trading.

You could also choose the $22.50 strike put option if you like. We see that the $22.50 strike put option is paying $125 for each put option contract you sell. In this case, you will be assigned the shares only if MSFT closes below $22.50 on the third Friday of January 2007. In this case, you'd have to buy 100 shares of MSFT for $22.50 per share (still lower than its current price of $22.63), but your real cost basis would be $21.25 ($22.50 strike minus $1.25 premium equals $21.25 cost basis).

DON'T FOCUS SOLELY ON THE OPTION PREMIUM

As I said earlier in the chapter, once you understand the strategy you might be tempted to look for stock options that pay a lot of money up front. This is a strategy for the gamblers and speculators. They are not interested in owning any stock. They just want to sell put options on stocks that pay big up front. Don't get sucked into this game unless you know what you are doing and you have long-term experience with selling naked put options. The stocks that pay high premiums up front are the true highfliers. These are very erratic stocks that can go up big or go down big in a heartbeat. You might be thinking that the high up-front premiums will cancel out any potential downside move in the stock. Don't be so sure. I've seen lots of stocks come out with devastating news that fall much farther than any option premium will protect them. *Only sell naked put options on stocks you want to own for the long term!*

A FEW REQUIREMENTS

In order to execute naked put selling in your brokerage account, you need to have a margin-type account, and also be approved by your brokerage to the options trading level that allows put selling. Some firms will not let novice traders sell put options right off the bat as they feel put selling is too risky a strategy. The risk is unlimited to the point where the stock can fall to zero after being assigned the shares (think of our MSFT example where we imagined it falling to $1).

There is no difference in risk between a put selling strategy and outright buying shares of stock. What's your risk when you buy shares of stock? The risk is that the stock can fall to zero, but the brokerage firms don't seem to put restrictions on anyone wanting to buy stock. Correct? Any joe out there can open a stock trading account and lose all his money on a long stock position. No one seems to stop investors from doing that.

It's the same with trading covered calls (which you'll read about in Chapter 10). The risk is also unlimited to the downside to the point of the stock falling to zero, yet the brokerages consider covered call trading one of the most conservative strategies out there. Go figure. Why would put option selling be considered riskier than buying stocks? To this day I still don't have the answer.

Also remember, if you are assigned on your put option, you must have enough money in your account to cover the cost of buying 100 shares of stock (one option contract). In our MSFT example, you would need to have at least $2,000 free cash available to pay for your new 100 shares of MSFT.

MARGIN REQUIREMENTS

While your short put position is open, your broker will require you to keep a certain amount of money on hand at all times in your account. What kind of money? It's called "margin money" or a "margin requirement." This is an amount of money you must keep accessible in your account at all times while you hold the naked short put option position. It's classified as good faith money to be used to cover yourself if the position starts to move against you.

The margin requirement is a fantastic deal for put sellers because you don't need to keep cash on hand to cover the full purchase price of the stock while the trade is open. In our example, we wouldn't need to have $2,000 available at all times to cover the cost of buying 100 shares of MSFT at $20. Instead, your broker will ask you to keep only a fraction of that $2,000 in your account. This is based on one option contract.

Each broker is different in regard to how much he needs for the margin requirement, but there is an industry standard that we can use as a good reference point. That standard is derived from a simple formula for calculating the margin requirement. It is 15 percent of the underlying price at time of trade plus the option's premium times 100. In the MSFT example, the margin requirement would be (.15 × $22.63) + ($.50) × 100 = $389.45.

So, from the outset of the $20 put-sell trade, your broker would ask you to keep a minimum $389.45 on hand in your account for every put option you sold. If you sold 10 put options, your requirement would be $3,894.50, but that's much better than having to hold $20,000 in your account (based on 1,000 shares of stock). Along with the almost 81 percent savings from the margin requirement (compared to holding the full purchase price of the stock), you could take some of that extra cash and invest it in other options, or keep it as cash and earn interest on it. Just another way to get rich with options.

PUT SELLING ON THE DOWNDRAFT

The reason I love this strategy so much is because I love having other people pay me money in addition to the opportunity to buy my favorite stock at a price of my choosing. One of my favorite put-selling scenarios is when a quality blue-chip stock gets hammered to the downside for one reason or another. Most of these initial, knee-jerk downside moves create incredible put-selling opportunities. Not only do most of the stocks recover pretty quickly (or at least don't fall much farther), but the implied volatility gets blasted upward, making the put options even more expensive. Remember, implied volatility has a direct effect on the price of an option. And when implied volatility goes up, so do the option prices. So now the put options are worth much more than usual, which gives us put sellers more money in our pockets. And if we get assigned the shares, then we truly got to buy one of our favorite blue chip stocks at an awesome price, and we got paid even better money to do it.

I want to show you some real-life examples of put-selling trades that I've done in the recent past. These are actual trades, and I'm including snapshots of my brokerage statements from Interactivebrokers .com to prove the authenticity. (See Figures 7.2 and 7.3.)

The two graphics depict a daily chart for Intel Corporation (INTC) and naked put sales I executed on that stock during the month of January 2006, as seen from my brokerage statement. In mid-January 2006, we see the gap-down opening on INTC, followed by its price continually falling all the way through to the middle of June. All of my actual naked put sales were done after that initial gap down. Little did I know that INTC would fall even further over the coming months. That didn't matter to me because I was determined to buy INTC well below where it had been trading. I chose $20 per share and lower as the levels at which I felt comfortable owning shares of INTC if I ever happened to get assigned.

Looking at my statement, I sold the INTC February 2006 $20 puts for $.10 and $.20 apiece, the April 2006 $17.50 puts for $.15, and the July 2006 $15 puts for $.10. Just from those INTC trades alone, I took in $51 in cold hard cash (including commissions) just for selling those put options. INTC never finished below any of my short put option strikes during any of those expiration periods. This was fine with me as I got to keep the $51 free and clear without ever being assigned the shares. Although I would have liked to have bought INTC cheaply, it never got down to my desired level. Also, with that initial gap down in January 2006, implied volatility spiked higher on the INTC options, making

TRANSACTIONS

Options						
USD						
Symbol	**Date Time**	**Exchange**	**Quantity**	**Price**	**Amount**	**Commission**
INTC FEB06 20 P (100)	2006-01-18, 12:42:06	ISE	-1	0.1000	10.00	-1.00
ISE FEB06 22.5 P (100)	2006-01-23, 11:08:57	PHLX	-1	0.0500	5.00	-1.00
INTC FEB06 20 P (100)	2006-01-23, 12:47:32	CBOE	-1	0.2000	20.00	-1.00
INTC JUL06 15 P (100)	2006-01-23, 12:48:25	CBOE	-1	0.1000	10.00	-1.00
INTC APR06 17.5 P (100)	2006-01-23, 14:34:28	CBOE	-1	0.1500	15.00	-1.00
Total					60.00	-5.00

Figure 7.2 Actual Put Sales, January 2006

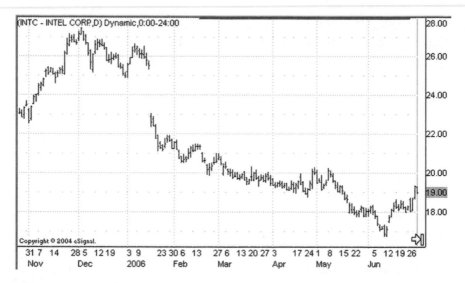

Figure 7.3 INTC Daily Chart
Source: eSignal.com.

the puts more expensive and allowing me to get a few more dollars than normal out of them.

To see more about put selling, following is a copy of an article I wrote for the Smartprofitsreport.com web site back in January 2006 after INTC had the big fall. The article corresponds to my brokerage statement shown in Figure 7.2.

Before I forget, I want to show you more real-life examples of put-selling activities in my own trading accounts. Figure 7.4 is a confirmation statement from my retirement account at Interactive brokers.com.

TRANSACTIONS

Options							
USD							
Symbol	Date Time	Exchange	Quantity	Price	Amount	Commission	
INTC APR06 17.5 P (100)	2006-03-03, 10:33:42	PHLX	−1	0.1000	10.00	−1.00	
ISE JUL06 22.5 P (100)	2006-03-16, 13:16:39	ISE	−1	0.1000	10.00	−1.00	
Total					**20.00**	**−2.00**	

Figure 7.4 IRA Brokerage Statement, March 2006

BUYING INTEL BELOW THE MARKET

Did you see the drubbing Intel (INTC) took the other day in the market? It's been knocked for a loop and had four points shaved off the price of its shares. That's what so-called bad earnings can do for a company. But for people like me who have never owned shares of INTC and have wanted to wait for the right time to get in, I think now's the time. But I'm doing it a little differently.

Time and time again, I've seen shares of good companies get hammered just like INTC, only to work their way back higher over the course of the next few weeks or months. This is the perma-bullish attitude of the majority of the market. But you can't argue with a company that controls about 95 percent of the chip market for every new PC manufactured. I like to take a chance on that kind of company.

Here's how I'm hoping to get into INTC in the next few weeks and months at even lower prices than where it's at today. I'm selling naked put options on INTC stock.

Figure 7.5 is a monthly chart of INTC going back nine years to 1997. The upper portion of the graphic is the actual chart of INTC while the lower portion shows the relative strength indicator (RSI) I use to help make directional assessments. Each vertical bar on the chart represents one full month of trading for INTC. Other than that dip down to about $12.95/share back in 2002, INTC's had pretty good support in the $15–$20 range. That's where I'm looking to try to buy my shares of INTC. This is based solely on my opinion and technical analysis of the market. Others might have a different view, but this is what I'm seeing. As of today, January 24, 2006, INTC is trading at $21.45/share. I'm looking to try to scale into shares of INTC between $15 and $20 via naked put sales. If I never get to buy shares of INTC at my prices, at least I will get compensated up front for the effort in the form of instant cash payments deposited into my trading account. Here's how it works:

You pick a price level for a stock that you would like to buy and then you sell put option contracts that correspond as closely to

(Continues)

BUYING INTEL BELOW THE MARKET (Continued)

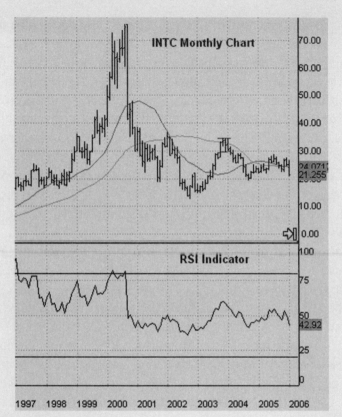

Figure 7.5 INTC Monthly Chart
Source: eSignal.com.

that level as possible. When you sell naked put options, you have an obligation to buy 100 shares of stock for every option contract you sell. Right now INTC is at $21.45/share, but if it trades lower than $20, I will be forced to buy 100 shares at $20 no matter how much lower INTC may be. If INTC falls down to $18, I'm still obligated to buy the shares at $20. But that's okay with me as that is my buy price. I'm also willing to sell put options at the $17.50 and $15 strike prices, which can potentially allow me to buy INTC for $15 and $17.50/share.

One of the great benefits of selling naked put options is that we collect the premium that we receive from the buyer. We get this money up front and it's deposited into our trading account. Once the trade is executed, all we have to do is wait to see if INTC falls below our strike price by option expiration. If it does, we will be assigned on our trade, meaning we will have to purchase 100 shares of stock at the stated strike price. If the stock does not fall below our strike price by option expiration, the trade is dead but we get to keep the premium we were paid up front. So at least we're compensated for our time waiting to see if we would ever get assigned the shares.

The three option expiration months that I'm selling INTC puts on are shown in Figures 7.6 through 7.8. I've sold the February 2006 $20 put options for an average price of $.15 per contract, the April 2006 $17.50 puts for $.15 per contract, and the July 2006 $15 puts for $.10 per contract. Since the option multiplier is $100, I've taken in $15 for each contract I sold for February and April, and $10 for each contract that I sold for July. Since I've sold a total of four option contracts, that theoretically puts me in a position to buy 400 shares of INTC from $20 down to $15. For my effort, I've taken in $55 (before commissions) in exchange for the opportunity to buy INTC below where it's trading now. Someone is actually giving me money today in exchange for the opportunity to buy INTC later. What a great deal.

			Puts					
Strike	Symbol	Last	Chg	Bid	Ask	Vol	OpInt	
INTC @ 21.44							Feb 06 Puts	
17.50	NQNW	0.05	0	0	0.05	0	62	trade
20.00	NQND	0.15	-0.05	0.15	0.20	4,937	21,280	trade

Figure 7.6 INTC Options, February 2006 Expiration
Source: OptionsXpress.

Be warned, this is not a strategy for everybody, and not everyone can be approved to sell naked options. The reason for the warning is because someone might get caught up in the frenzy of selling options just to take in the premium. Don't do this! Only sell naked puts on stocks that you definitely

(Continues)

BUYING INTEL BELOW THE MARKET (Continued)

INTC @ 21.44							Apr 06 Puts	
15.00	NQPC	0.05	0	0	0.05	0	35	trade
17.50	NQPW	0.15	0	0.10	0.15	5	2,950	trade

Figure 7.7   INTC Options, April 2006 Expiration
Source: optionsXpress.

INTC @ 21.44							Jul 06 Puts	
15.00	NQSC	0.10	0	0.05	0.10	0	329	trade
17.50	NQSW	0.35	+0.05	0.25	0.35	32	1,299	trade

Figure 7.8   INTC Options, July 2006 Expiration
Source: optionsXpress.

have a desire to keep in your portfolio. And don't sell more put option contracts than what you're comfortable owning. If you normally trade in 500-share stock increments, don't sell more than five put options.

The other issue is whether you can be approved for naked put selling in your trading account. Brokerage houses consider selling naked options taboo and have strict guidelines for the type of account you must have in order to do this. In my eyes, it's not a risky strategy as long as you don't abuse it. Also, it's no more risky than selling covered calls, and brokerage houses consider covered calls as safe as you can get. Ask your broker about that comparison and see how much he or she knows!

Good luck.

My wife and I both have retirement accounts in which we can sell naked put options. We execute this trade only for stocks that we are willing to have and hold (just like a marriage!). In this case, we sold OTM put options on INTC and the International Securities

Exchange (ISE). We both collected $20 in total premium up front while we waited to see if either stock would end up below the strike price at expiration. It turned out (as I proofread this section months after initially writing it) neither stock traded low enough for us to get assigned the shares. Not to worry, we still got some money out of it.

If you look at the confirmation statement, you'll see that our commissions are only $1 per contract. This is one of the cheapest in the industry. Since we spent $2 on commissions and took in $20 in option premium, the net cash given to us was $18. This might not seem like a lot, but any money is good money. If you do this trade enough times over the years with enough contracts with enough stocks, you will see your bank account add up quickly. One tip, though: Make sure you are paying cheap commissions so you can cover the premium you receive. If you are selling an option for $20 but are paying $25 in commissions, you will actually lose $5 on the trade. Make sure you account for all your costs!

TOUGH TIMES IN 2008

When I revised this put-selling chapter in January 2009, the U.S. economy was undergoing one of its toughest periods since the Great Depression. Between the bank credit crisis, the auto industry meltdown, the demise of some long-standing investment houses, the crash in the real estate market, the high unemployment rate, and even the Bernie Madoff scandal—it's now easy to see how and why the stock and commodity markets have taken a huge beating since the fall of 2008.

We've seen the implosion of many stocks, some of which have gone out of business. But on the other hand, this downdraft is giving the opportunity to possibly buy other bellwether, top quality stocks at levels that have not been seen in 10 to 15 years. This makes for the perfect scenario for implementing put option sales. Not only are stocks the cheapest they've been for over a decade, but the volatility levels have skyrocketed—making the options even more expensive, thus putting even more money in our put-selling pockets!

I executed a few put-selling trades for my own smaller account toward the end of 2008 on Citigroup and Disney. If you had been following the news around that time, you may have seen that Citigroup was getting pounded because the market felt that it would not survive the current financial crisis, just like some of the other investment houses such as Bear Stearns and Lehman Brothers, which had fallen victim to the carnage. Of course, at the last minute, the federal government stepped in and gave Citigroup a huge lifeline of funds. This, in turn, was able to stop the freefall and give the bank a bit of support. Figure 7.9 shows what the Citigroup chart looked like at the time.

As you can see in Figure 7.9, Citigroup fell all the way down to $3.05 per share on November 21, 2008. No doubt, this was a very scary event for the U.S. banking system, let alone the Citigroup shareholders. We saw lots of equity wiped out of many people's portfolios in just the last three months of 2008. This, of course, was not a fun time for many investors.

But just as ugly as things seemed to be at that time, there always lie opportunities for others. If you never held stock in many of these

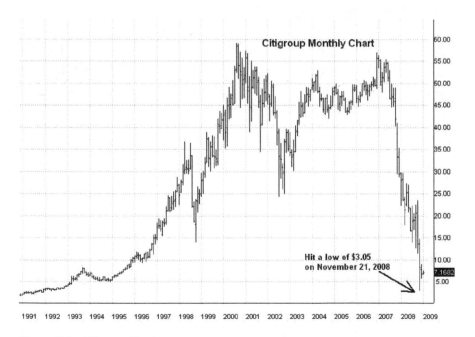

Figure 7.9 Citigroup Chart
Source: eSignal.com.

quality companies before, then you were witnessing a possible once-in-a-lifetime investing opportunity.

As for me, I decided to sell a put option contract on Citigroup the very day that it made its lowest price since 1992—17 years ago. (See Figure 7.11.) I sold a December 2008 $2.50 put option contract for $.70. Did you ever think that Citi would trade down below $5 per share again in our lifetimes? I certainly didn't. But when I sold the $2.50 put option for $.70, I was obligating myself to buy 100 shares of Citi for $2.50 per share. How much lower could it go? And with the $.70 that I received upfront ($70 of real money with the multiplier), my actual cost basis would have been $1.80 per share ($2.50 − $.70 = $1.80). How'd you like to buy Citi for $1.80?

It turns out that Citigroup never fell any lower than the $3.05 that it hit on November 21, 2008, and so the put option expired worthless in December 2008, leaving me with the $70 free and clear that I collected upfront. I didn't roll my put-sales into another expiration month because I still felt unsure about all the financial stocks in general.

Mickey on the Cheap

Next up was the Disney trade. Based on the chart in Figure 7.10, Disney was getting into very oversold levels, and reaching into areas that hadn't been seen in over five years. One of the things I like to do when deciding on which stocks to sell put options on, is to wait for them to get down to levels that haven't been touched in quite some time, and then sell even further OTM put options.

When Disney got down to $20 per share, I decided to execute my plan. I went ahead and sold the April 2009 $12.50 put options for $.75 per contract. (See Figure 7.11.) This trade would obligate me to buy 100 shares of Disney at $12.50 per share if Disney fell below that level by the option's expiration in April 2009. $12.50 per share is a price Disney has not seen since August 1993. And since I collected $.75 upfront from the option buyer, my real cost basis would be $11.75. Pretty sweet. This trade was still open when I wrote this section (January 2009), so I had no idea how it would pan out. If you've sold put options before (and even if you haven't), you can see

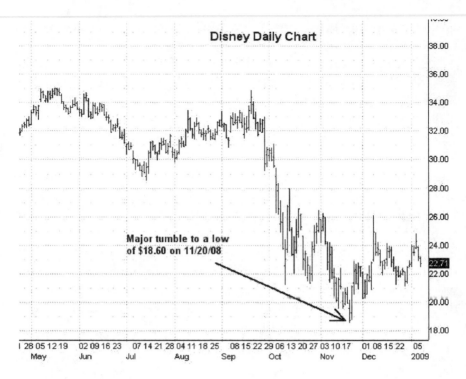

Figure 7.10 Disney
Source: eSignal.com.

Symbol	Date/Time	Exchange	Quantity	T. Price
Equity and Index Options				
USD				
C DEC08 2.5 P	2008-11-21, 10:26:23	-	-1	0.7000
DIS APR09 12.5 P	2008-11-17, 10:17:49	-	-1	0.7500

Figure 7.11 Put-Sell Confirmation
Source: Courtesy Interaction Brokers LLC. All Rights Reserved.

how you can sell options for decent premiums that can sometimes be up to 50 percent OTM from the current price of the stock.

Does It Always Work?

There's no guarantee though, that even if you sell put options on high quality stocks that they won't go down. All stocks go down at some point, as was demonstrated during the market slump in the final quarter of 2008. It's been tough for everyone. The fall in the stock market has brought much misery to many people as they look at their declining portfolio values. Some of the biggest drags on the stock market at that time were the financial stocks and automotive stocks. Many of the best and biggest banks, some that were considered mainstays of any successful portfolio, saw their share prices crushed by up to 90 percent. Companies such as Citigroup, Bear Stearns, Lehman Brothers, Morgan Stanley, and even Goldman Sachs, all had their share prices get walloped. The big three automakers—Ford, General Motors, and Chrysler were trading at their lowest levels in history, and at the time of this book's update (January 2009), had just received a big financial bailout plan from the U.S. government.

Even a great option strategy like naked put selling needs to be used with caution, especially in a declining market, because in the end, you can wind up owning shares of stock while they're still falling in price. But that might not be as bad as it seems, because if you sold put options far enough OTM, the price level of the stocks from which you're assigned (some of which that haven't been seen in 10 to 15 years) could be fantastic. I know that if I'm assigned on the Disney $12.50 put options, I'd be ecstatic to own Disney shares at that level.

Look at some of the INTC examples I gave a few pages back. In January 2009, INTC was trading for $14 per share. That's lower than any of the strike prices that I had sold back in 2006. If that were now, I could've been assigned on my options and had been forced to buy INTC anywhere from $15 to $20 per share. But remember, one of the things about options is that they all expire at some point. All those INTC options that I sold in 2006 have already expired, and I can now sell INTC put options at even lower strike prices—possibly the $7.50 or $10 put options. Could you imagine buying INTC that cheaply now?

Instant Money Trader

With the great success rate one can have with put selling, I've recently started a second option advisory service in November 2008 called the *Instant Money Trader.* This service focuses specifically on selling OTM put options on name brand, top quality, S&P 500 and Dow Jones Industrials stocks. We plan to build a diversified portfolio of these excellent stocks while at the same time get paid cash just for our efforts.

Figure 7.12 shows a sample of one of the actual alerts that we sent out in regard to selling puts.

This was one of the first IMT alerts received by subscribers after we launched in November 2008. Our first trade was a put option sale on Microsoft that expired in April 2009 in which we sold the $17.50 strike price for $1.15 per contract.

Anyone who sold 10 of these put option contracts collected $1,150 in their trading accounts on Day One, while obligating themselves to buy 1,000 shares of Microsoft for $17.50 per share by the April 2009 option expiration. At the time of the trade, MSFT was trading at $21.75 per share, so we were looking to buy MSFT at another 20 percent below its then-current value. If the stock didn't trade below $17.50 by the option's expiration, then we wouldn't get to buy any shares—but at least we got compensated with cold, hard cash up front. We couldn't know how the trade would turn out at the time this section was written in January 2009.

IN$TANT MONEY
─────TRADER─────

The Instant Money Trader
105 W. Monument Street
Baltimore, MD 21201

Thursday, November 6, 2008

Email - #3

Hello Instant Money Traders.

Yesterday we successfully implemented our first put-sell trade on Microsoft stock. We were able to sell the April 2009 $17.50 put options for a price of $1.15 per option. Some of you may have gotten more for that option depending on when you received the alert.

If you sold 10 options, you would receive $1150 into your trading account and will now have a margin requirement based on your broker's parameters. If we end up buying MSFT at $17.50 per share in April, you will be buying 1000 shares of it and have to pay for it in full at that time. If you sold less options, your obligation is for less shares, of course.

Currently, MSFT is now at $21.75 per share, still a full $4.25 higher than our targeted buy point. If you follow the option prices, you will see them fluctuate higher or lower depending on where MSFT is currently trading and how much time is left before option expiration. Our ultimate goal is to own the shares at $17.50. If that doesn't happen, then at least we get to keep the money we collected yesterday.

Here's a current monthly chart of MSFT with our targeted buy point drawn in.   *(Continues)*

Figure 7.12 Instant Money Trader Alert
Source: Mt. Vernon Research.

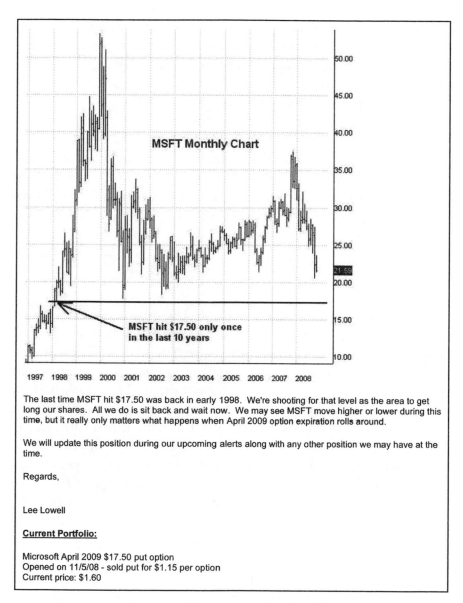

The last time MSFT hit $17.50 was back in early 1998. We're shooting for that level as the area to get long our shares. All we do is sit back and wait now. We may see MSFT move higher or lower during this time, but it really only matters what happens when April 2009 option expiration rolls around.

We will update this position during our upcoming alerts along with any other position we may have at the time.

Regards,

Lee Lowell

Current Portfolio:

Microsoft April 2009 $17.50 put option
Opened on 11/5/08 - sold put for $1.15 per option
Current price: $1.60

Figure 7.12 *(Continued)*

RISK MANAGEMENT

Once again, we want to talk about a risk management plan. In the case of the put–selling strategy, make sure that you don't sell too many options above your comfort zone. If you normally buy stock in 500-share lots, then don't sell more than five put option contracts. If you get assigned on the options, you will receive that many shares in your account and have to pay for them in full at that time. And as I mentioned previously, don't sell put options just to receive the premiums *unless* you are well aware of the risks and are able to watch your position at all times. Don't get caught! It can hurt badly.

Once you do get assigned on the options and end up with shares of stock, you're now going to be long stock in your account with full exposure to the market. Play that position as you would like any other stock you currently have. Do you have a stop-loss point, or are you just going to hold forever? You can re-read what I wrote in the risk management plan from Chapter 6 to get some ideas in setting steps on long positions. Whatever your choice, make sure you have a plan.

WRAPUP

Let's wrap it up in a nutshell. If you want to buy shares of stock cheaper than where they currently trade, you can place a limit buy order and wait, hoping that it comes down in price—not a very efficient way to use your time. Or, you can be a smart option trader and sell some put options at a strike price below the current price of the stock (OTM) and wait to see what happens. At expiration, either you will be assigned the shares of stock and will have to pay for them at that time, or the option will be abandoned and expire worthless, in which case you do not get to buy the stock. But, in either scenario, you always get to keep the premium that the buyer pays to you at the beginning of the transaction. If you are not assigned, you have the luxury of repeating the process all over again next month. Look at the strategy as a double winner. You get to buy the stock at a discount and/or you get to keep the money for your time and effort. How great is that? It's just another way to help you get rich with options.

Remember, there is no guarantee with this strategy that you will be able to buy the stock at a lower price. That's only going to happen if the stock falls below your strike price by expiration. But that's okay, because you've set your buy levels at a predetermined point. If it never gets there, then fine. So be it. But at least you know you're taking a proactive approach with your money and doing something with it. None of us should ever be sitting idle with our money when there are other ways to increase it. Why not have someone hand you cash today that can sit in your account earning interest while you wait to see if you can buy your stock at a little cheaper price down the road? Just do it!

I truly believe this strategy is one that anyone can master with a little time and effort. Learning how to trade options will not happen overnight. It is something that you must research and learn how to do just like any other skill. But it is something that you can do right out of your own home, just as I do every day. You just need to figure out what stock you like and then must figure out which put options you want to sell. If you have a home computer and a connection to the Internet, you have all the tools necessary. This can be a great part-time or full-time home business for anyone willing to put forth the effort.

As a final tip, you should always concentrate on selling OTM put options as this will allow you to compensate for large falls in the stock price, and to potentially allow you to buy the stock at very attractive, historical levels.

CHAPTER 8

OPTION CREDIT SPREADS: THE ALL-STAR STRATEGY

This is it, my favorite "option-selling" strategy of all time. This is #3 of the group and it's the trade that I execute more than any other for my personal accounts. I can't say enough good things about the option credit spread. I feel so strongly about this method that I'm willing to use it with almost every trade. It not only gives a nice cushion for directional error, but it also lets you collect income due to the "selling" nature of the strategy, and lastly, it has a limited loss feature. Option credit spreads fall mostly into the income-producing category, but they have hedging and speculation features as well. The option credit spread can be used at any time, in any market scenario, and for any type of security. It's that diverse!

Option credit spreads can give you the best of all worlds when taking a position. For example, how many times have you bought a stock or option and it immediately moves in the wrong direction, or doesn't go far enough in the right direction? Too many times, I bet. Selling option credit spreads can help alleviate that problem. One of the greatest benefits of the option credit spread is the cushion it gives you in case of incorrect directional prediction. How awesome is that? The way it accomplishes that is by concentrating on selling out-of-the-money (OTM) strike prices within the spread.

Here again, we are going to take advantage of the option buyers who concentrate on risking their money on the low-probability, short-term, OTM options. We will be selling these options to them, but not as single, unlimited-risk types of trades. We will be selling them as option spreads, which have a defined limited risk, as well as a limited reward feature. I'm going to show you so many real-life examples that your head will spin in amazement at how simple and lucrative this strategy can be. I want to open your eyes to the fact that option selling can be one of your best allies in the marketplace.

THE FIRST STEPS

In order to take advantage of this strategy, you need to open up your mind to the fact that you're not going to try to predict where the market **will go to** in the allotted time frame (expiration month), but where the market likely *won't go to* in the allotted time frame. There's a huge difference in those two approaches. In the first approach (the one we don't want to take), you're making a guess at where you think the market will end up at the end of option expiration. As I've been saying throughout this book, that is the hardest game to win. Nobody is that good at figuring out the where and when of a market move. But, if you are somewhat good at having at least a general idea of which way the market is headed (either higher or lower), you can also make a pretty good guess as to where the market probably *won't* end up at option expiration.

With this approach, you'll have more than one way to win. When you sell options, your only concern is for the market to **NOT** go past the OTM option strike that you sold. That's the key, and that's what this strategy will focus on. When you sell an OTM option, or an OTM option spread, you can win in three different market scenarios as opposed to the buyer only having one winning scenario.

So the first step is to pick a stock or commodity that you have a general idea of where it might be headed. Now, let's make sure we're on the same page here. I'm assuming that when you make an investment or a trading decision, you have done a fair amount of research and analysis on the specific stock or commodity, allowing you to make a fairly educated decision on its future direction. We don't want to be taking these trades as a result of gut feelings, tips from friends, chat room suggestions, or any other dubious sources. I want you to have a concrete, well-thought-out idea of where the underlying security might be headed. And that goes for every other strategy I discuss in the book as well.

After you have picked the stock or commodity and the direction in which you believe it will move, it's time to pick the strike prices and the expiration date. Since we are selling options in this strategy, we will be taking advantage of the "time decay" factor. If you remember, time decay is the process by which an option will lose a little bit of its value day after day, regardless of which direction the underlying security moves and regardless of whether it moves in your favor or not. The one characteristic of time decay I want to impress upon you is the fact that time decay will accelerate the closer you get to option expiration day. This means that the option will lose value faster as it nears expiration day. Even though the option is losing value every day, the value gets lost faster as expiration draws near.

For example, if you bought a six-month option for $5.00, the value lost in the first month might only be $1.00, but the value lost in the last month before expiration day might be $3.00 (if it still remained OTM). In this case, the time value decay was three times as big in the last month even though it happened in the same amount of time (one-month intervals). So, when selling option credit spreads, we want to concentrate on picking shorter-term expiration months—not more than 90 days in length—and option strikes that are OTM.

Back up for one second. Just to clarify the actual mechanics of the trade, an option credit spread entails the buying and selling of the same amount of options as a single transaction for a single price. You don't have to worry about trying to buy one option first and then selling the other option at a later time. It's all done together. The options are done in the same expiration month with different strike prices and are either both call options or both put options. It is called a credit spread because you will be selling the more expensive of the two options, which will yield a cash credit to your account. When you buy the more expensive option, it is called a "debit" spread because money is taken out of your account. We like the idea of having money deposited into our account.

Option credit spreads come in two flavors:

1. *Bear call option credit spread*—a neutral/bearish directional option spread used with call options.
2. *Bull put option credit spread*—a neutral/bullish directional option spread used with put options.

Throughout the rest of the chapter I will refer to each spread as either "bear call" or "bull put."

HOW THE OPTION CREDIT SPREAD WORKS

The best way to see how the strategy works is with good old-fashioned examples. All the examples that you will see in this chapter are actual trades that I've done in one of my smaller commodity trading accounts. These trades constitute one part of my overall trading portfolios. Not only will I show you the chart that I used to make the initial assessment, but I'll also include the confirmation statements from my broker. There are no hypotheticals or fluff here. These are all real trades.

Before I get into the actual trades, I want to show you the mentality of the how and why of the option credit spread and why it works so well. Figure 8.1 is the type of chart that you will see throughout this chapter. This one happens to be a daily chart of sugar futures from September 2005 to February 2006. The top panel is the actual sugar chart with three different moving average lines and the lower panel is the RSI technical indicator that I use to help with my directional assessment.

There's no doubt that sugar has been in a solid uptrend. Any smart trader who wants to get involved with sugar would probably be best served by sticking with that bullish attitude. But what's the best option play? I think many traders would try to buy a call option at a strike price above the current price of sugar hoping that it would get there by the option expiration date. These traders are trying to predict where sugar might **"go to"** by that date. With option credit spreads,

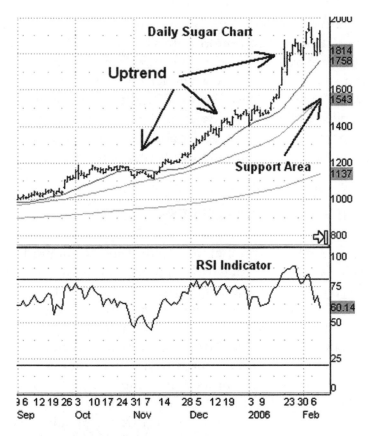

Figure 8.1 Sugar Daily Chart
Source: eSignal.com.

we're trying to predict where the market probably **"won't go to"** by the expiration date. Let's explain that.

Since I want to go with the trend, I would pick a bullish option strategy. But instead of picking an area higher on the chart, I would pick an area lower on the chart where I don't think sugar will go back down to by option expiration. Understand that? I do this by using my technical analysis indicators. On the chart, I would feel pretty strongly that sugar will not go below the 1600 level over the short term. So with that prediction in mind, I would sell an **OTM bull put option credit spread**. This is a bullishly oriented strategy that has defined risk and defined reward parameters.

I would sell the 1600 put and simultaneously buy the 1550 put as a single transaction and receive an up-front option premium payment from the buyer. The 1600 level is lower than where the current price of sugar is (1814 level as seen on right side of chart). As long as sugar does not retrace back down below the 1600 level by option expiration, our credit spread trade will be a winner because both options of the spread will expire worthless. We would get to keep the full premium that we collected from the buyer at the beginning of the trade. That's how it works. And the great thing about the option credit spread is that we can use it in bullish and bearish environments.

REAL-LIFE TRADE EXAMPLES

Read on to see how typical option credit spreads can produce winning trades without having to be pinpoint accurate with market direction. Based on technical chart patterns, I initiated the following option credit spread trades for the commodities indicated. I had an initial idea about the general direction of the market and the option credit spread helped me take advantage of that prediction. All of the option credit spreads that I executed were out-of-the-money (OTM) to begin with, which gave me a cushion and margin for error in case I was wrong on the direction. Time decay worked in my favor as the OTM options (and all options) lost a little bit of value every day. I count on that value loss to add to my overall profitability.

Remember, the idea of selling options is to let time decay erode the option price so we can buy it back cheaper for a nice profit, or to let all strikes expire worthless so we can keep all the money that we received up front from the option buyer. I'm not looking to predict where the market will go to in the allotted time. I'm just looking for the market to not go through my short option strike (which happens to be well away from the current price of the security). This is the driving force in succeeding with option-selling tactics.

Option Credit Spread #1

Figure 8.2 is a daily cotton chart spanning from August 2003 to March 2004. Each single black vertical bar in the top panel represents one day's worth of trading in the cotton futures market. The top of each bar represents the high of the day for the market and the bottom of

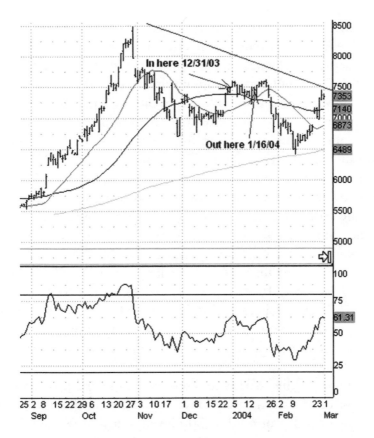

Figure 8.2 Daily Cotton Chart
Source: eSignal.com.

each bar represents the low of the day for cotton. Each bar also has a small dash mark on the left side and one on the right side. The left dash mark represents where the futures opened up for trading on that day and the right dash mark represents where the futures market closed on that specific day of trading. I explain this to you so you have an idea of what the chart represents.

My option credit spread was initiated on 12/31/2003. Here is what I saw on that day when cotton was trading around the 7500 mark (values are located on the right side of the chart): Cotton seemed to have finished the pullback from its uptrend that started in September. Since I felt that cotton was going to continue higher, I opted to sell a bull put option credit spread, which is a neutral to bullish play. I sold the 7000/7100 put option credit spread on 12/31/2003 for 32 points, which equates to $160 in the cotton market. Each commodity works on a different point system. In the cotton market, each point is worth $5. The actual mechanics of the option credit spread trade involved selling the 7100 put strike and buying the 7000 put strike both together in one transaction for a net credit of 32 points.

This was an OTM put spread with roughly a 400-point cushion. This means that the cotton futures were 400 points away from my spread seeing any danger. The strike price I sold was at the 7100 level, well below the current cotton price of 7500. Since I was bullish and expecting cotton to move higher, I felt that cotton would not turn on me and move lower 400 points to turn the trade sour. Instead of trying to predict how high or how far cotton might go up to, I was making a guess as to where cotton most likely *won't go to*. Sixteen days later, on 1/16/2004, I bought the spread back for 16 points ($80) to close out the trade. When I bought the spread back, I bought the 7100 strike put and sold the 7000 strike put together in a single transaction for 16 points. This closed out the whole trade and I now had no position. Nice and clean!

If you look at the chart, you'll see the main benefit of option selling. The price of cotton barely moved at all during the time our position was open (still around the 7500 level), but due to time decay, we were able to close out the spread for a profit of $80 per spread. This was a quick 23.6 percent return on margin money in 16 days. (See Figure 8.3.)

Option Credit Spread #2

Figure 8.4 is a daily chart of coffee futures from late 2003 to May 2004. Before our trade, coffee had a big move up on January 5, 2004, which formed a "flagpole" pattern. The next few days formed the rest of the bullish part of the flag pattern, which was my signal to go long. I opted for a bullish OTM bull put option credit spread. On 1/8/04, coffee was trading near the 6800 mark and I sold the 6250/6500 put spread, which gave me roughly 300 points of cushion. You calculate the cushion amount by subtracting the short strike of the spread from the current price of the commodity (6800 − 6500 = 300).

```
*  *  *  *  *  *  *  *  *  *   C O N F I R M A T I O N   *  *  *  *  *

THE FOLLOWING TRADES HAVE BEEN MADE THIS DAY FOR YOUR ACCOUNT AND RISK.

TRADE    SETTL   AT     BUY          SELL        CONTRACT DESCRIPTION          EX TRADE PRICE CC
-------  ------- --  -------------- ------------ ------------------------------ -- ----------- --
12/31/3          F1           1                  PUT  MAR 04 NYC COTTON    7000 13     1.10    US
                                                 SPREAD
                 F1           1*                 EX- 2/06/04                     COMMISSION US
                 F1                                                          CLEARING FEES US
                 F1                                                          EXCHANGE FEES US
                 F1                                                              NFA FEES US
                 F1                                                             BROKERAGE US
                 F1                                         PREMIUM / GROSS AMT US

12/31/3          F1                         1    PUT  MAR 04 NYC COTTON    7100 13     1.42    US
                                                 SPREAD
                 F1                         1*   EX- 2/06/04                     COMMISSION US
*  *  *  *  *  *  *  *  *  *   C O N F I R M A T I O N   *  *  *  *  *

THE FOLLOWING TRADES HAVE BEEN MADE THIS DAY FOR YOUR ACCOUNT AND RISK.

TRADE    SETTL   AT     BUY          SELL        CONTRACT DESCRIPTION          EX TRADE PRICE CC
-------  ------- --  -------------- ------------ ------------------------------ -- ----------- --
1/16/4           F1                         1    PUT  MAR 04 NYC COTTON    7000 13      .30    US
                                                 SPREAD
                 F1                         1*   EX- 2/06/04                     COMMISSION US
                 F1                                                          CLEARING FEES US
                 F1                                                          EXCHANGE FEES US
                 F1                                                              NFA FEES US
                 F1                                                             BROKERAGE US
                 F1                                         PREMIUM / GROSS AMT US

1/16/4           F1           1                  PUT  MAR 04 NYC COTTON    7100 13      .46    US
                                                 SPREAD
                 F1           1*                 EX- 2/06/04                     COMMISSION US
```

Figure 8.3   Cotton OTM Bull Put Option Credit Spread—Open and Closed

Data Source: Commodity trading statements.

Once again, I chose to sell the strike price at a level lower than where coffee was trading at the time of execution. Since I was bullish, I didn't think coffee would retrace back down below 6500 before offsetting the trade.

I sold the spread for 70 points ($262.50) and then bought it back for 35 points ($131.25) on 1/20/04. Coffee has a point multiplier of $3.75 per point. Again, the mechanics of the trade involved selling the more expensive strike (6500 strike) and buying the cheaper strike (6250 strike) in one single transaction. Since you are selling a more expensive option, you get to receive that money into your account. We aren't taking on unlimited-risk trades here. The reason I execute spread trades is to keep my potential losses capped and known ahead of time. Remember, you don't have to always buy options to be successful. We make profits on credit spreads by using our technical analysis

Figure 8.4 Daily Coffee Chart
Source: eSignal.com.

abilities and capturing time decay. The trade worked well quickly not only due to the time decay but also because the coffee market moved higher as I had expected. It was a quick 19.4 percent return on margin money in just 12 days. (See Figure 8.5.)

```
*   *   *   *   *   *   *   *   *   *   C O N F I R M A T I O N   *   *   *   *   *

THE FOLLOWING TRADES HAVE BEEN MADE THIS DAY FOR YOUR ACCOUNT AND RISK.

TRADE   SETTL  AT    BUY           SELL       CONTRACT DESCRIPTION        EX TRADE PRICE CC
------- ------ --  -------------- ---------   ---------------------------- -- ----------- -- .
1/08/4         F1                  1          PUT  MAR 04 CSC COFFEE C  625 06    .70    US
                                              SPREAD
               F1                  1*         EX- 2/13/04                      COMMISSION US
               F1                                                             CLEARING FEES US
               F1                                                             EXCHANGE FEES US
               F1                                                                NFA FEES US
               F1                                                                BROKERAGE US
               F1                                                     PREMIUM / GROSS AMT US

1/08/4         F1                  1    PUT  MAR 04 CSC COFFEE C  650 06    1.40   US
                                       SPREAD
               F1                  1*  EX- 2/13/04                      COMMISSION US
*   *   *   *   *   *   *   *   *   *   C O N F I R M A T I O N   *   *   *   *   *

THE FOLLOWING TRADES HAVE BEEN MADE THIS DAY FOR YOUR ACCOUNT AND RISK.

TRADE   SETTL  AT    BUY           SELL       CONTRACT DESCRIPTION        EX TRADE PRICE CC
------- ------ --  -------------- ---------   ---------------------------- -- ----------- -- .
1/20/4         F1                  1    PUT  MAR 04 CSC COFFEE C  625 06    .15   US
                                       SPREAD
               F1                  1*  EX- 2/13/04                      COMMISSION US
               F1                                                      CLEARING FEES US
               F1                                                      EXCHANGE FEES US
               F1                                                         NFA FEES US
               F1                                                         BROKERAGE US
               F1                                              PREMIUM / GROSS AMT US

1/20/4         F1                  1          PUT  MAR 04 CSC COFFEE C  650 06    .50   US
                                              SPREAD
               F1                  1*         EX- 2/13/04                      COMMISSION US
```

Figure 8.5   Coffee OTM Bull Put Option Credit Spread—Open and Closed
Data Source: Commodity trading statements.

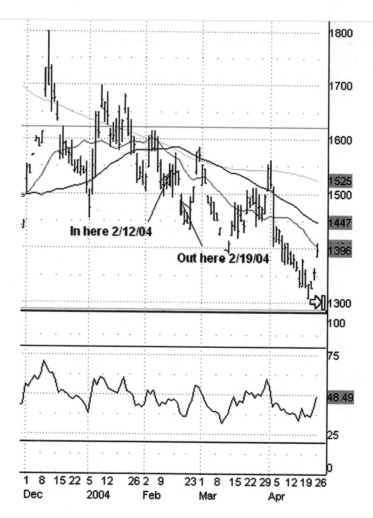

Figure 8.6   Cocoa Daily Chart
Source: eSignal.com.

ITM Option Spread #1

Figure 8.6 is a daily chart of cocoa futures from December 2003 to May 2004. Cocoa was in a nice downtrend and I opted to buy an in-the-money (ITM) put option debit spread this time. This was a slight divergence from my usual credit spread activity, but I felt very strongly about cocoa making a quick move downward. Buying ITM helps to minimize time decay and increases the delta, which helps to realize

```
*  *  *  *  *  *  *  *  *     C O N F I R M A T I O N     *   *   *   *   *

THE FOLLOWING TRADES HAVE BEEN MADE THIS DAY FOR YOUR ACCOUNT AND RISK.

TRADE    SETTL   AT      BUY          SELL       CONTRACT DESCRIPTION           EX TRADE PRICE CC
-------  ------  --  ---------------  ---------- ------------------------------ -- ------------ -- -
2/12/4           F1                        1     PUT  APR  04  CSC  COCOA-MTR 1450 06       .15    US
                                                 SPREAD
                 F1                       1*      EX- 3/05/04                         COMMISSION US
                 F1                                                                 CLEARING FEES US
                 F1                                                                 EXCHANGE FEES US
                 F1                                                                      NFA FEES US
                 F1                                                                      BROKERAGE US
                 F1                                                          PREMIUM / GROSS AMT US

2/12/4           F1       1                      PUT  APR  04  CSC  COCOA-MTR 1500 06       .30    US
                                                 SPREAD
                 F1      1*                       EX- 3/05/04                         COMMISSION US
*  *  *  *  *  *  *  *  *     C O N F I R M A T I O N     *   *   *   *   *

THE FOLLOWING TRADES HAVE BEEN MADE THIS DAY FOR YOUR ACCOUNT AND RISK.

TRADE    SETTL   AT      BUY          SELL       CONTRACT DESCRIPTION           EX TRADE PRICE CC
-------  ------  --  ---------------  ---------- ------------------------------ -- ------------ -- -
2/19/4           F1       1                      PUT  APR  04  CSC  COCOA-MTR 1450 06       .35    US
                                                 SPREAD
                 F1      1*                       EX- 3/05/04                         COMMISSION US
                 F1                                                                 CLEARING FEES US
                 F1                                                                 EXCHANGE FEES US
                 F1                                                                      NFA FEES US
                 F1                                                                      BROKERAGE US
                 F1                                                          PREMIUM / GROSS AMT US

2/19/4           F1                        1     PUT  APR  04  CSC  COCOA-MTR 1500 06       .60    US
                                                 SPREAD
                 F1                       1*      EX- 3/05/04                         COMMISSION US
```

Figure 8.7   Cocoa ITM Put Option Debit Spread—Open and Closed
Data Source: Commodity trading statements.

gains much faster if the directional call is correct. To capitalize on my prediction that cocoa would keep moving lower, I bought the 1500 put and sold the 1450 put as a spread on 2/12/04 for 15 points ($150) and sold it out on 2/19/04 for 25 points ($250). It was a quick $100 gain per spread or 66 percent return on invested money in just seven days. (See Figure 8.7.)

Option Credit Spread #3

Continuing on with my bearish cocoa outlook, I then initiated an OTM 1450/1500 bear call credit spread sale on 5/3/04 for 14 points ($140) by selling the 1450 call and buying the 1500 call. I then bought

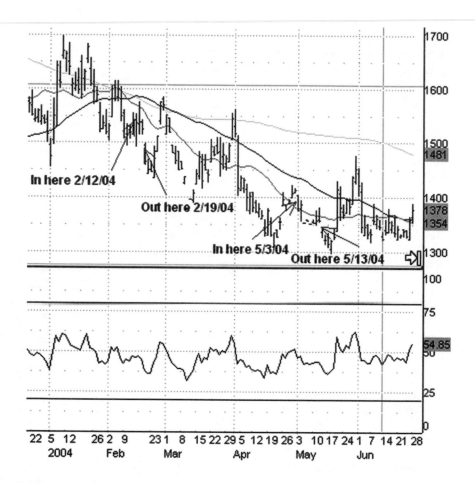

Figure 8.8 Daily Cocoa Chart
Source: eSignal.com.

back the spread for 7 points ($70) on 5/13/04 for a quick 19.4 percent return on margin money in 10 days. (See Figure 8.8.)

In this case, the short strike (1450) in the spread was above the market price of cocoa, so cocoa could move up slightly against our prediction and we'd still make money on the trade. The mechanics of the trade had me selling the more expensive 1450 call and buying the less expensive 1500 call in a single net credit transaction for 14 points ($140).

Every OTM option credit spread has three ways to win. All we need to do is watch time decay eat away at the option prices and/or have the

```
*  *  *  *  *  *  *  *  *     C O N F I R M A T I O N     *  *  *  *  *

THE FOLLOWING TRADES HAVE BEEN MADE THIS DAY FOR YOUR ACCOUNT AND RISK.

TRADE   SETTL  AT    BUY          SELL          CONTRACT DESCRIPTION            EX TRADE PRICE CC
------- ------ --  ------------  ------------  ----------------------------    -- ----------- -- .
5/03/4         F1                 1  CALL JUL 04 CSC COCOA-MTR 1450 06           .36    US
                                     SPREAD
               F1                1*  EX- 6/04/04                          COMMISSION     US
               F1                                                       CLEARING FEES    US
               F1                                                       EXCHANGE FEES    US
               F1                                                            NFA FEES    US
               F1                                                           BROKERAGE    US
               F1                                            PREMIUM / GROSS AMT         US

5/03/4         F1    1                 CALL JUL 04 CSC COCOA-MTR 1500 06           .22    US
                                       SPREAD
               F1   1*                  EX- 6/04/04                       COMMISSION     US
5/13/4         F1    1                 CALL JUL 04 CSC COCOA-MTR 1450 06           .14    US
                                       SPREAD
               F1   1*                  EX- 6/04/04                       COMMISSION     US
               F1                                                       CLEARING FEES    US
               F1                                                       EXCHANGE FEES    US
               F1                                                            NFA FEES    US
               F1                                                           BROKERAGE    US
               F1                                            PREMIUM / GROSS AMT         US

5/13/4         F1                 1  CALL JUL 04 CSC COCOA-MTR 1500 06           .07    US
                                     SPREAD
               F1                1*  EX- 6/04/04                          COMMISSION     US
               F1                                                       CLEARING FEES    US
```

Figure 8.9 Cocoa OTM Bear Call Option Credit Spread—Open and Closed
Data Source: Commodity trading statements.

commodity move in the correct direction so we can take profits even faster. In this case, cocoa could move lower and we'd be making money. Cocoa could stay at the same level and we'd profit from time decay. And the best part is that cocoa could even move higher, against our initial directional call, and we'd still be able to make money on the trade. As long as cocoa didn't move up past the 1450 level (our short option strike), we'd be in good shape. That's why it's important to sell OTM spreads. This is what gives you the cushion. You're giving yourself three scenarios to have a profitable trade. That's nice! (See Figure 8.9.)

Speculative Call Buy #1

Just to prove the point that selling options isn't my only form of trading, here is one of my purely "speculative" trades that I executed in the

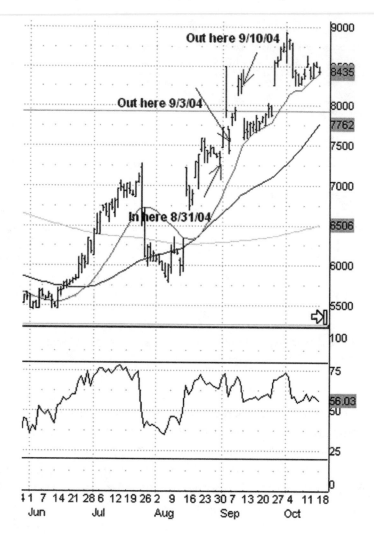

Figure 8.10 Daily Orange Juice Chart
Source: eSignal.com.

orange juice market back in 2004. (See Figure 8.10.) I live in Florida so
I'm well aware of the hurricane season. This trade was executed during
the first or second of the hurricanes that swept through the state that
summer. I bought two 9000 strike calls on 8/31/04 for 90 points ($135)
each and sold them out on two dates, 9/3/04 and 9/10/04, for 225
points ($337.50) and 350 points ($525), respectively. Not only did the

```
*   *   *   *   *   *   *   *   *   *    C O N F I R M A T I O N    *   *   *   *   *

THE FOLLOWING TRADES HAVE BEEN MADE THIS DAY FOR YOUR ACCOUNT AND RISK.

TRADE   SETTL  AT       BUY           SELL         CONTRACT DESCRIPTION              EX TRADE PRICE CC
-------  ------- --  --------------- ---------------  -------------------------------- -- ----------- -- .
8/31/4         F1            2                      CALL NOV 04 NYC FRZN O J  9000 13    .90    US
               F1            2*                     EX-10/15/04                        COMMISSION US
               F1                                                            CLEARING/PRCSNG FEES US
               F1                                                            PREMIUM / GROSS AMT US


9/03/4         F1                         1    CALL NOV 04 NYC FRZN O J  9000 13   2.25   US
               F1                         1*   EX-10/15/04                        COMMISSION US
               F1                                                       CLEARING/PRCSNG FEES US
               F1                                                       PREMIUM / GROSS AMT US

*   *   *   *   *   *   *   *   *   *    C O N F I R M A T I O N    *   *   *   *   *

THE FOLLOWING TRADES HAVE BEEN MADE THIS DAY FOR YOUR ACCOUNT AND RISK.

TRADE   SETTL  AT       BUY           SELL         CONTRACT DESCRIPTION              EX TRADE PRICE CC
-------  ------- --  --------------- ---------------  -------------------------------- -- ----------- -- .
9/10/4         F1                         1    CALL NOV 04 NYC FRZN O J  9000 13   3.50   US
                                                SPREAD
               F1                         1*   EX-10/15/04                        COMMISSION US
               F1                                                       CLEARING/PRCSNG FEES US
               F1                                                       PREMIUM / GROSS AMT US
```

Figure 8.11 Orange Juice Directional Call Buy—Open and Closed

Data Source: Commodity trading statements.

direction help me profit on this trade but the emotional volatility helped just as much. When people panic, it adds more value to the options and their prices will increase even if the commodity doesn't move. I had a quick 150 percent and 289 percent return on invested money in 3 to 11 days' time. (See Figure 8.11.)

Figure 8.12   Coffee Daily Chart
Source: eSignal.com.

Option Credit Spread #4

Here is another quick bullish play in the coffee market. Figure 8.12 shows coffee futures from July 2004 to November 2004. I sold the 7000/7250 bull put spread for 75 points ($281.25) on 9/20/04 and bought back the spread on 9/22/04 for 45 points ($168.75). I got in and got out for a quick 17 percent return on margin money in two

```
*  *  *  *  *  *  *  *  *  *  *    C O N F I R M A T I O N    *  *  *  *  *

THE FOLLOWING TRADES HAVE BEEN MADE THIS DAY FOR YOUR ACCOUNT AND RISK.

TRADE    SETTL   AT    BUY          SELL       CONTRACT DESCRIPTION           EX TRADE PRICE CC
-------  ------- --  -------------- ---------- ------------------------------- -- ----------- -- .
9/20/4           F1         1                  PUT  DEC 04 CSC COFFEE C  700 06      1.00      US
                                               SPREAD
                 F1                 1*         EX-11/12/04                         COMMISSION US
                 F1                                                        CLEARING/PRCSNG FEES US
                 F1                                                        PREMIUM / GROSS AMT US

9/20/4           F1                       1    PUT  DEC 04 CSC COFFEE C  725 06      1.75      US
                                               SPREAD
                 F1                      1*    EX-11/12/04                         COMMISSION US
                 F1                                                        CLEARING/PRCSNG FEES US
                 F1                                                        PREMIUM / GROSS AMT US

9/22/4           F1                       1    PUT  DEC 04 CSC COFFEE C  700 06       .40      US
                                               SPREAD
                 F1                      1*    EX-11/12/04                         COMMISSION US
                 F1                                                        CLEARING/PRCSNG FEES US
                 F1                                                        PREMIUM / GROSS AMT US

9/22/4           F1         1                  PUT  DEC 04 CSC COFFEE C  725 06       .85      US
                                               SPREAD
                 F1                 1*         EX-11/12/04                         COMMISSION US
                 F1                                                        CLEARING/PRCSNG FEES US
                 F1                                                        PREMIUM / GROSS AMT US
```

Figure 8.13   Coffee OTM Bull Put Option Credit Spread—Open and Closed

Data Source: Commodity trading statements.

days. The coffee point multiplier is \$3.75 per point. Coffee futures were trading for roughly 7850 at the time of the trade, which gave me at least 600 points of cushion to be incorrect in directional bias. As long as coffee didn't go below 7175 before option expiration, I would make money on the trade. (See Figure 8.13.)

One thing I haven't mentioned fully is that the cushion for directional error is even larger than the difference between the short option strike and the current price of the futures market. Since we're selling the spread, our breakeven price is calculated by taking the credit we receive from the buyer and subtracting it from our short option strike. As I mentioned, the breakeven on this trade was at the 7175 level (7250 short strike − 75 points = 7175). At that point, the coffee futures were almost 700 points away from me being in danger! In the case of option credit spreads, the breakeven point is where we will start to lose money. We want that point to be far away from the current price of the futures market. You can go back and look at every trade I've shown you here and see the large cushion that I started with. That's the beauty of selling OTM spreads—you can be wrong on your direction and still make money.

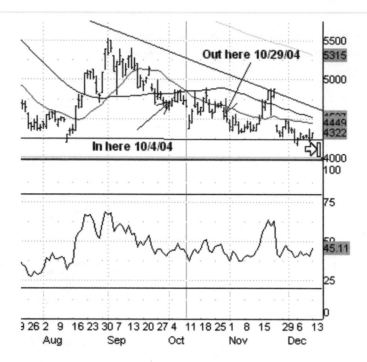

Figure 8.14   Daily Cotton Chart
Source: eSignal.com.

RETURN ON MARGIN

You might have noticed that when I mention the profit gain on the trade, I describe the results as "return on margin money." This is due to the fact that when you sell an option, you are not actually paying, or investing, any money in the trade. Someone is giving you money instead. So, in order for your broker to hold the trade for you, the broker will require you to deposit some good faith money, or margin money, to keep on hand while the position is open. There is a certain formula used to figure out how much margin is needed, and I've taken that into consideration when I present my return figures here. When selling options, your return on margin is calculated by dividing how much you made on the trade by how much initial margin was required by your broker at

```
10/04/4        F1                          1   CALL DEC 04 NYC COTTON    4900 13      1.50    US
                                               SPREAD
               F1                          1*  EX-11/12/04                       COMMISSION US
               F1                                                       CLEARING/PRCSNG FEES US
               F1                                                       PREMIUM / GROSS AMT US

10/04/4        F1              1               CALL DEC 04 NYC COTTON    5000 13      1.20    US
                                               SPREAD
               F1              1*              EX-11/12/04                       COMMISSION US
               F1                                                       CLEARING/PRCSNG FEES US
               F1                                                       PREMIUM / GROSS AMT US

*   *   *   *   *   *   *   *   *   *   C O N F I R M A T I O N   *   *   *   *   *

THE FOLLOWING TRADES HAVE BEEN MADE THIS DAY FOR YOUR ACCOUNT AND RISK.

TRADE    SETTL  AT     BUY            SELL        CONTRACT DESCRIPTION          EX TRADE PRICE CC
-------  -----  --  -------------- -------------- ---------------------------- -- ----------- --
10/29/4        F1              1               CALL DEC 04 NYC COTTON    4900 13      .08     US
                                               SPREAD
               F1              1*              EX-11/12/04                       COMMISSION US
               F1                                                       CLEARING/PRCSNG FEES US
               F1                                                       PREMIUM / GROSS AMT US

10/29/4        F1                          1   CALL DEC 04 NYC COTTON    5000 13      .15     US
                                               SPREAD
               F1                          1*  EX-11/12/04                       COMMISSION US
               F1                                                       CLEARING/PRCSNG FEES US
               F1                                                       PREMIUM / GROSS AMT US
```

Figure 8.15   Cotton OTM Bear Call Option Credit Spread—Open and Closed
Data Source: Commodity trading statements.

the beginning of the transaction. In the coffee example, my margin requirement was $656.25. Since I made $112.50 on the trade, my return on margin (ROM) was 17 percent ($112.50/$656.25 = 17%).

Option Credit Spread #5

Going with the downtrend in cotton, I sold the 4900/5000 bear call option credit spread on 10/4/04 for 30 points ($150) and bought the spread back on 10/29/04 for 7 points ($35). (See Figure 8.14.) I netted $115 per spread. This may not seem like much, but if you do multiple spreads, it can add up quickly. I like to get in and out of many trades just like this one: a quick 32.9 percent return on margin money in 25 days.

At the time of initiation of this particular spread, the current price of cotton futures was at about the 4750 level, which gave me a minimum of 150 cotton points cushion for the market to move against me before having to institute a contingency plan. You can always breathe easier knowing that you have many scenarios with which to be correct when selling options. (See Figure 8.15.)

Figure 8.16   Daily Cotton Chart
Source: eSignal.com.

Option Credit Spread #6

Continuing with the cotton market (Figure 8.16), I saw an upside
breakout toward the end of December 2004. I opted for a bullish
trade this time and sold the 4100/4200 bull put spread on two occa-
sions, 1/12/05 and 1/18/05, for 18 points ($90) and 17 points ($85),
respectively. This meant that I sold the 4200 strike put options and
bought the 4100 strike put options in a single spread transaction on
each of two separate dates. The cotton market multiplier is $5 per
point. The market moved against me initially by trending lower in
January 2005, but eventually turned around higher and moved in my

1/12/5	F1		1		PUT MAY 05 NYC COTTON SPREAD	4100 13	.50	US
	F1	1*			EX- 4/15/05		COMMISSION	US
	F1						CLEARING/PRCSNG FEES	US
	F1						PREMIUM / GROSS AMT	US
1/12/5	F1			1	PUT MAY 05 NYC COTTON SPREAD	4200 13	.69	US
	F1			1*	EX- 4/15/05		COMMISSION	US
	F1						CLEARING/PRCSNG FEES	US
	F1						PREMIUM / GROSS AMT	US

* * * * * * * * * * *   C O N F I R M A T I O N   * * * * *

THE FOLLOWING TRADES HAVE BEEN MADE THIS DAY FOR YOUR ACCOUNT AND RISK.

TRADE	SETTL	AT	BUY	SELL	CONTRACT DESCRIPTION	EX TRADE PRICE	CC
1/18/5	F1		1		PUT MAY 05 NYC COTTON SPREAD	4100 13 .53	US
	F1	1*			EX- 4/15/05	COMMISSION	US
	F1					CLEARING/PRCSNG FEES	US
	F1					PREMIUM / GROSS AMT	US
1/18/5	F1			1	PUT MAY 05 NYC COTTON SPREAD	4200 13 .70	US
	F1			1*	EX- 4/15/05	COMMISSION	US
	F1					CLEARING/PRCSNG FEES	US
	F1					PREMIUM / GROSS AMT	US

* * * * * * * * * * *   C O N F I R M A T I O N   * * * * *

THE FOLLOWING TRADES HAVE BEEN MADE THIS DAY FOR YOUR ACCOUNT AND RISK.

TRADE	SETTL	AT	BUY	SELL	CONTRACT DESCRIPTION	EX TRADE PRICE	CC
2/28/5	F1			2	PUT MAY 05 NYC COTTON SPREAD	4100 13 .04	US
	F1			2*	EX- 4/15/05	COMMISSION	US
	F1					CLEARING/PRCSNG FEES	US
	F1					PREMIUM / GROSS AMT	US
2/28/5	F1		2		PUT MAY 05 NYC COTTON SPREAD	4200 13 .10	US
	F1		2*		EX- 4/15/05	COMMISSION	US
	F1					CLEARING/PRCSNG FEES	US
	F1					PREMIUM / GROSS AMT	US

Figure 8.17 Cotton OTM Bull Put Option Credit Spread—Open and Closed

Data Source: Commodity trading statements.

favor. I closed out the spreads on 2/28/05 by buying them back for 6 points ($30) each. This meant that I bought back my short 4200 strike put options and sold out my long 4100 strike put options. You will notice the previous cotton trade was a bearish play, while this one was bullish. That's the great thing about the markets; you can trade from either camp. (See Figure 8.17.)

Figure 8.18 Coffee Daily Chart
Source: eSignal.com.

Option Credit Spread #7

Another bullish trade in coffee via selling put option spreads is shown in
Figure 8.18. I sold the 9500/9750 bull put spreads for 55 and 77 points
respectively ($206.25 and $288.75) on 10/26/05 and 10/27/05 and
bought them back on 11/3/05 for 15 and 20 points ($56.25 and $75.00)
for a quick 20.6 percent and 33 percent return gain on margin money
in seven and eight days' time. You'll notice that the coffee market was
essentially in the same place price-wise when I closed out the trade, yet
I was able to book a profit due to time decay. (See Figure 8.19.)

```
*   *   *   *   *   *   *   *   *   *   C O N F I R M A T I O N   *   *   *   *   *
THE FOLLOWING TRADES HAVE BEEN MADE THIS DAY FOR YOUR ACCOUNT AND RISK.

  TRADE   SETTL  AT    BUY           SELL       CONTRACT DESCRIPTION          EX TRADE PRICE CC
-------  ------- --  -------------- ----------- ------------------------------ -- ----------- -- .
10/26/5          F1           1                 PUT  DEC 05 CSC COFFEE C   950 06     1.35    US
                                                 SPREAD
                 F1          1*                  EX-11/11/05                        COMMISSION US
                 F1                                                         CLEARING/PRCSNG FEES US
                 F1                                                         PREMIUM / GROSS AMT US

10/26/5          F1                         1    PUT  DEC 05 CSC COFFEE C   975 06     1.90    US
                                                 SPREAD
                 F1                        1*    EX-11/11/05                        COMMISSION US
                 F1                                                         CLEARING/PRCSNG FEES US
                 F1                                                         PREMIUM / GROSS AMT US
*   *   *   *   *   *   *   *   *   *   C O N F I R M A T I O N   *   *   *   *   *
THE FOLLOWING TRADES HAVE BEEN MADE THIS DAY FOR YOUR ACCOUNT AND RISK.

  TRADE   SETTL  AT    BUY           SELL       CONTRACT DESCRIPTION          EX TRADE PRICE CC
-------  ------- --  -------------- ----------- ------------------------------ -- ----------- -- .
10/27/5          F1           1                 PUT  DEC 05 CSC COFFEE C   950 06     1.00    US
                                                 SPREAD
                 F1          1*                  EX-11/11/05                        COMMISSION US
                 F1                                                         CLEARING/PRCSNG FEES US
                 F1                                                         PREMIUM / GROSS AMT US

10/27/5          F1                         1    PUT  DEC 05 CSC COFFEE C   975 06     1.77    US
                                                 SPREAD
                 F1                        1*    EX-11/11/05                        COMMISSION US
                 F1                                                         CLEARING/PRCSNG FEES US
                 F1                                                         PREMIUM / GROSS AMT US
*   *   *   *   *   *   *   *   *   *   C O N F I R M A T I O N   *   *   *   *   *
THE FOLLOWING TRADES HAVE BEEN MADE THIS DAY FOR YOUR ACCOUNT AND RISK.

  TRADE   SETTL  AT    BUY           SELL       CONTRACT DESCRIPTION          EX TRADE PRICE CC
-------  ------- --  -------------- ----------- ------------------------------ -- ----------- -- .
11/03/5          F1                         1    PUT  DEC 05 CSC COFFEE C   950 06      .40    US
                                                 SPREAD
11/03/5          F1                         1    PUT  DEC 05 CSC COFFEE C   950 06      .70    US
                                                 SPREAD
                 F1                        2*    EX-11/11/05                        COMMISSION US
                 F1                                                         CLEARING/PRCSNG FEES US
                 F1                                                         PREMIUM / GROSS AMT US

11/03/5          F1           1                 PUT  DEC 05 CSC COFFEE C   975 06      .60    US
                                                 SPREAD
11/03/5          F1           1                 PUT  DEC 05 CSC COFFEE C   975 06      .95    US
                                                 SPREAD
```

Figure 8.19 Coffee OTM Bull Put Option Credit Spread—Open and Closed
Data Source: Commodity trading statements.

Figure 8.20   Cocoa Daily Chart
Source: eSignal.com.

Option Credit Spread #8

I think you may be getting the picture here of the option credit spread strategy. I'm taking my initial directional assessment and applying that to an OTM bull put or bear call credit spread. This trade was a quick bullish opportunity to sell put spreads in the cocoa market on 01/24/06

```
*  *  *  *  *  *  *  *  *  *    C O N F I R M A T I O N    *  *  *  *  *

THE FOLLOWING TRADES HAVE BEEN MADE THIS DAY FOR YOUR ACCOUNT AND RISK.

 TRADE    SETTL   AT    BUY          SELL        CONTRACT DESCRIPTION            EX TRADE PRICE CC
-------  ------- --  --------------- ------------ -------------------------------- -- ----------- --
 1/24/6          F1          1                    PUT  MAR 06 CSC COCOA-MTR 1400 06     .08    US
                                                  SPREAD
                 F1          1*                   EX- 2/03/06                      COMMISSION US
                 F1                               CLEARING/PRCSNG FEES US
                 F1                               PREMIUM / GROSS AMT US

 1/24/6          F1                     1         PUT  MAR 06 CSC COCOA-MTR 1450 06     .20    US
                                                  SPREAD
                 F1                     1*        EX- 2/03/06                      COMMISSION US
                 F1                               CLEARING/PRCSNG FEES US
                 F1                               PREMIUM / GROSS AMT US

*  *  *  *  *  *  *  *  *  *    C O N F I R M A T I O N    *  *  *  *  *

THE FOLLOWING TRADES HAVE BEEN MADE THIS DAY FOR YOUR ACCOUNT AND RISK.

 TRADE    SETTL   AT    BUY          SELL        CONTRACT DESCRIPTION            EX TRADE PRICE CC
-------  ------- --  --------------- ------------ -------------------------------- -- ----------- --
 2/01/6          F1                     1         PUT  MAR 06 CSC COCOA-MTR 1400 06     .02    US
                                                  SPREAD
                 F1                     1*        EX- 2/03/06                      COMMISSION US
                 F1                               CLEARING/PRCSNG FEES US
                 F1                               PREMIUM / GROSS AMT US

 2/01/6          F1          1                    PUT  MAR 06 CSC COCOA-MTR 1450 06     .08    US
                                                  SPREAD
                 F1          1*                   EX- 2/03/06                      COMMISSION US
                 F1                               CLEARING/PRCSNG FEES US
                 F1                               PREMIUM / GROSS AMT US
```

Figure 8.21 Cocoa OTM Bull Put Option Credit Spread—Open and Closed

Data Source: Commodity trading statements.

for 12 points ($120) and to buy them back on 02/01/06 for 6 points ($60). The market didn't move too much directionally between my buy and sell dates, but time decay did! It was a quick 15.8 percent ROM in eight days. (See Figures 8.20 and 8.21.)

Figure 8.22   Feeder Cattle Daily Chart
Source: eSignal.com.

Option Credit Spread #9

I don't get to trade feeder cattle all that often, but this one worked out too. (See Figure 8.22.) I was banking on the continuation of the downtrend as it hugged the moving average line. I sold the OTM 1100/1120 bear call spreads on 03/20/06 for 50 points ($250) and bought them back on 03/29/06 for 27.5 points ($137.50). The feeder cattle contract has a $5 point value system. The short strike of the

```
*  *  *  *  *  *  *  *  *  *   C O N F I R M A T I O N   *  *  *  *  *
THE FOLLOWING TRADES HAVE BEEN MADE THIS DAY FOR YOUR ACCOUNT AND RISK.
 TRADE   SETTL  AT      BUY           SELL      CONTRACT DESCRIPTION        EX TRADE PRICE CC
-------  -----  --  --------------  ----------  ----------------------------  -- ----------- --
3/20/6          F1                       1     CALL MAY 06 CME FD CATTLE 1100 02   1.00     US
                                               SPREAD
                F1                      1*     EX- 5/25/06                     COMMISSION US
                F1                                                   CLEARING/PRCSNG FEES US
                F1                                                   PREMIUM / GROSS AMT US

3/20/6          F1          1                  CALL MAY 06 CME FD CATTLE 1120 02    .50     US
                                               SPREAD
                F1         1*                  EX- 5/25/06                     COMMISSION US
                F1                                                   CLEARING/PRCSNG FEES US
                F1                                                   PREMIUM / GROSS AMT US

*  *  *  *  *  *  *  *  *  *   C O N F I R M A T I O N   *  *  *  *  *
THE FOLLOWING TRADES HAVE BEEN MADE THIS DAY FOR YOUR ACCOUNT AND RISK.
 TRADE   SETTL  AT      BUY           SELL      CONTRACT DESCRIPTION        EX TRADE PRICE CC
-------  -----  --  --------------  ----------  ----------------------------  -- ----------- --
3/29/6          F1          1                  CALL MAY 06 CME FD CATTLE 1100 02    .50     US
                                               SPREAD
                F1         1*                  EX- 5/25/06                     COMMISSION US
                F1                                                   CLEARING/PRCSNG FEES US
                F1                                                   PREMIUM / GROSS AMT US

3/29/6          F1                       1     CALL MAY 06 CME FD CATTLE 1120 02  .22 1/2 US
                                               SPREAD
                F1                      1*     EX- 5/25/06                     COMMISSION US
                F1                                                   CLEARING/PRCSNG FEES US
                F1                                                   PREMIUM / GROSS AMT US
```

Figure 8.23   Feeder Cattle OTM Bear Call Option Credit Spread—Open and Closed

Data Source: Commodity trading statements.

spread (1100) was 500 points away from the current price of the market at the time of the trade, giving me a nice cushion if the market decided to turn higher for a while. I got out of this trade a little early; as you can see the market tanked just days after I offset the trade. I would've been able to buy back the spread for less, but a profit is a profit! (See Figure 8.23.)

Figure 8.24   Silver Daily Chart
Source: eSignal.com.

Option Credit Spread #10

Silver had a huge tumble on April 20, 2006, in which it came down to one of my moving average lines as seen in Figure 8.24. It had been in an uptrend before that decline and I felt that it would rebound and continue higher despite the setback. I opted for a bullish trade and sold the 1075/1100 bull put spread on 04/24/06, collecting 5 points ($250).

```
*  *  *  *  *  *  *  *  *  *   C O N F I R M A T I O N   *  *  *  *  *
THE FOLLOWING TRADES HAVE BEEN MADE THIS DAY FOR YOUR ACCOUNT AND RISK.
  TRADE   SETTL  AT      BUY          SELL       CONTRACT DESCRIPTION           EX TRADE PRICE CC
-------  -------  --  ----------------  ----------------  --------------------------------- --  ----------- -- -
 4/24/6         F1            1                          PUT  JUN 06 CMX SILVER  1075 04    15.00    US
                                                         SPREAD
                F1            1*                         EX- 5/25/06                    COMMISSION US
                F1                                               CLEARING/PRCSNG FEES US
                F1                                               PREMIUM / GROSS AMT US

 4/24/6         F1                             1         PUT  JUN 06 CMX SILVER  1100 04    20.00    US
                                                         SPREAD
                F1                             1* EX- 5/25/06                    COMMISSION US
                F1                                               CLEARING/PRCSNG FEES US
                F1                                               PREMIUM / GROSS AMT US

*  *  *  *  *  *  *  *  *  *   C O N F I R M A T I O N   *  *  *  *  *
THE FOLLOWING TRADES HAVE BEEN MADE THIS DAY FOR YOUR ACCOUNT AND RISK.
  TRADE   SETTL  AT      BUY          SELL       CONTRACT DESCRIPTION           EX TRADE PRICE CC
-------  -------  --  ----------------  ----------------  --------------------------------- --  ----------- --
 5/08/6         F1                             1         PUT  JUN 06 CMX SILVER  1075 04     3.00    US
                                                         SPREAD
                F1                             1* EX- 5/25/06                    COMMISSION US
                F1                                               CLEARING/PRCSNG FEES US
                F1                                               PREMIUM / GROSS AMT US

 5/08/6         F1            1                          PUT  JUN 06 CMX SILVER  1100 04     5.00    US
                                                         SPREAD
                F1            1*                         EX- 5/25/06                    COMMISSION US
                F1                                               CLEARING/PRCSNG FEES US
                F1                                               PREMIUM / GROSS AMT US
```

Figure 8.25 Silver Bull Put Option Spread—Open and Closed
Data Source: Commodity trading statements.

At the time, silver was trading at roughly $12 per ounce, which gave me a full dollar cushion above my short strike ($11). You will notice that the figures I use to quote the strike prices don't always match up with what you see on the charts. In this case, the charts quote the silver prices with five digits, whereas I use the numbers that correspond with how prices are quoted by traders and how they are presented in the trading confirmations you see in Figure 8.25.

In this trade, the silver bulls came roaring back into the market soon after and I liquidated the spread on 05/08/06 for 2 points ($100) for a quick 15 percent ROM in 14 days.

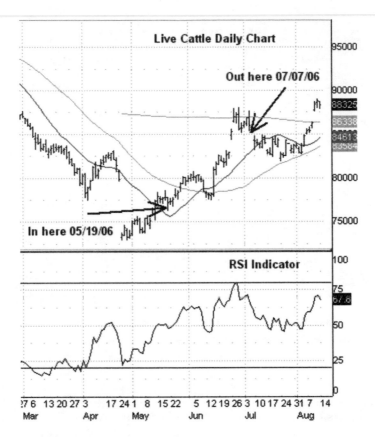

Figure 8.26   Live Cattle Daily Chart
Source: eSignal.com.

Option Credit Spread #11

Live cattle took a plunge toward the end of April 2006 and started heading higher from there. (See Figure 8.26.) You'll notice that the RSI indicator in the lower panel didn't make a new low point on that same day cattle plunged. That's what's called "bullish divergence" between the chart and the RSI. A sign like that is often a good indicator that the commodity has made a low and is about to turn higher. And that's exactly what the cattle market did.

I entered a bullish trade on 05/19/06 and sold the 7300/7400 bull put spread for 20 points ($80). The current price of the futures market at the time of execution was roughly 7700, which gave me a nice

5/19/6	F1	1			PUT AUG 06 CME CATTLE SPREAD	730 02	.90	US
	F1	1*			EX- 8/04/06		COMMISSION	US
	F1					CLEARING/PRCSNG FEES		US
	F1					PREMIUM / GROSS AMT		US
5/19/6	F1		1		PUT AUG 06 CME CATTLE SPREAD	740 02	1.00	US
	F1		1*		EX- 8/04/06		COMMISSION	US
	F1					CLEARING/PRCSNG FEES		US
	F1					PREMIUM / GROSS AMT		US

```
*   *   *   *   *   *   *   *   *    C O N F I R M A T I O N    *   *   *   *   *
THE FOLLOWING TRADES HAVE BEEN MADE THIS DAY FOR YOUR ACCOUNT AND RISK.
 TRADE   SETTL  AT    BUY            SELL       CONTRACT DESCRIPTION               EX TRADE PRICE CC
-------  ------ --  ------------  ------------  ------------------------------  -- ----------- -- -
```

7/07/6	F1		1		PUT AUG 06 CME CATTLE SPREAD	730 02	.12 1/2	US
	F1		1*		EX- 8/04/06		COMMISSION	US
	F1					CLEARING/PRCSNG FEES		US
	F1					PREMIUM / GROSS AMT		US
7/07/6	F1	1			PUT AUG 06 CME CATTLE SPREAD	740 02	.17 1/2	US
	F1	1*			EX- 8/04/06		COMMISSION	US
	F1					CLEARING/PRCSNG FEES		US
	F1					PREMIUM / GROSS AMT		US

Figure 8.27 Live Cattle Bull Put Option Spread—Open and Closed
Data Source: Commodity trading statements.

300-point cushion for directional error. This trade actually took me a very long time to unwind and consequently lasted much longer than most of my trades. Even though the market moved in my favor from day one, I had problems getting filled at my profit price. I believe the market makers just didn't want to deal with my order. Regardless, I eventually got filled on 07/07/06 at 5 points ($20) for a locked-in gain of $60 per spread with a ROM of 18.75 percent in 49 days. Not much of a profit, but still a profit. (See Figure 8.27.)

Figure 8.28   Gold Daily Chart
Source: eSignal.com.

Option Credit Spread #12

This trade in Figure 8.28 was very similar to the previous silver spread. Metals move in tandem, so gold bounced just as well after falling down to one of the moving average lines. I was bullish and sold the 525/530 bull put spread on 06/19/06 for 100 points ($100). The short 530 strike price was roughly $45 away from where gold

```
*  *  *  *  *  *  *  *  *  *      C O N F I R M A T I O N      *  *  *  *  *  *
THE FOLLOWING TRADES HAVE BEEN MADE THIS DAY FOR YOUR ACCOUNT AND RISK.
  TRADE    SETTL   AT      BUY              SELL        CONTRACT DESCRIPTION              EX TRADE PRICE CC
-------- -------- --  ---------------  --------------- ------------------------------- -- ----------- -- -
 6/19/6            F1             1                     PUT  AUG 06 CMX GOLD            525 04     5.00    US
                                                        SPREAD
                   F1            1*                     EX- 7/26/06                           COMMISSION US
                   F1                                                          CLEARING/PRCSNG FEES US
                   F1                                                          PREMIUM / GROSS AMT US

 6/19/6            F1                             1     PUT  AUG 06 CMX GOLD            530 04     6.00    US
                                                        SPREAD
                   F1                            1*  EX- 7/26/06                              COMMISSION US
                   F1                                                          CLEARING/PRCSNG FEES US
                   F1                                                          PREMIUM / GROSS AMT US
```

Options On Futures

USD

Symbol	Date Time	Exchange	Qty	Price	Amount
ZG AUG06 540 P	2006-07-06, 10:29:30	ECBOT	1	0.3000	-30.00
ZG AUG06 535 P	2006-07-06, 10:30:35	ECBOT	-1	0.2000	20.00

Figure 8.29 Gold OTM Bull Put Option Credit Spread—Open and Closed
Data Source: Commodity trading statements.

was trading at the time ($575 per ounce). Whenever you are selling option credit spreads, you will always sell the more expensive option and buy the less expensive option. In this case, I sold the 530 put option and bought the 525 put option.

I opted to offset this trade using the electronic version of the gold market instead of the pit-traded contract. This was executed in one of my other trading accounts. Gold futures and options have been pit-traded for years and years but the electronic futures and options were launched not that long ago. I love electronic markets because they put everyone on equal footing. Nothing against my former comrades who still work on the exchanges, but the electronic markets are the wave of the future. I bought the put option spread back on 07/06/06 for 10 points ($10) for a quick 22.5 percent ROM in 18 days. (See Figure 8.29.)

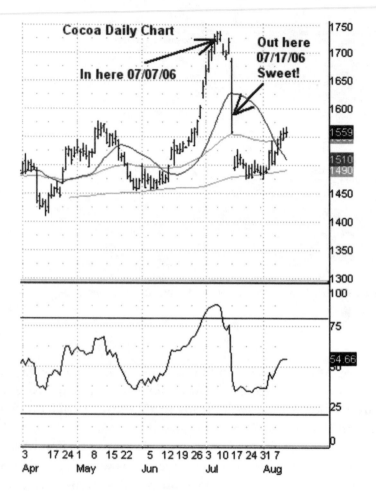

Figure 8.30   Cocoa Daily Chart
Source: eSignal.com.

ITM Option Spread #2

Cocoa futures were making an extreme up move and could not sustain that kind of momentum for too much longer. (See Figure 8.30.) This was a pure case of gravity having to take over sooner or later. Due to my bearish outlook for the immediate future, I bought the ITM 1700/1750 bear put debit spread on 07/07/06 for 27 points ($270). In this specific trade, I bought the more expensive ITM 1750

```
7/07/6        F1                        1  PUT  SEP 06 CSC COCOA-MTR 1700 06       .50   US
                                           SPREAD
              F1                        1* EX- 8/04/06                    COMMISSION US
              F1                                             CLEARING/PRCSNG FEES US
              F1                                             PREMIUM / GROSS AMT US

7/07/6        F1          1                PUT  SEP 06 CSC COCOA-MTR 1750 06       .77   US
                                           SPREAD
              F1          1*               EX- 8/04/06                    COMMISSION US
              F1                                             CLEARING/PRCSNG FEES US
              F1                                             PREMIUM / GROSS AMT US

*   *   *   *   *   *   *   *   *   *     C O N F I R M A T I O N   *   *   *   *   *
THE FOLLOWING TRADES HAVE BEEN MADE THIS DAY FOR YOUR ACCOUNT AND RISK.
  TRADE    SETTL   AT       BUY            SELL      CONTRACT DESCRIPTION         EX TRADE PRICE CC
------- ------- --  --------------- ---------------  -------------------------- -- ------------ --
7/17/6        F1          1                PUT  SEP 06 CSC COCOA-MTR 1700 06      1.00   US
                                           SPREAD
              F1          1*               EX- 8/04/06                    COMMISSION US
              F1                                             CLEARING/PRCSNG FEES US
              F1                                             PREMIUM / GROSS AMT US

7/17/6        F1                        1  PUT  SEP 06 CSC COCOA-MTR 1750 06      1.40   US
                                           SPREAD
              F1                        1* EX- 8/04/06                    COMMISSION US
              F1                                             CLEARING/PRCSNG FEES US
              F1                                             PREMIUM / GROSS AMT US
```

Figure 8.31 Cocoa ITM Bear Put Debit Spread—Open and Closed

Data Source: Commodity trading statements.

strike put option and sold the less expensive 1700 strike put option. Look at that free fall 11 days later on 07/17/06. That's a trader's dream come true scenario. I closed out the trade by selling it for 40 points ($400), netting a 48 percent return (sold the 1750 put option and bought the 1700 put option). (See Figure 8.31.)

Figure 8.32 OJ Daily Chart
Source: eSignal.com.

Option Credit Spread #13

And lastly, one more OJ spread. In this case (Figure 8.32), I was just
going along with the trend of the market. OJ had been hugging the
moving average line all the way up and I felt that it would continue to
do so. I sold the 13500/14000 put spread on 07/14/06 for 100 points
($150). At the time, OJ was trading at the 15900 level, which was well

```
*  *  *  *  *  *  *  *  *  *    C O N F I R M A T I O N    *  *  *  *  *
THE FOLLOWING TRADES HAVE BEEN MADE THIS DAY FOR YOUR ACCOUNT AND RISK.
  TRADE    SETTL  AT      BUY          SELL     CONTRACT DESCRIPTION         EX TRADE PRICE CC
------- ------- -- ---------------- ---------------- ---------------------------- -- ----------- -- .
  7/14/6         F1            1                  PUT  NOV 06 NYC FRZN O J 13500 13    2.00     US
                                                  SPREAD
                F1            1*                  EX-10/20/06                  COMMISSION US
                F1                                        CLEARING/PRCSNG FEES US
                F1                                        PREMIUM / GROSS AMT US

  7/14/6         F1                          1   PUT  NOV 06 NYC FRZN O J 14000 13    3.00     US
                                                  SPREAD
                F1                          1* EX-10/20/06                  COMMISSION US
                F1                                        CLEARING/PRCSNG FEES US
                F1                                        PREMIUM / GROSS AMT US
*  *  *  *  *  *  *  *  *  *    C O N F I R M A T I O N    *  *  *  *  *
THE FOLLOWING TRADES HAVE BEEN MADE THIS DAY FOR YOUR ACCOUNT AND RISK.
  TRADE    SETTL  AT      BUY          SELL     CONTRACT DESCRIPTION         EX TRADE PRICE CC
------- ------- -- ---------------- ---------------- ---------------------------- -- ----------- --
  8/01/6         F1                          1   PUT  NOV 06 NYC FRZN O J 13500 13     .50     US
                                                  SPREAD
                F1                          1* EX-10/20/06                  COMMISSION US
                F1                                        CLEARING/PRCSNG FEES US
                F1                                        EXCHANGE FEES US
                F1                                        NFA FEES US
                F1                                        BROKERAGE US
                F1                                        PREMIUM / GROSS AMT US

  8/01/6         F1            1                  PUT  NOV 06 NYC FRZN O J 14000 13     .25     US
                                                  SPREAD
                F1            1*                  EX-10/20/06                  COMMISSION US
                F1                                        CLEARING/PRCSNG FEES US
                F1                                        EXCHANGE FEES US
```

Figure 8.33   OJ Bull Put Option Credit Spread—Open and Closed

Data Source: Commodity trading statements.

above the danger zone for the spread. I closed out the trade on 08/01/06 for 25 points ($37.50) netting an 18.75 percent ROM in 17 days. (See Figure 8.33.)

RISK MANAGEMENT

You've seen my actual results of the option credit spreads. I can't emphasize enough how easy it is to sell options as well as buy them. You just need to get yourself into the mind-set of taking the other side of the trade. As great as the strategy is, I want to inform you of the risk/reward profile so you know ahead of time what you can make and what you can possibly lose. Make no mistake, no strategy will win every time; but for me, the option credit spread is as good as it gets.

Any time you execute an option "spread" play, where you buy and sell the same amount of options in the same trade, there is a limited risk and limited reward feature of the position. You will not be exposed to an unlimited loss potential nor will you have the opportunity to have an unlimited type of gain. That's just the nature of any options spread. But, when done correctly, the limited rewards that we can achieve from the option credit spread can add up significantly over time.

I've shown you examples of all winning trades, but not every trade you make will work out to be positive. You can rest easy knowing your loss is capped, but that still doesn't force you to hold onto a potential loser all the way to the end. There are no rules here. You can unwind the trade at any point you like. If the trade is just not moving in your favor and you feel it won't turn around, then by all means close it. Don't hope and pray for it to turn around. Be decisive. It's better to lock in a smaller loss today than a bigger loss tomorrow.

As I've stated in most of these trade examples, each commodity has a different point and dollar value. It's advisable to keep a cheat sheet of each commodity so you won't be surprised when you see the numbers in your account. With the option credit spread, you will be taking in money right off the bat. This is the most you will ever be able to make with the spread if you hold it all the way to option expiration. If you unwind the trade early, as I've done many times, your profit will be less than the maximum. But that's okay because a profit is still a profit.

On the flip side, there is a defined maximum loss you can suffer if the trade moves against you and you hold out all the way to option expiration. As you'll know ahead of time what this full dollar amount of loss can be, you can plan accordingly. Some traders will risk the entire amount, while others will set stop-loss levels at predetermined points along the way. Some traders will also close out the trade if the market moves to the short strike of the spread, while others will close it out if the cost of the spread doubles in price. Whichever method you choose, just make sure you stick to it.

Lastly, I want to show you the formula to use to figure out what your maximum loss can be with any option credit spread. Since we're selling the spread, we know what our maximum gain can be. It's whatever we sell the spread for. In order to find the potential maximum loss, you need to subtract the credit received (in point value) from the difference between the strike price levels of the spread.

Example: In the last orange juice credit spread, we sold the 13500/14000 put spread for 100 points. Even though we pronounce the strikes as 135/140, they're really calculated as 13500/14000. This is something that you'll learn from experience or by talking to your broker. The difference between those strike prices is 500 points (14000 − 13500 = 500). Since we received 100 points for selling the spread, the most we can ever lose then is 400 points (500 points − 100 points = 400 points). Maximum gain is 100 points and maximum loss can be 400 points. Orange juice has a $1.50 multiplier, so maximum gain is $150 and maximum loss is $600.

I know some of you might be thinking, "Wait a minute, I'm going to risk 400 points just to make 100 points? Why would I want to do that? That's a 4:1 risk/reward ratio. Who in their right mind would take a trade like that?" Us, that's who! And every other smart option seller. Let me stress again the point I've been making throughout this book: The probability of our being successful on an option-selling type of trade is so overwhelmingly skewed to our advantage that it makes up for that unconventional risk/reward scenario. Just look at all the results I've shown.

All of my option credit spreads took advantage of the low-probability, close-to-expiration, out-of-the-money strikes that had almost no chance of being profitable. And in the investing world, when your chances of winning are high, you usually have to give up something in return. That something happens to be the risk/reward ratio.

In most cases, our chances of being successful will be in the 80 to 90 percent probability range (look back at all the probability calculator graphics from earlier in the book). So, you either have a very low chance to win more dollars or you have a very high chance to win fewer dollars. My 17 years of experience have shown me which one to choose. What about you? Of course, my goal is to give you the strategy and show you how it works. Every person must make their own decisions and do what is right for them. No one will take care of your money more than you. Make sure you're okay with every nuance of a trade before you execute it.

With our orange juice credit spread, the breakeven price occurred at the 13900 price level. At the time of execution, November 2006, OJ futures were trading at the 15900 level. (See Figure 8.34.) You can verify this by looking back at any OJ chart. The volatility level was around the 30 percent mark and there were 98 days to option expiration.

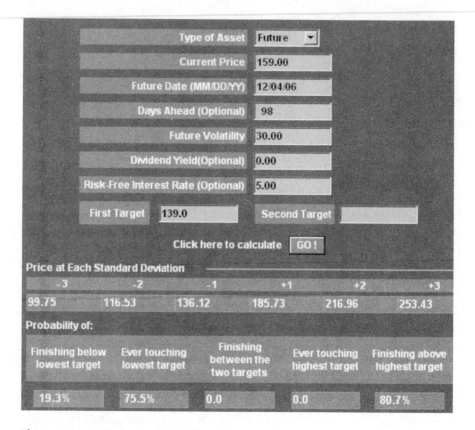

Figure 8.34   OJ Trade—Probability Calculator
Source: © Copyright Optionvue Systems International, Inc.

Given these parameters, we had an 80.7 percent probability that OJ would stay above the breakeven price for the duration of the trade. That's a good probability. And the odds got even higher knowing that we'd probably offset the trade early. Less time in the trade means less time for us to see an adverse move.

2007 AND 2008 CREDIT SPREAD UPDATE

Once again, as I'm revising this book in 2009, I am offering you some more real-time trade recommendations that were made in 2007 and 2008, because most of the previous option credit spread examples were from 2006. These newer examples all come from my commodity option advisory and are the actual trade alerts that my members received by e-mail.

Crude Oil Option Credit Spread

The first trade here was an option credit spread that we executed in the crude oil option market. We were bullish, so we went ahead and initiated a bull put option credit spread. (See Figure 8.35.)

Figure 8.36 (on page 165) shows the offset to that trade, which came just five days later.

Coffee Option Credit Spread

This next example is for another bullish trade in the coffee market in which we executed a bull put option credit spread. (See Figure 8.37 on page 167.)

Figure 8.38 (on page 168) shows the offset to that trade, which came just one week later.

GOLD AND ORANGE JUICE OPTION CREDIT SPREADS

Figure 8.39 (on page 169–171) shows the last alert e-mail I will show you because I'm sure you're getting tired of seeing these and I bet you see by now how lucrative these types of spreads can be.

You may have noticed the name change at the top of this last e-mail. We decided to give the service a fresh look with a new name starting in the fall of 2007. Here's the offset e-mail for the gold option spread, which came just a few short weeks later. We like to get in and out and book our profits quickly! (See Figure 8.40 on page 171.)

SUMMARY

As you can probably tell, I'm a **huge** fan of the option credit spread. No doubt it is the strategy that I employ more than any other in my own trading business. In the financial markets, where choosing the correct direction of an investment is the main driving force behind having a profitable trade, I like the fact that an options-selling strategy gives you the most leeway to navigate that directional call.

DELTA FORCE
TRADER

A SPECIAL PUBLICATION OF MT. VERNON RESEARCH

White List Us | Mt. Vernon Research | Archives

You are receiving this email as a part of your subscription to The Delta Force Trader. Should you have any questions or wish to change your e-mail settings, please reference the contact information at the bottom of this e-mail.

February 22, 2007

Email #52

A Slick Oil Spread

Great job today DEFT subscribers! Our timing was impeccable with the crude oil option spread today. We sold the May 2007 $58/$56 put option credit spread for 60 points ($600) per spread right before the market blasted higher. Since we're bullish, our put spread will get cheaper as the oil market moves higher. That's what we want. We either want the spread to expire worthless or to buy it back cheaper than what we sold it for.

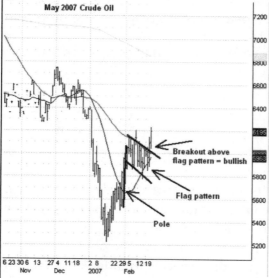

Look at the crude oil chart above. Although we missed getting in at the bottom around $52 (nobody is that good!), we waited for precise signals to let us know the correct time to strike. In my chart analysis, the pattern that I drew is called a bullish flag pattern. You have the long uptrending "pole" with a slightly bearish "flag" pattern. Once the market moves up and out above the flag portion, you should take that as your cue to get long. All we do now is wait and see what happens.

Since we sold the $58 put option and bought the $56 put option as a spread, our maximum gain on the spread can only be what we sold it for – 60 points ($600) per spread. As long as the crude oil market stays above our breakeven level, we won't lose on the trade. In this case, the breakeven level is $57.40 (looks like 5740 on the chart).

The way to calculate the breakeven is to take the premium received from the spread and subtract it from the short strike of the spread ($58.00 - $.60 = $57.40). The market would need to retrace a decent bit and stay down there in order for us to get into trouble. Time will tell.

Regards,

Lee Lowell

Figure 8.35   Crude Oil Option Spread

Courtesy: Mt. Vernon Research.

DELTA FORCE
——TRADER——

A SPECIAL PUBLICATION OF MT. VERNON RESEARCH

White List Us | Mt. Vernon Research | Archives

You are receiving this email as a part of your subscription to The Delta Force Trader. Should you have any questions or wish to change your e-mail settings, please reference the contact information at the bottom of this e-mail.

February 27, 2007

Urgent Alert #54

Congratulations *DEFT* Subscribers!

Once again, our timing was right on the money as we locked in another profitable trade today. We bought back our May 2007 crude oil $58/$56 put option spread for 40 points just as the market was making its high for the day (that was good for us).

The order was to buy the spread for 40 points or cheaper, and some of you may have gotten it for 38 or 39 points. Regardless of the fill price, we all cashed in again. Lucky that we got out when we did, as the stock market plunge has affected the oil market as well, and is now trading about $1.60/barrel cheaper than when we were filled on our trade. That would put our spread at about 50 points right now.

We locked in a gain of 20 points ($200) per spread, which represents a 14.3% return on margin in just the five short days we were involved with this trade. Short, quick stabs just as I mentioned earlier.

And regarding the return on margin, I'm using the worst-case scenario to yield our results. As it stands, the margin requirement varies from broker to broker. Some allow customers to maintain the minimum as set by the exchanges, while others add a "premium" to the minimum requirements.

What does this all mean? Well, when we sell an option spread, we don't have any money invested in the play. We're the ones actually collecting the money from the option buyer. So, how are the brokers supposed to keep us in check if the trade starts to move against us? If we were the option buyer, we'd pay all the money upfront, and that's all we could lose.

But, when you sell an option or option spread, the broker needs you to put some money aside to guarantee you'll cover the trade in case it goes sour. The money that's put aside is called your "margin requirement." This money isn't taken out of your account or anything like that. The money stays put, but the broker will restrict you from putting on more trades that might infringe on that margin requirement.

How does the broker calculate margin? Through a software program called SPAN. This software takes into account all the parameters of the trade at time of execution, taking into account the price of the futures, time to expiration, strike price and volatility. SPAN will then tell the broker how much money needs to be put aside for our option spread.   *(Continues)*

Figure 8.36   Crude Oil Option Trade

Courtesy: Mt. Vernon Research.

In the specific case of our crude oil option spread, we took in 60 points on the spread and we had 140 points at risk. We calculate the risk by taking the difference between the strike prices and subtracting the option premium from it. Since we sold the $58.00/$56.00 put spread, there is 200 points between those strikes. We subtract the 60 points from that to equal our margin of 140 points (200 - 60 = 140). So 140 (-$1400) is our worst-case scenario margin requirement.

Our worst-case scenario would have us losing 140 points ($1400) per spread. This is what I calculate our return on. Since we made 20 points, we need to divide that by the margin of 140. (20/140 = 14.3%). Get it?

But, 140 points is not what the brokers initially require us to put aside when executing this spread. SPAN most likely calculated us needing something like 10 - 15% of the worst-case scenario. So, in reality, we only needed to put aside $140 - $210 per spread to execute this trade. That makes a big difference in our return numbers. If we divide the $200 profit by the $210 margin requirement, then we just booked ourselves about a 100% return on margin (ROM). But, since not everyone uses the same broker, I have to be fair and use a uniform number to calculate returns. I've opted to use the worst-case scenario for this purpose.

I'm in the process of getting my hands on the SPAN software so I can always give you an accurate idea of what our margin would actually be. Since we sometimes have money invested in many plays at once, the numbers get jumbled together, and it's hard to keep track of what each individual position would cost on a margin-basis.

Now, here's another little tidbit of information. Most commodity brokers will not pay you interest on your free cash balances that you hold in your commodity account. This is unlike regular bank and stock brokerage accounts which "sweep" your free cash into an interest-bearing money market account. But there's a way to get around this.

You can use the cash in your commodity account to purchase a short-term T-Bill, which the brokers allow you to use for 95% worth towards margin requirements. Plus, you will receive all the interest from the T-Bill once it matures. Bonus! This is a well-kept secret that many commodity investors don't know about. I usually do a rolling T-Bill purchase program for my commodity account by investing in 3-month T-Bills. This keeps it short and lets me take advantage of high short-term rates.

My one piece of advice, though, is that you need to hold the T-Bill to maturity to ensure all the interest and to not potentially have to sell it at a loss. So, if you have $25,000 in your account for example, maybe you should buy $20,000 worth of T-Bills. It's always good to have some free, liquid cash on hand in case of emergencies. Just another little tip from the resident DEFT editor.

Congrats again everyone.

Regards,
Lee Lowell

Figure 8.36 *(Continued)*

DELTA FORCE
——TRADER——

White List Us | Mt. Vernon Research | Archives

You are receiving this email as a part of your subscription to The Delta Force Trader. Should you have any questions or wish to change your e-mail settings, please reference the contact information at the bottom of this e-mail.

Wednesday, May 30, 2007

Email #94

Your *DEFT* Questions Answered

Hello *DEFT* subscribers.

Ok, I just got confirmation from the NYBOT (New York Board Of Trade) floor and from some of you that we've been filled on our August coffee $1.05/$1.00 put option credit spread for 70 points. Great job!

This will bring in an immediate $262.50 into your trading accounts for every spread you sold. Remember, we sold the spread, so someone is paying us the money. We didn't pay any money to anyone. All we do now is wait for either the coffee market to go up and/or for time decay to kick in on the options. Everyday that the position is open, both options in this spread will lose a little bit of their value regardless of which way the coffee market moves. As the options decay and the market movement obliges us, the spread will get cheaper and cheaper, allowing us to either buy it back for a profit, or to have it expire worthless entirely. Remember, when you sell something at Price X, you want it to get cheaper to Price Y, so you can buy it back for a profit. That's what we do when we sell option spreads. Get it?

We don't necessarily need the coffee market to go up, we just need it to stay above our breakeven price of $1.0430, which is 900 points lower than where coffee is currently trading. So, coffee can move higher, stay flat, or even move lower against our directional call (but not more than 900 points lower), and we'll walk away a winner. That's the beauty of option credit spreads - we can win in many different market scenarios.

As far as margin requirements to hold this trade, my broker gave me an initial margin figure of $363 per spread to be kept on hold. Your maximum risk in this trade is $1612.50, which is not what you have to keep on hold. If we end up taking profits on this trade, I will always show the dollar gain plus the percentage gain based on the margin requirements. I like to show the dollar gain because, bottom line, it really is about how much you make or lose on each trade, in my opinion.

That's it for now. Thanks for writing in.

Regards,

Lee Lowell

Figure 8.37 Coffee Option Spread

Courtesy: Mt. Vernon Research.

DELTA FORCE
——TRADER——

A SPECIAL PUBLICATION OF MT. VERNON RESEARCH

White List Us | Mt. Vernon Research | Archives

You are receiving this email as a part of your subscription to The Delta Force Trader. Should you have any questions or wish to change your e-mail settings, please reference the contact information at the bottom of this e-mail.

Thursday, June 7, 2007

Email #97

The Rich Aroma of Our Coffee Spread

Congratulations *DEFT* subscribers. We just locked in another profitable position this morning. Great job everyone.

We were filled on our coffee put option credit spread for 20 points. We originally sold this spread for 70 points on May 30, and bought it back today for 20 points, locking in a gain of 50 points. Coffee options are worth $3.75/point, so that represents a gain of $187.50 for every spread you sold. <u>This also represents a gain on initial margin of 55% in just 8 days time</u> . So it looks like "three-times-a-charm" for us in the coffee market, as this was the third consecutive-winning bullish put option credit spread that we executed in the last two months alone.

For any new subscribers that did not happen to get involved with this trade, do not try to enter this trade anymore as it is now officially closed out.

I'm currently searching for the next profitable trade and of course will keep you informed of any new developments.

That's it for now.

Regards,

Lee Lowell

Figure 8.38 Coffee Option Spread

Courtesy: Mt. Vernon Research.

Why am I getting this?

White List Us | Mt. Vernon Research | Archives

A SPECIAL PUBLICATION OF MT. VERNON RESEARCH

You are receiving this email as a part of your subscription to The Triple-Zone™ Profit Trader. Should you have any questions or wish to change your e-mail settings, please reference the contact information at the bottom of this e-mail.

Friday, December 14, 2007

Alert #182

TZP Probability Charts

Hello *TZP* Members.

We had a busy day yesterday with both of our open orders getting filled. We've been filled on the gold option spread at $1.50 and on the orange juice spread at 100 points. With both markets selling off yesterday, this gave us the move we needed to get filled.

At this point, we just watch and wait. Although establishing put option credit spreads is a bullish strategy, we don't necessarily need the markets to go up. We just need the markets to stay above our breakeven levels.

The breakeven level for the gold spread is $778.50 and $129 for orange juice. At the time of initiation, gold was trading at the $808 level and oj was at the $146 level. This gives us some breathing room in case each market makes a temporary move lower. In order to find the breakeven levels, all you need to do is take how much we collected for the option spread and subtract that from the short strike of the spread.

Gold: $780 strike - $1.50 = $778.50

OJ: $130.00 strike - 1.00 points = $129.00

The probabilities of profiting on each trade is currently 80% for OJ and 70% for gold. Take a look at the calculators below.

Here's the probability chart for orange juice:

(Continues)

Figure 8.39 Gold and Orange Juice Option Spreads

Courtesy: Mt. Vernon Research.

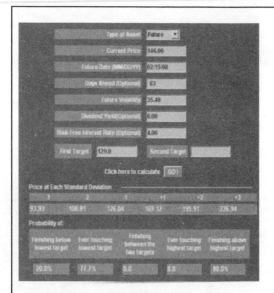

And here's the probability chart for gold:

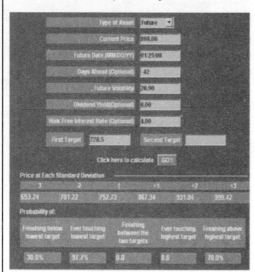

Just as a reminder, our maximum profit for the gold spread is $150 per spread and the maximum loss could be $350 per spread. The oj spread has a maximum profit of $150 per spread and a maximum loss of $600 per spread.

When I give these calculations, it is always based on using the minimum number of contracts per

Figure 8.39 (*Continued*)

trade. **So these numbers are based on 1 spread only** . If you do 5 gold spreads, your potential maximum gain goes up to $750, but your potential maximum loss goes up to $1750. Please plan accordingly.

The initial margin for the gold spread is $161 per spread and $168 for orange juice per spread. Although the maximum loss is larger than the margin requirements, your broker is still only asking you to put up that smaller amount to hold the trade.

Regards,

Lee Lowell

Figure 8.39 *(Continued)*

Why am I getting this?

TR|PLE ZONE PROFIT TRADER

A SPECIAL PUBLICATION OF **MT. VERNON RESEARCH**

White List Us | Mt. Vernon Research | Archives

You are receiving this email as a part of your subscription to The Triple-Zone™ Profit Trader. Should you have any questions or wish to change your e-mail settings, please reference the contact information at the bottom of this e-mail.

Wednesday, January 2, 2008

Email #192

TZP Update

Congratulations TZP Members.

We just closed out another profitable position today - our first one of 2008. I'm getting reports from the floor that we're getting fills on the gold spread at our recommended price of 30 cents. Gold kept rallying during the day, which allowed us to get filled.

This represents a profit of $120 for every spread traded and a return on initial margin of 74.5%. Great job everyone!

Let's keep it going.

Regards,

Lee Lowell

Figure 8.40 Gold Option Spread
Courtesy: Mt. Vernon Research.

The beautiful thing about selling OTM option credit spreads is the margin of error it allows you. Your directional bias can be faulty to a degree and the trade can still come out ahead. You can win if the market moves in your favor, if it moves sideways, or if it moves slightly against you. It's just a better way to increase your chances of profitability. You're aiming to keep the initial credit that you take in at the outset of the trade by having all options expire worthless, or, at a minimum, at least to buy back the spread for a locked-in profit (as I've done in every example). The most you can make when selling credit spreads is that initial premium, but the chances are high that you will be able to keep most of it. There's no unlimited loss potential when doing spread trades, and that's helpful in keeping your sanity in the markets.

Although all of these examples have been with commodity options, I know there are opportunities that exist in the stock options market as well. I've only concentrated on commodity options because I've been involved with that market for such a long time. I also believe that they offer great chances of success because you call sell the spreads at good distances OTM.

Lastly, another thing to remember is that most of the real trades described in this chapter are for short-term option expiration periods. A majority of my option credit spread trades will be executed in the first few months before expiration. This is the ideal time to take advantage of the time decay element of options, which is so crucial to the success of an option-selling strategy. Use it to your advantage!

CHAPTER 9

A DAY IN
THE LIFE OF THE
MARKET MAKER

I _____ r break before diving into the last of my
_____ you something fun to read about. I get
n_____ ds and acquaintances about what life was
like _____ er. For one thing, life was never dull. Every
day was _____ he floor, and I certainly will never forget the
times and _____ I met along the way. So, in order for you to get
a feel for how ____ time was spent, enjoy reading this chapter.

WHO IS THE MARKET MAKER?

For many years I was a market maker in the crude oil and natural gas
options pits on the floor of the New York Mercantile Exchange
(NYMEX). These are commodity options, not stock options. I know
many of you are somewhat familiar with, or at least have heard about,
the market makers from the stock exchanges, and I believe those stock
option pits function a little differently from the commodity option pits.
Those guys get more airtime from the media, so that's why the public

hears more about them. All the stories that I tell you here relate only to my time spent on the NYMEX.

The market-maker generally comes in two types: One that works for a market-making firm or one that works for themselves. I had the distinction to do both. A market-making firm can be a large company, a single wealthy individual, or a group of individuals who will hire traders to become market makers for them in different commodity pits. Examples of firms like this are Susquehanna Investment Group (SIG), Chicago Research & Trading (CRT), and the one I was employed by, First Continental Trading, Inc. (FCT). FCT was started by an individual who made lots of his money by trading in the Chicago markets. He in turn then hired other traders to work for and make money for him.

The market-making firms would put up the financial backing for these other traders. That means the market makers needed to have trading accounts opened up in order to trade on the exchange, and those accounts needed to be funded. The firm would put the money in an account and let the market maker do his or her thing. A typical agreement would have the market maker earning a small monthly draw for living expenses and then all the trading profits (if there were any) would usually be split 50–50 after expenses were deducted. This was a pretty sweet deal to have someone drop a few hundred thousand dollars into an account for you to try to make more of it. It takes a very confident (and wealthy) person to allow others to use his or her money on market-making activities.

The market makers would be spread out among the various pits on the exchanges so the firms could have a wide exposure to all the different markets. I worked in the options pit, but we had guys working in the futures pit as well. Most of the futures traders were there to help facilitate the option traders' efforts to lay off their directional risk. By this I mean, when an option trader makes an option trade, he or she will have an initial directional position. Most option market makers are taught to have nondirectional trades, so in order to offset that initial option position, the option trader will make an opposing directional trade using futures contracts. That's where our futures guys fit into the equation. They would take orders from the option traders via hand signals and fill the trade.

The other type of market maker, as I mentioned earlier, works for themselves and uses their own money for financial backing. When FCT and I parted ways in late 1995, I had enough experience at the time to think about being in business for myself. I had enough money built up that I didn't need to rely on anyone to fund me with cash, and now I could keep 100 percent of my profits. It was an exciting but scary endeavor, to say the least. I now had no one giving me a small salary, no type of company health insurance, and no other co-workers to share the load with. But it was all worth it. When you become a self-employed market maker like I was, you were usually referred to as a floor "local." This just denotes that you are an individual and not associated with any bigger firm.

The way that the market maker gets hired, or actually gets to be a market maker, is different for each company. But the one thing that market makers all have in common is that they have to start out as floor clerks. If you get hired by one of the bigger market-making firms, your time as a floor clerk could be years. Most of them give the clerks intensive training on their trading philosophy and how to actually learn the mechanics of being a market maker. The firm I worked for was one of the smaller companies and the time spent as a clerk was short. But I will say being a floor clerk was probably one of the most emotionally stressful jobs I've ever lived through. One flash of the wrong hand signal can cause a loss of hundreds, if not millions, of dollars. Gulp!

MARKET-MAKER SURVIVAL

As a floor clerk, there was no better feeling than learning that you were being promoted to trader. You were being moved into another echelon of stature. That was the goal and I was happy to be there. But I want to give you the breakdown of how a market maker thinks, acts, and operates when an option order hits the pit. This will enable you to get an understanding of who's taking the other side of your trade and why that person isn't always trying "to take you." Remember, these facts and stories apply only to my experience during my days on the NYMEX.

First, we need to understand the makeup of the options pit and how market makers fit into that arena. Believe it or not, there is a type of hierarchy, or caste system that prevails in the options and futures pits.

The days of a newbie market maker are not all that much fun. You are essentially the low man on the totem pole in your designated pit. You need to prove yourself not only to the other market makers, but to the brokers as well.

An options or futures pit (if none of you have seen an exchange floor) is made up of three or four concentric circles, with each circle elevated higher and wider than the one below it. There are guys (and girls) standing on higher or lower steps in relation to their front-side or back-side neighbors. Just think of it as looking like a sports stadium without the seats where everyone has to stand instead of sit.

These steps form the basis of the pit hierarchy. The brokers are the ones who get to be on the highest step. This is because they need to be near their phones, which are installed in small wooden booths that line the outer edge of the top step. The brokers are the ones who have all the orders. They get their orders either from retail customers (you and me), from their in-house traders who take positions for the firm (Goldman Sachs, Merrill Lynch, Citibank, etc.), or from other big institutional firms.

Make no mistake, you want to be in good with the brokers, and you want to be as close to them physically as possible. A market maker is only as good as the amount of orders he or she can get involved with. If you're a market maker and you don't make any trades, how are you going to make any money? The brokers have the orders, so you want to be near them. Your mission as a market maker (besides just trying to survive) is to eventually move yourself up in the pit to be as accessible to the brokers as possible. This may sound easy, but it's not. You have to contend with other market makers who have been standing in the same spot for years, and they're certainly not going to let some new green rookie take their place. I remember the first two words I heard the very first day I stepped into the pit as a market maker: "fresh meat." That's right, market makers and brokers will prey on the new guy as a sort of initiation. It happened to me and will most likely happen to every other new guy as well.

Most new market makers start on the lowest step, which is the farthest place from the brokers, or they just try to squeeze into a space wherever they can. Being timid or shy at this point is not a good thing. You need to assert yourself as quickly as possible. I think the exchanges are one of the last places in the work field where being physically big and loud has a huge advantage for you. That is what gets you noticed. That's why sometimes you'll see many former ball players getting jobs as brokers or other types of floor traders. Nevertheless, all new marker makers will be feeding off the scraps of orders that were not taken by all the bigger, faster, louder, and more senior traders in the ring. You take what you can get at first and work your way up from there. It's tough being at the bottom at first, but if you're good, you can move up quickly.

THE TRADER'S MIND-SET

Here's a topic that I know is on the minds of most off-floor investors and traders: Got a bad fill on a trade? Must've been the market makers playing their games. Got filled on a stop-loss order right at the bottom, only to see the market turn around and go in your favor without you? Must've been the market makers playing their games again. Well, I'm here to tell you that it's not always the market makers who are playing the games. I should know, as I was one of them. For six years I slugged it out in the pits on the floor of the NYMEX. Being a market maker or local, as we're sometimes called, doesn't always get a good rap. Let me give you the skinny on the life of these guys.

As a refresher, the NYMEX is a global center for the trading of energy futures and options. These energy contracts consist of such products as crude oil, heating oil, unleaded gasoline, and natural gas. The NYMEX also houses the Commodities Exchange (COMEX), which trades in metal futures and options consisting of gold, silver, copper, platinum, and palladium.

So what does a market maker actually do? In the simplest terms, a market maker helps facilitate the execution of a trade by providing a continuous bid and ask market for a futures or options contract to any interested party. You want to buy a futures contract for July natural gas? Who do you think gives your broker a quote for the most current price of that contract? Looking to get a market on the April crude oil $78/$79 call spread? It's the options market makers who provide you with a bid/ask quote on that call spread.

In stark contrast to how most off-floor retail players trade, the market makers usually don't trade with a prediction about the direction of a particular market. The market makers are there purely to try to buy a contract on their bid price, and then try to either sell that same contract on their offer price or hedge their delta risk immediately if they can't offset the original trade. When you ask your broker for a quote from the floor (which you should always do before placing *any* futures option trade), the market makers don't know whether you want to buy or sell, so they aren't "out to get you." They don't have a hidden agenda in which they try to rob you of all your money. In fact, the market makers try really hard to give good, accurate, and fair quotes, because quite frankly, the ones who give the best markets are the ones who get involved with the most trades.

But, if you're the type who gives very wide bid/ask quotes, or someone who doesn't "honor their markets" if a broker wants to buy or sell from you, then you won't be around for very long. Honoring their markets means the market maker will trade with the broker with the bid/ask quote just given by that market maker. Sometimes market makers can give inaccurate quotes for whatever reason (busy market, checked the wrong option sheets, etc.), and the broker (and the broker's customer) will be upset if they can't get a trade done at the prices that the market maker just gave them. If you want to be a good market maker, you have to be able to stand by the quote you just gave because a broker could come back to you at any moment and want to trade with you based on the quote you gave him or her. If you get the reputation of backing away or not honoring your bid/ask quotes, no one will ever want to trade with you.

It's a market maker's job to be involved with as many trades as possible and get a small edge with each one of those trades. The tighter and fairer you make a quote, the more the brokers will trade with you. This is how market makers earn a living—by providing continuous, tight, and fair quotes. It is a privilege to trade on an exchange. And for that privilege, the market makers must either buy their own seat on that exchange outright or they must lease a seat. The last time I checked (July 2006), a seat lease on the NYMEX cost about $18,000 a month, and to buy a seat cost $3 million! If you're a market maker who leases a seat, you're already in the hole $18,000 come the first of the month. That's a tough nut to crack month after month. That's why it's in the best interests of the market makers to provide a continuous flow of good, fair, and quality quotes. So the next time you get a bad fill on a trade, think twice before blaming the market maker.

2009 Update: Since the first printing of this book, the NYMEX has been bought out by the CME (CHICAGO MERCANTILE EXCHANGE). For updated seat prices, check www.nymex.com

PIN RISK AND LOPSIDED POSITIONS

Continuing on with the story about pit market makers, I'd like to share with you some of the hardships that these traders face in their day-to-day operations. I'm sure this will make many of you feel better, as most of us assume the market maker is the enemy and the sole cause of our trading losses. (Gotta blame somebody, right?)

I'd like to share two trading situations that can wreak havoc on the option market maker. They are the "one-way" positions, and "pin risk." During my time in the NYMEX options pit, these two issues were personally some of my biggest stresses.

When an options market maker does a trade, they usually do the transaction with a pit broker, and sometimes with other market makers. That initial position will give you a long or short directional bias that you then would offset with a futures transaction to keep the directional risk neutral. Besides keeping the directional (delta) risk neutral, option traders also need to balance out their gamma, vega, and theta risk. I won't go into detail on these, but suffice it to say, these are just as important measures of risk as delta.

Many times, different brokers in the pit will get very similar orders from their customers to take positions in the same options. It is the market makers' job to take the other side of those trades. When many of the brokers are doing the same trades for their customers, the market makers can end up with lopsided positions heavily weighted in one direction with respect to delta, gamma, vega, and theta. This means that a market maker's position can be heavily weighted to being short or long options, and that can be very damaging to his or her profit/loss scenario. But the market makers have no choice. They have to make the markets and trade with the brokers. If the markets end up doing what the brokers' customers thought it would, the market makers would be on the other side of those trades and the losses could be significant.

So what's the market maker to do in this case? Many times they have no choice but to ride out the storm and see if the market helps or hurts them, or wait to see if the brokers decide to turn tail and unwind all the positions they just initiated. Other times, the market makers are forced to do trades that will balance out their lopsided positions, but at unattractive prices. At the NYMEX, we did what was best at the time.

The second issue that can cause concern to an option market maker is that of "pin risk." This can occur when the market maker has a sizable stake in a conversion or reversal position. These are three-sided trades that include a long and short option position of the same strike, offset by a corresponding futures trade. The trader can be either long a call option and short a put option at the same strike with a short futures trade, or short a call and long a put at the same strike with a long futures position. These are riskless trades that the market makers put on for fractions of points; they can get in trouble only when the futures contract settles exactly at the strike price level on options expiration day. Let me explain.

Let's say the current price of the November crude oil futures contract is $63.77. Our market maker is long 100 crude oil $64 calls, short 100 crude oil $64 puts, and short 100 futures contracts. On expiration day, if the futures price is above $64, he will exercise his long 100 $64 calls, which will be offset by his short 100 futures contracts, leaving him with a zero position. If the futures price is below $64 on options expiration day, he will be assigned on his 100 short puts, requiring him to become long 100 futures contracts. Again, this will be offset by his short 100 futures contracts already in the account, thus leaving him with a zero position.

But what happens when the futures price settles exactly at $64 on options expiration day? This is why it's called "pin risk"—because the market gets pinned right at the $64 strike price. Does the market maker exercise his long calls, or does he think that he will get assigned on his short puts? Nobody knows. And the problem is that this must be done by a cutoff time and there is no way of knowing beforehand what the other side is going to do. If the market maker decides to exercise his long calls but also gets assigned on his short puts, he will have a position of long 200 futures contracts that will be offset only by his original short 100 futures position, thus leaving him with an open position of long 100 futures contracts. This is a very dangerous situation. Nobody wants to be left with a large open position like that over the weekend (if options expiration occurs on a Friday afternoon).

If this situation arises, the market maker is forced to make a judgment call between how many contracts he thinks he will be assigned versus how many of his long calls he should exercise. He has only 100 futures contracts in this case, so he needs to balance out the amount he thinks he should exercise against what he thinks he will be assigned. Sometimes this is done on a Friday expiration day and you won't find out until Monday morning what position you're left with. It can be very hairy at times.

So those are two of the most stressful position management situations that I've had to contend with during my days as an options market maker, and they still are to many of the traders working on the exchanges today. You might think the market makers are always out to get you, but they have bigger problems to deal with sometimes.

THE SLOW DAYS

The futures and options pits are usually loud, hectic, and very stressful places to be. A majority of the time you'll see frantic traders yelling and screaming and flashing hand signals to buy and sell securities. On a busy day, many of them will not even have time to take a bathroom break, let alone catch a bite to eat.

Well, on the rare day that things get really slow in the pit, market makers come up with some very interesting things to do to pass the time. Let me share with you some of the more fun moments I observed during my time in the options pits on the floor of the NYMEX.

Don't tell them it's your birthday—unless you're a glutton for punishment. I usually took the day off on my birthday, which is in the middle of the summer, not only because I feel everyone has that right, but because of my fear of what might happen to me in the pit. I saw it time and time again. The unsuspecting birthday boy—could be a market maker, could be a broker—is there just doing his job of filling customer orders when all of a sudden, here comes the plastic bag filled with shaving cream. Creeping up behind him is the sinister prankster with everyone else aware of what's about to happen. *Blam!* The bag gets pulled over the birthday boy's head and he's doused with shaving cream from top to bottom. The crowd goes wild and the roar sounds like someone just hit a home run to win the World Series. Happy birthday!

Have you ever seen a real live New York City–sized cockroach? Well, I have, and they're scary. We're talking grandpa-size roaches as big as rats. I never thought they could be worth more than the pleasure I'd get from stomping on them with my size 11 shoe. But when traders take up a collection of $500 in cash for someone to eat the insect, it makes you think a little more. I passed on the idea but there was someone else who was up for the challenge. The money was collected and the trader stood in the middle of the option pit that day. Three bites and it was down. First, he took off the head, crunched it up, and swallowed. The midsection followed, and you could actually see some stringy things pulling apart. Finally, the rear section. He washed it down with a Coke and called it a day. Some nice lunch money. Yuck!

How about $1,000 in cash to shave your head? Yes, that was another way to kill some downtime in the options pit. I added $20 to that pot. The victim was a longtime member of the exchange and was known for being that type of risk taker. Someone went out and bought an electric razor, shaving cream, and some disposables as well to make sure it was a clean job. And it was. The guy looked like Freddy Krueger when it was over, not a very good look for him. I heard his wife wasn't too happy when he went home that night.

Next story: I never understood how I ended up with funny drawings on my sneakers and the back of my trading jacket until I became a more seasoned trader in the pit. One of the brokers, who has also been mentioned in another part of this chapter, would actually slink along the floor of the pit and doodle on everyone else's shoes. It was funny for a while until it would happen to you. When you're in the heat of the battle making trades, you are very focused on that one task and you aren't aware of what might be happening to other parts of your body. I mean, catching an elbow in the eye from a fellow trader is an everyday occurrence in the pit, as well as getting spit on and stabbed in the arm multiple times with your neighbor trader's pen. So as those distractions held my attention, there was our friend drawing pictures on my shoes and jacket, and I never felt a thing. I went through many pairs of sneakers during my tenure, and it wasn't always because they were worn out!

Those were some of the funnier moments I can recall from my time in the pits. As crazy and stressful as it is on the exchange, everyone needs a good laugh from time to time. It helps keep you sane.

CHAPTER 10

PUT YOUR STOCKS TO WORK—SELL COVERED CALLS

If you own shares of stock (minimum 100 shares) and you're not selling call options against them, then you are throwing away free money. How's that? Well, there are other traders out there who will give you money today for the right to take your stock away from you if it reaches a much higher price. Selling "covered calls" is such a great strategy for padding your bank account that I still can't believe there are investors who aren't taking advantage of it. It's one of the best ways to take in extra cash flow that you never thought you could have. Covered calls get their name from the fact that the long shares you own will cover you against any adverse movement by the short call that you sell.

I tell all my friends and associates who own stock that they *must, must, must* sell covered calls against their stock to bring in easy extra income. After many years of nudging, I finally got my parents into the process of selling covered calls. They're hooked now and think it's one of the greatest ways to earn passive income. That's right, we're talking about earning income just for the fact that you happen to be long stock in your portfolio. Why not do something to inflate your portfolio while you "hope and wait" for your stock to go up in price? If I can get my parents to do it, I know I can convince you to as well. So take heed; here is strategy #4, and it's the last of my core option-selling strategies, one that falls into the hedging and income-producing categories.

Before I discuss the tactics, I just want to say that I think the reason why my parents didn't sell covered calls for so long, and why many others still don't for that matter, is because they're not aware of or familiar with the strategy, or maybe they're just outright scared to try it. So my goal in this chapter is not only to get you up to speed on what selling covered calls is all about, but also to get you to see why it's such an easy way to produce passive income. You'll be surprised to see, once you've employed this strategy for a few months, how fast the cash will start to add up.

WHAT IS IT?

Let's break it down. There are two ways to approach covered calls:

1. You can sell one call option against every 100 shares of stock you already have in your portfolio.
2. You can opt to buy stock and sell calls against it all in one transaction. This is typically called a "buy-write" because you buy the stock and write the calls against the stock at the same time in the same trade.

I want to focus specifically on the first version of covered call writing, as this is where investors are missing out on the free money. I want you all to understand that you can be much more proactive with your portfolio and add incredible amounts of passive income to it every few months of the year. You need to understand that there are people who are willing to give you money today just because you happen to own stock. The money that I'm talking about is the option premium that the call buyer will pay you.

When you sell covered calls, you are giving someone the right to possibly take your stock away from you sometime in the future. Now, before you close this chapter and run away because you don't want to risk losing your long stock, hear me out. We're going to focus on the best way to sell covered calls that minimizes the danger of losing your stock. The buyer of that call option (you are the seller of that call option) pays you cash today (the option premium) for the opportunity to **possibly** take your stock away. Many of these buyers, though, are purchasing short-dated, out-of-the-money (OTM), low-probability calls that I've been telling you to sell all along. Time decay will be eating away at them, so that's why we use them against our long stock positions.

But still, why would anyone want to take that chance of losing their stock and potentially miss out on future upward movement? For two reasons:

1. Someone is giving you good money for it.
2. Like I said, your chance of losing your stock will be low with our OTM strategy.

The fabulous thing about selling covered calls is that it allows you to passively accumulate income over time by having someone else pay you money. You become the option seller. For every 100 shares of stock you own, you can sell one option contract. Another great benefit of covered calls is that they help reduce your cost basis of the stock by the amount of the option you sold. Every time you sell a call option, the premium you receive acts as a reduction in the price you paid for the stock. If you bought stock at $25 and the first covered call you sell brings in $.50 in premium, you've just reduced your cost basis down to $24.50. Pretty sweet. It's like someone is giving you a rebate on your long shares. If you sell enough covered calls over time, your cost basis could eventually be zero! Read on.

HOW DO WE DO IT?

Let's run through an example and then I'll explain the finer points. Say you own 500 shares of Intel (INTC) that you bought in 1997 for $25.50 per share. How have you done? Well, if you didn't sell any during the tech bubble that ended in the year 2000, then you are just breaking even as of today (January 2006) as INTC is trading for about $26 per share. Bummer—all that time and you still haven't made any money on it.

You probably could've used that money to invest in something else, or at least buy yourself something nice after all that time. Who knew? Nobody knows how an investment will turn out over time. But you're still optimistic and hope the price will go back up.

I've included a monthly chart of INTC along with an option chain for the April 2006 expiration date (Figures 10.1 and 10.2). The last price for INTC was $25.97 (upper right corner of Figure 10.2). We want to concentrate on selling OTM call options. Again, an OTM call option is one whose strike price is higher than the current price of

Figure 10.1   INTC Monthly Chart

Source: eSignal.com.

Bid	Ask	Last	Change	Prev	ip Vol(E	ip Vol(A	High	Low	OpInt	Delta	Symbol
11.00	11.20	11.60	+0.10	11.50	72.82	82.87	11.60	11.60	535	100	APR06 15.00
8.50	8.70	8.60	-0.20	8.80	54.44	62.98	8.60	8.60	1.46K	99	APR06 17.50
6.10	6.30	6.10	0.00	6.10	42.11	48.66	6.10	6.10	3.99K	95	APR06 20.00
3.90	4.00	4.03	+0.03	4.00	34.45	36.81	4.03	4.03	8.68K	82	APR06 22.50
2.00	2.10	2.00	-0.05	2.05	28.11	29.92	2.20	2.00	34.3K	61	APR06 25.00
0.80	0.85	0.80	0.00	0.80	25.35	26.28	0.90	0.80	40.1K	39	APR06 27.50
0.25	0.30	0.25	0.00	0.25	24.16	25.62	0.25	0.25	15.1K	21	APR06 30.00
0.05	0.10	0.10	0.00	0.10	22.63	25.90	0.10	0.10	3.47K	10	APR06 32.50
0.00	0.05	0.10	0.00	0.10		28.30	0.10	0.10	1.95K	4	APR06 35.00

INTEL CORP. Bid: 23.97 High: 26.15 Last: 25.97 c Ask: 27.00 Low: 25.88 Change: 0.00

Figure 10.2   INTC Option Chain, April 2006 Expiration

Source: eSignal.com.

the stock. In this case we'll focus on the $30 strike calls. Ultimately, which-ever OTM strike you choose is entirely up to you, but for this strategy it should be at a level that you don't think the stock will reach by the expiration date. Or even better, it can be at a level where you would feel comfortable having it taken away from you (if it comes down to that). Picking OTM strikes increases your buffer zone for not losing your stock, plus it gives you extra price appreciation possibilities.

We see from the "Bid" column in the option chain that the $30 calls will yield $.25 each. This means that for every $30 call you sell, you will take in $25 ($.25 × $100 multiplier). Since you own 500 shares, you can sell five option contracts and net a take-home pay of $125. The $125 will show up in your trading account after you execute the call sale.

Selling the OTM $30 call allows you more upside gain on the stock while limiting the possibility of having the stock called away. If you really like the stock and want to keep it in your portfolio, then that's why you concentrate on selling OTM options since the stock has to move a good deal higher for you to possibly have to give it up. Do you understand that? This is the concept that I've been hammering at throughout the book. As long as you sell OTM options, your chances of success are greater. In the case of covered calls, as long as the price of your stock doesn't go up past the OTM strike you sold, you won't have to worry about giving up your stock.

Okay, you're long 500 shares of INTC and you sell five $30 calls for $.25 each. Once the trade is executed, your broker will deposit $125 into your account. What happens next? You sit and wait to see where INTC goes. If INTC trades above $30 by the April 2006 expiration date and stays above $30, you will be forced to sell your INTC shares to someone for $30 per share. It's called "getting assigned on your short options." But, is that a bad thing? Well, considering that INTC hasn't been above $30 in two years, then I don't think it's a bad bet. Plus, the trade is good only until April 2006. If INTC doesn't get above $30 per share by the April 2006 expiration, then the trade is over and you get to keep the $125 free and clear, and you also still have your long INTC shares intact. You can now repeat the trade for a different expiration month and collect more money.

ASSIGNMENT?

Don't fret. If you happen to get assigned on your call options and are forced to sell the stock, then so be it. Your broker will take the shares out of your account and you won't see the position anymore in your portfolio. But you've still come out ahead. Not only did you make $125 from the options, but you also have a gain on the stock from your original purchase price of $25.50 to the sale price of $30. That's a $2,250 gain on the stock.

Selling OTM covered calls forces you to take some profits along the way (assuming you are selling calls with strike prices above your initial stock buy price). You have to realize that you're still gaining price appreciation on your long stock up to the point of the stock price hitting your short call option. Like I said, you've just made $4.50 per share of appreciation from your original buy price of $25.50 to the short call strike price of $30. Once you hit the $30 mark, you will no longer gain any appreciation on your long shares. But that's something you knew ahead of time and were okay with that idea. And in the event that the stock never reaches the short call strike, you've still reduced the cost basis by $.25 to $25.25 per share. You can look at the result and see it as either locking in a nice gain or reducing your cost basis.

INTC Price	Long Shares P/L	Short Call P/L	Total P/L
$0.00	($12,750.00)	$125.00	($12,625.00)
$5.00	($10,250.00)	$125.00	($10,125.00)
$10.00	($7,750.00)	$125.00	($7,625.00)
$15.00	($5,250.00)	$125.00	($5,125.00)
$20.00	($2,750.00)	$125.00	($2,625.00)
$25.00	($250.00)	$125.00	($125.00)
$30.00	$2,250.00	$125.00	$2,375.00
$35.00	$4,750.00	($2,375.00)	$2,375.00
$40.00	$7,250.00	($4,875.00)	$2,375.00
$45.00	$9,750.00	($7,375.00)	$2,375.00

Figure 10.3   INTC Covered Call Profit/Loss Spreadsheet

The spreadsheet in Figure 10.3 shows the results of the long 500 shares position from its $25.50 cost basis, with the five short calls against it. The calls brought in an initial premium of $125. As we already noted, the calls will slightly cushion a fall in the price of the stock and will eventually cap your profits once the stock gets above the $30 strike price level. No matter how high INTC may go, you'll have a guaranteed locked-in gain of $2,375 for the whole position. If INTC is above $30 at expiration, you would be assigned and have to give up your shares.

If you had been selling covered calls all along, maybe once every three months taking in $125 or so, you could have netted a nice small sum while the stock lingered at the same price for several years. And you can do that every few months going forward. The call premium you receive is like getting a consolation prize while you wait to see if your stock ever moves higher. By selling covered calls, you're taking a more proactive approach with your money (just like I've said with the other strategies) and gaining income on the trade. Sure, there's a chance your stock might be called away, but that chance will be small because you're selling OTM options. And even if your stock is called away, you're going to make money not only from the option premium but from the stock price appreciation as well. Listen, people, these are great ways to use options. Always think about ways to add extra income to your account. Selling covered calls is one of them.

WHAT, ME WORRY?

Some investors will worry about two things:

1. Missing out on higher prices once assigned.
2. Causing a capital gains tax event.

If you are truly worried about missing out on future price appreciation after your stock has been taken away from you (if that happens), then you have four choices:

1. You can just not be involved with covered call trading (not my preferred choice).
2. You can pick a further OTM strike to give you more cushion.
3. You can offset the option trade at any time by buying back the option itself.
4. You can buy more shares again after being assigned. What's stopping you from doing that?

The other worry is the pain of having to pay Uncle Sam if you are assigned and forced to sell some shares. That's a legitimate concern, but in my opinion it's better to take a profit somewhere along the way than no profit at all. I like to hear the register ring. Would you rather not sell your stock for a profit just to avoid the Internal Revenue Service (IRS)? Look at all the stocks that have imploded since the 2000 meltdown and the current crash of 2008. I'm sure there are many folks kicking themselves for not selling at some point, either through a regular stock sale or by an option assignment. But since most people want to keep their stock, this is why we concentrate on selling OTM call options. There's less of a chance for assignment.

STRIKE PRICE VERSUS COST BASIS

One item to note that I just briefly mentioned before, on page 190 in regard to picking calls, is selling at strike prices below your cost-basis point. Don't do this, because it could lock you into a realized loss.

Let's go back and examine the hypothetical buy of 500 shares of INTC at $25.50 in 1997. As of the date this chapter was updated in

January 2009, take a look at the current chart of INTC so we can see where it's been since I first wrote this chapter a few years ago. (See Figure 10.4.)

You can see from the chart (Figure 10.4) that INTC has gone from the $25 area (which is where it was when I first wrote this chapter) to a high of $28 in late 2007, to its new low price of $12, which was just hit in late 2008 (courtesy of the current economic meltdown in the United States).

If you decided to hold on to INTC to weather the storm because you still believe in its long-term viability, selling covered calls now would not be a good idea. Since you would currently be about $12 per

Figure 10.4 Intel Weekly Chart

Source: eSignal.com.

share underwater (paper loss), there would not be any strike prices you could pick that would give you current income without taking on the risk of being assigned at unfavorable prices.

Let me show you what I mean. Look at the current option chain in Figure 10.5, which lists the call options available for the April 2009 option expiration. If you chose to sell five of the $17 calls for $.33 each (splitting the bid–ask), you would receive $165 in your trading account.

If INTC happened to trade above $17 per share come the April 2009 expiration, you would be forced to give up your shares to the option buyer at a price of $17 per share, thus locking you in to a realized loss of roughly $8 per share based on your initial cost basis of $25.50 per share.

Do you see how that happened? Even though you were being proactive and selling covered calls to bring in current income, the strike price of the options you sold ($17 strike) was too far below your original cost-basis level. Once you're assigned on the options, you're forced to sell INTC at a price well below your $25.50 cost basis.

Now, if INTC doesn't get above $17 by the April 2009 expiration, those $17 call options will expire as worthless and you'll have

INTEL CORP		c				BSize: 1	Bid: 11.75 Ask: 15.49	ASize: 3		Last: 13.74 Change: + 0.45	
BSize	Bid	Ask	ASize	Last	Change	Prev	High	Low	T	Time	Symbol
377	8.55	8.85	392	8.90	+ 0.70	8.20	8.90	8.90	c	Jan16	APR09 5.00
633	4.75	4.90	72	5.35	0.00	5.35	5.35	5.35	c	Jan16	APR09 9.00
114	3.90	4.00	14	3.95	+ 0.42	3.53	4.00	3.95	c	Jan16	APR09 10.00
831	3.05	3.20	207	3.00	+ 0.10	2.90	3.26	2.91	c	Jan16	APR09 11.00
61	2.37	2.42	19	2.32	+ 0.07	2.25	2.41	2.21	c	Jan16	APR09 12.00
117	1.75	1.81	359	1.75	+ 0.18	1.57	1.94	1.60	c	Jan16	APR09 13.00
28	1.23	1.28	569	1.25	+ 0.15	1.10	1.39	1.10	c	Jan16	APR09 14.00
249	0.82	0.85	89	0.85	+ 0.10	0.75	0.97	0.72	c	Jan16	APR09 15.00
375	0.52	0.54	2	0.54	+ 0.06	0.48	0.64	0.46	c	Jan16	APR09 16.00
25	0.12	0.37	25	0.00	0.00	0.00	0.00	0.00	c	Nov06	APR09 17.00
91	0.32	0.34	88	0.32	0.00	0.32	0.40	0.30	c	Jan16	APR09 17.00
25	0.06	0.31	25	0.00	0.00	0.00	0.00	0.00	c	Nov06	APR09 18.00
346	0.18	0.20	61	0.20	0.00	0.20	0.25	0.19	c	Jan16	APR09 18.00
25	0.04	0.29	25	0.00	0.00	0.00	0.00	0.00	c	Nov06	APR09 19.00
225	0.10	0.12	150	0.12	0.00	0.12	0.13	0.10	c	Jan16	APR09 19.00
25	0.01	0.26	25	0.00	0.00	0.00	0.00	0.00	c	Nov06	APR09 20.00

Figure 10.5   Intel Options Chain

Source: eSignal.com.

no more obligation to sell the shares at $17 anymore. But be careful going forward, because you don't want to take the chance of getting assigned and having to sell shares below your original buy point.

At this point, since you still own your shares and are currently underwater from your cost basis of $25.50, you would need to wait for INTC to move higher again so you could sell call options with strike prices above $25.50.

I GOT MY FOLKS IN ON THE ACTION!

Let me show you two recent actual covered call trades we did for my parents' trading accounts. They are each long 800 shares of IBM and 1,200 shares of Dell. When I left the floor of the New York Mercantile Exchange (NYMEX), I was able to concentrate my trading efforts not only on the commodity option markets but on the stock option markets as well. I approached my parents and asked them if they had been selling covered calls against their stock. They had no idea what I was talking about. For years they watched both stocks go up and down without much to show for their efforts. Look at the charts of IBM and Dell in Figures 10.6 and 10.7.

The big Internet boom started to occur in 1998 and we all know what happened to most equities during that time—an incredible run-up into the year 2000 only to be followed by the collapse of everything. In eight years' time, they've seen IBM go up to $140 per share only to trade all the way back down to where it is now at $76 per share. Look at Dell—all the way up to $60 per share and all the way back down. You'd hope that holding onto something for eight years would give you a decent return. Dividends helped a little but not nearly as much as covered calls could have.

I want to dissect their covered call trade and show you how we did it. As a side note, the only reason why my parents finally "gave in" and decided to do the trade was because they had an opportunity to hear my colleagues and I speak at a stock and option trading conference. For whatever reason, hearing all these smart traders talk about the benefits of options trading got them excited to join in on the action.

In March 2006, with IBM at $83 per share, we sold eight of the January 2007 $95 calls for $1.95 each. That brought an immediate

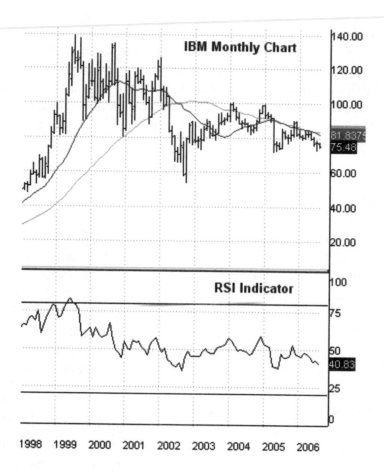

Figure 10.6 IBM Monthly Chart
Source: eSignal.com.

$1,560 (before commissions) into each of my parents' accounts. We chose the $95 strike price level as an area that my folks felt comfortable about finally unloading their IBM stock if they happened to be assigned on the short call options. Let me remind you that the trade is good only for the 10-month time span from March 2006 to expiration day in January 2007. If IBM doesn't end up above $95 by expiration, the call options will expire worthless and my folks will get to keep their shares intact. We'd be ready to possibly repeat the process for another expiration period. Total premium received between both accounts was $3,120—money that would never have been received if we didn't execute the trade.

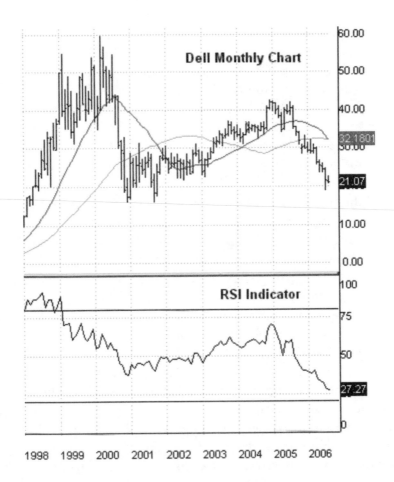

Figure 10.7 Dell Monthly Chart
Soruce: eSignal.com.

Here's the scenario with Dell. My parents bought a bunch of their stock in mid–1998 at approximately $14 per share (split adjusted). Eight years later, Dell is slightly higher than where they purchased it. What have they got to show for their efforts of holding through the ups and downs? Not too much price appreciation, that's for sure. I know my folks are not happy sharing the composition of their portfolios, but they are a great example to use because I know there are thousands, if not millions, of other investors who are in the same situation.

So in March 2006 we also sold covered calls on their Dell holdings. They each sold 12 of the January 2007 $35 strike calls for $1.15. That brought an immediate $1,380 (before commissions) into both of my parents' trading accounts. Comparable to the IBM trade, we chose the $35 strike price level as an area that my folks felt comfortable about selling their Dell stock if they happened to be assigned on the short call options. Total premium received between both accounts for the Dell trade was $2,760. Add that to the $3,120 from the IBM calls and my folks just took in a cool $5,880 in a matter of minutes. They were so excited! I'll take my commission, please.

Let me tell you what we did a few months later as we took the covered call trade one step further. As you know, you're not obligated to hold the option contract to expiration. You can buy and sell at will as it's totally up to you when to offset an option trade. You can hold it for minutes, days, weeks, or months—it doesn't matter. In our case, both IBM and Dell started trading lower right off the bat, which meant the options were getting cheaper. There was nothing holding us back from taking profits on just the option side of the trade. The stocks were heading lower and so were the option premiums. We bought back all the IBM and Dell call options for $.15 each.

We locked in $1.80 per contract, or $1,440 per person for the IBM options and $1.00 per contract, or $1,200 per person for the Dell options. When we originally sold the options, we brought in a combined total of $5,880. When we bought the options back, we had to pay $300 per person for the offset, netting us a grand total of $5,280 of locked-in pure profit. At this point my parents had no more obligation to sell their shares at the stated strike prices because the options were no longer in their accounts. They are now just long stock again, waiting to sell some more call options at my recommendation.

What was the reasoning behind offsetting the option trade before expiration? A couple of things. When an option trade moves in your favor as quickly as this one did, it's usually a good idea to take the money off the table. We bought the options back for $.15 each. The lowest price an active option can trade for is $.05, so we pretty much took all the money out of the option side of the trade. Even though we were losing money on the stocks themselves, as IBM and Dell were trading lower, we made money on the options and locked that gain in.

I also felt that both IBM and Dell might have hit a bottom when we bought back the options. If in fact both stocks did turn around and move higher, the option prices would move higher as well, not allowing us to buy them back as cheaply as we did. I was in a sense trying to pick a bottom in those two stocks.

Make no mistake, IBM and Dell were falling in price during this time, giving my folks a paper loss in their portfolios. They were losing money on their stock shares. But having sold the options gave them more than $5,000 in cushion money to soften the fall. See that? Selling covered calls gives you cushion and income to make you feel better while you watch your stocks fall in price. Think about all those times while *you* watched your long stock fall in price and had no buffer against it. I'll bet you might be interested in the covered call strategy now!

I want to show you graphically what the numbers can look like while having a covered call position in place. In the spreadsheet in Figure 10.8, I've incorporated the numbers that we used to figure the profit/loss scenario for the Dell covered call play. My folks bought 1,200 shares of Dell for $14 per share. With the sale of the call options, they received $1.15 per option contract, which reduced their cost basis to $12.85 per share. Once the short $35 strike price level would be hit, the profits would be capped and my parents would be forced to sell their Dell shares at $35 each. But that would have been fine with them, as they had determined ahead of time that $35 per share was acceptable.

Stock Price	Per Share Gain/Loss	$ Profit/Loss
$0.00	($12.85)	($15,420.00)
$5.00	($7.85)	($9,420.00)
$10.00	($2.85)	($3,420.00)
$15.00	$2.15	$2,580.00
$20.00	$7.15	$8,580.00
$25.00	$12.15	$14,580.00
$30.00	$17.15	$20,580.00
$35.00	$22.15	$26,580.00
$40.00	$22.15	$26,580.00
$45.00	$22.15	$26,580.00
$50.00	$22.15	$26,580.00

Figure 10.8 Dell Profit/Loss Breakdown

TRADE UPDATE

Let's see what's happened to my parents' IBM and Dell shares since we unwound the original covered call trades in July 2006. Here's the current (January 2009) weekly charts of both. (See Figures 10.9 and 10.10.)

Looking at the IBM chart (Figure 10.9), you can see that it made a low in July 2006 (after we bought back the call options) and continued to move higher after that point. One of the things you can do is sell more call options when you feel that a stock may have reached a

Figure 10.9   IBM Weekly Chart

Source: eSignal.com.

Figure 10.10   Dell Weekly Chart
Source: eSignal.com.

high point, or it reached a point where you'd feel comfortable selling them, if assigned.

We ended up selling more call options on IBM when it got above $90 per share in October 2006. We sold 16 (eight for each account) of the July 2007 $100 calls for $3 each. This brought in another $4,800 for the two accounts combined and obligated my parents to sell all of their IBM stock for $100 per share if IBM finished above that level at the July 2007 expiration.

As you can see in the chart (Figure 10.9), IBM moved above $115 per share by the July 2007 expiration, and thus my parents had to depart with their shares for $100 each. Even though IBM went up to $115, my parents still had to sell them at $100. Although they were a little disappointed to see IBM shoot past $100, they were still comfortable with the gain they had made because this was part of their decision from a long time ago.

They felt a little more vindicated in January 2009 because IBM's price moved back down to a low of $70 in November 2008 to its then-current price of $85. They were able to sell their shares at $100 and glad that they did, because IBM was then languishing below that.

As far as Dell goes (Figure 10.10), the story doesn't have as happy an ending. After we unwound the first set of covered calls in July 2006, Dell moved higher just as IBM did until it peaked above $30 in November 2007. We were examining some more calls to sell at that point but never pulled the trigger. Unfortunately for my folks, Dell never recovered back to the $30 level again (the area where they wanted to sell the calls) and has continued lower down to a price of $10 per share.

This has been a little disheartening, watching Dell move so much lower, especially below their cost-basis price of $14. Not only that, but they missed out on selling at least two more possible sets of call options, which could have brought in more passive income. Lesson learned. The bottom line is, make sure you sell calls against your stock because you never know when your shares will decline in price. Selling the calls will at least buffer part of the decline if you opt to hold on to the shares, just as my parents have done.

RISK MANAGEMENT

The risk management plan with a covered call strategy is no different than your normal "long stock" plan. This is because no matter how much the calls will shield you from a down move in the stock, it won't shield you from a total loss if the stock falls to zero. If you own shares of stock, what's your choice of action? Do you have a stop-loss point? Do you have a profit-taking point? Are you watching support and resistance levels on the charts? Whatever your plan is, make sure you follow it. Everyone has a different situation, so everyone's plan can be different.

SUMMARY

In summary, selling OTM calls against long stock is a way to gain sideline income while you wait for an eventual profit-taking sell price (you do have a sell point, don't you?). If you are adamant about keeping the stock forever, then you concentrate on selling OTM calls because that lessens the chance of assignment. The continual selling in exchange for premium income, and hopefully the expiration of worthless options, will allow you to repeat the process many times during the year, lowering your cost basis each time.

As a hedging mechanism, covered calls are a prudent play. We all are going to go through the ups and downs while owning stock. That's inevitable. You might as well have an outlet to bring you some extra cash every few months to buffer a potential fall and to pad your bank account along the way. Take the money. It's waiting there for you.

The real-life examples of my parents covered call trades with IBM and Dell should give you a good idea of how it can be done. Although they have opted to hold onto Dell because of their long-term commitment, they will continue to sell call options against it once Dell moves back higher a bit.

CHAPTER 11

A BONUS
STRATEGY: RATIO
OPTION SPREADS

In the introduction of this book I promised you a bonus. I've decided to offer you an extra option strategy to contemplate. What's another tactic between friends? This is an option-selling strategy that I used almost exclusively while trading on the New York Mercantile Exchange (NYMEX) floor. Be warned, this is a highly speculative play that entails unlimited risk, so it is not to be taken lightly and it may not be suitable for all readers. But, to offset the unlimited risk, this strategy offers incredible opportunities to make excellent profits with a high margin for error and a high probability of profit.

The strategy is called the **"ratio option spread."** It entails buying an out-of-the-money (OTM) option and selling multiple less-expensive, farther out-of-the-money options against it in one single spread trade. The trick is to sell enough OTM options to give yourself a net credit on the trade, even factoring in commissions. The distance between the long and short strikes should be large enough to compensate for any adverse move by the underlying security. The greatest part of the ratio option spread is that you can make good money if the market moves in favor of your long strike. And even if all options happen to expire worthless, you end up a winner due to the credit you received at the outset of the trade.

During the latter part of my floor-trading career, I used this trade almost exclusively with the crude oil options as they were so ripe for this kind of trade. One of the reasons why it was so profitable was because of the implied volatility skew structure of the crude oil options. The skew structure, if you remember from Chapter 3, is the discrepancy between implied volatility (IV) levels of each individual option in the same trading month on a specific stock or commodity. The skew structure can make certain patterns that tell you the best way to take advantage of the situation. For a very long time, crude oil options presented a "smiling skew" pattern, which meant that all OTM options traded at a higher IV level than the at-the-money (ATM) options.

The smiling skew pattern helped in this situation because it meant I would not need to sell an exorbitant amount of OTM options to offset the cost of the long option. Remember, volatility has a direct effect on the price of any option. If the volatility level is high, then that option will be more expensive on an IV basis than an option with a lower volatility level. In the case of crude oil, the OTM options always had a higher IV than the ATM options, which made it prime for this kind of trade. The larger the discrepancy in IV levels, the better the trade.

The smiling skew chart in Figure 11.1 plots the IV of each call option at its respective strike price. The strikes are listed along the horizontal axis and the IV levels are listed along the vertical axis. When you connect the dots, the pattern forms a smile. This IV structure reflects the fact that the ATM options are cheaper on an IV basis when compared to both the OTM and ITM options.

A smiling skew is not a prerequisite, though, for achieving profitability with the ratio spread. You can have a commodity that exhibits a forward or reverse skew as well. A forward skew is one in which all the call options have higher IV levels the farther you move OTM, whereas the reverse skew has all the OTM puts showing larger IV levels. I've learned over time that concentrating on selling put ratio spreads is probably better from a risk/reward standpoint because a stock or commodity can only go to zero, whereas call options can theoretically go up forever. But that doesn't mean selling call ratio spreads is out of the picture. Far from it. I'll show you specifically how

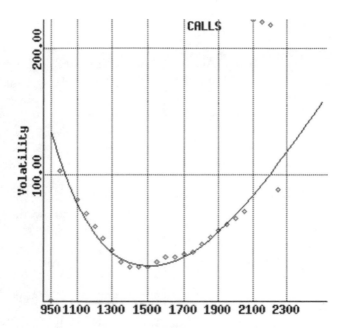

Figure 11.1 Smiling Skew Chart
Source: Chart provided by Optionetics, Inc.

the soybean market is one of the best to trade with this strategy, especially during the summer growing months.

The option chain in Figure 11.2 lists the available call options for soybeans that expire in November 2006. Soybean options are great to trade during the summer months, especially with a ratio spread strategy. The growing season occurs at this time and the market is prone to violent price swings due to weather factors. These weather scares produce a huge upside volatility skew in which the really far OTM call options have a higher IV than the closer ATM call options. What we want to do is find the right combination of expiration month and strike prices that will allow us to take advantage of the best IV differential.

Figure 11.3 is a typical "forward implied volatility skew" chart that depicts how the IV levels of each strike price get larger as you move farther OTM in respect to the call options. There is such a pervasive fear that soybean futures can explode to the upside during the summer because of possible drought conditions that could reduce the size of the soybean crop. The most common way to alleviate the potential

BSize:		Bid:				Last: 6046		Prev: 5984
		Ask:		ASize:		Change: +62		

Last	Change	Prev	High	Low	T	Time	Symbol
3046	+62	2984	3046	3022	s	14:57	NOV06 300
							NOV06 400
							NOV06 460
							NOV06 480
							NOV06 500
54	+53	1	54	54	+	Jul22	NOV06 520
672	+52	620	672	672	s	14:57	NOV06 540
515	+44	471	515	515	s	14:57	NOV06 560
386	+35	351	386	386	s	14:57	NOV06 580
284	+26	256	290	264	s	14:57	NOV06 600
210	+17	191	214	200	s	14:57	NOV06 620
155	+14	141	164	150	s	14:57	NOV06 640
115	+10	105	124	112	s	14:57	NOV06 660
90	+7	81	94	86	s	14:57	NOV06 680
67	+5	62	74	66	s	14:57	NOV06 700
53	+3	50	54	53	s	14:57	NOV06 720
43	+3	40	50	43	s	14:57	NOV06 740
35	+3	32	40	34	s	14:57	NOV06 760
30	+1	27	30	30	s	14:57	NOV06 780
24	0	24	26	24	s	14:57	NOV06 800
21	0	21	22	21	s	14:57	NOV06 820
17	+1	16	20	17	s	14:57	NOV06 840
15	+1	14	15	13	s	14:57	NOV06 860
13	0	13	16	13	s	14:57	NOV06 880
10	0	10	10	10	s	14:57	NOV06 900

Figure 11.2 Soybean Option Chain, November 2006 Expiration
Source: eSignal.com.

for a disruption in the supply of a product is to increase its price. That's the law of supply and demand.

As speculators enter the soybean option market in the spring, they tend to favor buying OTM call options because of their cheap price and the huge leverage they can offer. It's the same every year. If soybeans go ballistic, those call buyers will be very happy. Once the volume starts picking up in the option market, the market makers are forced to keep raising the prices, this inflates the IV levels, which in turn keeps propping up the prices. It's an endless cycle until the crop is ready and the beans are harvested.

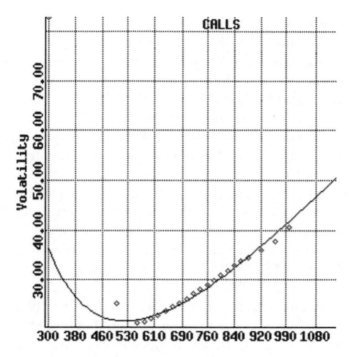

Figure 11.3 Soybean Options Forward IV Skew
Source: Chart provided by Optionetics, Inc.

MAKING THE TRADE

Look back at the option chain in Figure 11.2. The November soybean futures were at $604\frac{3}{4}$ per bushel at the time of writing. I use eSignal as my data provider and each vendor has a different way of presenting commodity quotes. At the top of the option chain, look for the "Last" price of soybeans and you will see the number 6046. Soybean futures are quoted in eighths of a cent, but move in quarter-point intervals ($\frac{1}{4}$, $\frac{1}{2}$, $\frac{3}{4}$), so the last price is equivalent to $604\frac{6}{8}$, with the bottom of the fraction getting dropped. The price gets shortened to 6046, which is the same as $604\frac{3}{4}$. Crazy, I know!

If you look at the November 640 calls, you will see the "Last" price as 155. Soybean options are also quoted in eighths of a cent, but actually do move in eighths ($\frac{1}{8}$, $\frac{1}{4}$, $\frac{3}{8}$, $\frac{1}{2}$, $\frac{5}{8}$, etc.) so that price is the equivalent of $15\frac{5}{8}$ or 15.625 cents. In dollar terms, one full soybean cent or point equals $50 and one-eighth of a full cent or point equals $6.25.

Don't worry yourself right now about how each commodity is quoted. I know you're probably thinking, "How can a cent equal $50?" Exactly. Have I confused you enough yet? See what we commodity option traders have to deal with? But it's all worth it! So our option price of 15.625 cents equals $781.25 ($15\,^5/_8 \times \$50 = \$781.25$).

All right, what do we do now? In order to take advantage of a bullish expectation and to execute the perfect ratio option spread, we need to find the right combination of strikes to maximize the skew discrepancy and keep a large distance between the strikes that we will buy and sell. In this example, we're going to buy one of the November 2006 680 calls for 90 cents (that's really 9.0 cents) and sell five of the November 2006 820 calls for 21 cents (that's really 2.125 cents or $2\,^1/_8$ cents) for a total credit of $1\,^5/_8$ cents. That credit would equate to $81.25 ($1\,^5/_8 \times \$50 = \$81.25$). We've put on a ratio of 5:1, being short five of the 820 calls and long one of the 680 calls. That's a full $1.40 (or 140 points, in trader lingo) between the strike prices, which is a very large move in the soybean market. The five short options have completely paid for the one long option and then some. With a commission structure of $5 per option (I will talk about this in Chapter 13 on Brokers and Commissions), this trade would cost us $30 ($5 $\times$ 6 options = $30). That would leave us with a net credit of $51.25. You'll notice with soybeans currently at 604^3/_4$, our long strike is roughly 75 points OTM and our short strikes are a full 215 points OTM. That's a nice cushion.

Now that we have the trade set up, what do we do? We watch and wait to see where the soybeans might go. You will find with this trade, just like the option credit spread, we can win in three market scenarios. If soybeans tank and all of our options expire worthless, we still walk away with our $51.25 credit. If soybeans stay flat and our options are still OTM, we'll still walk away with our initial credit. Once soybeans start to move higher, then we can begin to see some substantial gains. The trade can be very profitable as long as one scenario doesn't occur. We don't want the beans to go screaming higher past our short strike of 820. This is the one and only way to lose. That upward move has to be swift, though, for us to see a loss.

Our best-case scenario for the trade is for soybeans to slowly move up over time toward our short strike of 820. This will allow our long 680 call to appreciate in value while the 820 calls start to lose value due to time decay. To see the numbers in action, look at the spreadsheet in Figure 11.4, which gives us our profit/loss (P/L) breakdown at various prices at expiration.

The spreadsheet gives us an idea of how much we can make or lose at various soybean prices at expiration. A down move in the market still allows us to profit, as we'll end up keeping the initial $81.25 credit (commissions not included). You can see how our profit starts to rise as we move higher past our long 680 strike price and tops out right at our short 820 strike. The ideal scenario would be to have the soybean market close for trading on expiration day right at the 820 level.

Our breakeven point, or the area where we'll start to lose money if soybean prices rise too far, is right around the 856 level. You can also see that the losses will start to accumulate rather quickly once we pass that level as our naked short options will really kick in. At the current soybean price of 604¾, we have a tremendous profit zone spanning from $0 to $855. Even a move from 604¾ to our breakeven price of 856 is *huge* for the soybean market, which makes us feel very comfortable with our profit zone.

We want the market to go higher due to our bullish bias, but not too much too fast. From our historical, fundamental, and technical

Soybean Price	680 Call P/L	820 Call P/L	Total P/L
500	($450.00)	$531.25	$81.25
550	($450.00)	$531.25	$81.25
600	($450.00)	$531.25	$81.25
650	($450.00)	$531.25	$81.25
680	($450.00)	$531.25	$81.25
700	$550.00	$531.25	$1,081.25
750	$3,050.00	$531.25	$3,581.25
800	$5,550.00	$531.25	$6,081.25
820	$6,550.00	$531.25	$7,081.25
850	$8,050.00	($6,968.75)	$1,081.25
855	$8,300.00	($8,218.75)	$81.25
860	$8,550.00	($9,468.75)	($918.75)
900	$10,550.00	($19,468.75)	($8,918.75)
950	$13,050.00	($31,968.75)	($18,918.75)

Figure 11.4 Soybean Ratio Option Spread Profit/Loss Breakdown

analysis, we estimate that the $850 per bushel level is a good ceiling for now. Once again, our best-case scenario is for the soybean market to gradually ride up to $820 per bushel over the life of the spread, which expires on October 27, 2006, just over three months from time of execution. The chart in Figure 11.5 shows the soybean market going back over two years' time (as of mid-July 2006). We can decipher from the chart that soybeans haven't been above the $815 level in that time and we feel very strongly that they won't get above that level while we're in the trade.

Lastly, another reason why we chose these particular strike prices was because of the IV skew discrepancy between them. The larger the skew, the better the trade can be. This year has been quite tame in terms of soybean movement, so the skew is smaller than what has

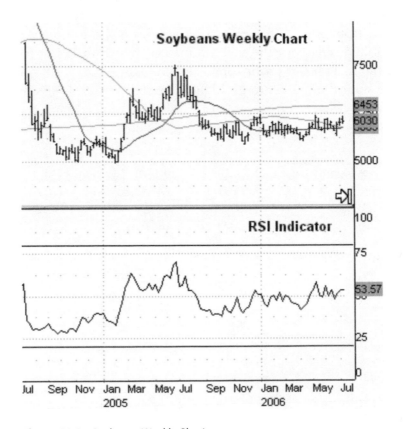

Figure 11.5   Soybeans Weekly Chart
Source: eSignal.com.

Strike Price	Option Price	Dollar Amount	IV Level
Long 1 680 Call	9 Cents	($450)	25.11%
Short 5 820 Calls	2⅛ Cents	$531.25	36.26%

Figure 11.6 Soybean Option IV Skew Discrepancy

been seen in the past, but nonetheless one still exists. The spreadsheet in Figure 11.6 shows the IV for each strike. There's an 11-point difference in IV levels, which isn't bad, but I've seen summers where strikes like this would have at least a 40-point difference between IV levels. For a case like that to occur, the soybean market would need to have already been blasting higher with more potential for dry weather conditions. This year, the soybean crop has been progressing well and the November bean futures have been trending lower. Once the market starts to come off (meaning the market is moving lower), so do the implied volatility and skew discrepancies.

The call ratio option spread is an incredible way to take advantage of a bullish directional bias without having to shell out any money for the trade. If we are correct and the market starts to move higher, we can see some significant gains add up. Since our short strikes are very far out-of-the-money, we have a nice cushion before getting into any danger. And if the market did start to move higher, we would already have a nice profit built up. This could allow us to liquidate our short calls and still walk away a winner.

2009 SOYBEAN UPDATE

In 2009, let's see how a current soybean ratio call option spread would fare at this time. Based on soybean's current $2.50 per bushel move higher in the last month and a half (which is a large move in that short time), I'll bet we can enter an even better spread because of larger absolute volatility levels of the new strike prices. As I had mentioned earlier, once the soybean futures start to make a good upside move, the IV levels really start to kick in.

Look at the following chart (Figure 11.7) of the July 2009 soybean futures contract. You can see the huge tumble it took starting in July 2008, because this was the time when most commodity and stock

Figure 11.7   Soybean Daily Chart, July 2009

Source: eSignal.com.

markets were just beginning to unravel from the fallout of the U.S. credit crisis. The soybeans made a low in early December 2008 and rallied a good $2.50 per bushel in about six weeks' time.

Let's see what the option prices are giving us. Look at the following option chain (Figure 11.8), which is for the July 2009 soybean call options. Currently, July 2009 soybean futures last traded at 1038.5 per bushel (10384 or 1038 4/8) as seen at the top of the option chain.

We can buy one of the July 1120 calls, which would require us to pay out 89.375 cents ($4,468.75) and sell three of the July 1400 calls in which we would receive 33.5 cents ($5,025). In this case, we'd be

BSize:	Bid:					Last: 10384	
	Ask:			ASize:		Change: +252	

Last	Change	Prev	High	Low	T	Time	Symbol
1276	+167	1276	1150	1150	s	Jan16	JUL09 1020
1192	+160	1192	1100	1100	s	Jan16	JUL09 1040
1112	+152	1112	990	985	s	Jan16	JUL09 1060
1033	+141	1033	1033	1033	s	Jan16	JUL09 1080
960	+130	960	865	960	s	Jan16	JUL09 1100
893	+125	893	801	893	s	Jan16	JUL09 1120
832	+123	832	742	832	s	Jan16	JUL09 1140
774	+120	774	686	774	s	Jan16	JUL09 1160
722	+117	722	635	722	s	Jan16	JUL09 1180
672	+114	672	587	672	s	Jan16	JUL09 1200
625	+110	625	543	625	s	Jan16	JUL09 1220
582	+104	582	503	582	s	Jan16	JUL09 1240
542	+100	542	465	542	s	Jan16	JUL09 1260
504	+94	504	431	504	s	Jan16	JUL09 1280
470	+90	470	397	470	s	Jan16	JUL09 1300
437	+85	437	370	437	s	Jan16	JUL09 1320
410	+81	410	342	410	s	Jan16	JUL09 1340
382	+76	382	315	382	s	Jan16	JUL09 1360
356	+73	356	293	356	s	Jan16	JUL09 1380
334	+70	334	271	334	s	Jan16	JUL09 1400
					c	Jan16	JUL09 1420
293	+62	293	233	293	s	Jan16	JUL09 1440
					c	Jan16	JUL09 1460
257	+55	257	257	257	s	Jan16	JUL09 1480
242	+52	242	242	242	s	Jan16	JUL09 1500

Figure 11.8 Soybean Option Chart, July 2009
Source: eSignal.com.

taking in roughly $560 credit for the trade (before commissions) while having an even smaller ratio than the previous soybean trade—meaning we had to sell only three option contracts to offset our one long option contract. When doing ratio spreads, the fewer contracts you have to sell to offset the long contract, the better. And to take it a step even further, the spread difference between the strike prices is a full 280 points ($2.80 per bushel), whereas in the previous example, we had only a 140-point cushion. This sounds like a great candidate for a ratio spread.

Strike Price	Option Price	Dollar Amount	IV Level
Long 1 1120 Call	89 3/8 Cents	($4,468.75)	44.50%
Short 3 1400 Calls	33 1/2 Cents	$5,025.00	47%

Figure 11.9 IV Skew Discrepancy, July 2009 Soybean Options

To see why this would make such a great spread, there must be higher IV levels of the options or a larger difference in the IV skew between the strike prices than in our previous example. Let's check Figure 11.9.

As it turns out, the skew differential was smaller than before (only a 2.5 percent difference now between strikes), but it was the absolute level of implied volatility that caused the options to make for a better spread. In the preceding table, the current volatility levels of 44.5 percent and 47 percent are a solid 9 to 19 percent higher than our previous example. That jump in implied volatility can have a large effect on the price of each option.

While looking at the following P&L spreadsheet (Figure 11.10), our maximum profit potential occurs once again if the soybean

Soybean Price	1120 Call P/L	1400 Call P/L	Total P/L
900.00	($4,468.75)	$5,025.00	$556.25
950.00	($4,468.75)	$5,025.00	$556.25
1000.00	($4,468.75)	$5,025.00	$556.25
1050.00	($4,468.75)	$5,025.00	$556.25
1100.00	($4,468.75)	$5,025.00	$556.25
1120.00	($4,468.75)	$5,025.00	$556.25
1150.00	($2,968.75)	$5,025.00	$2,056.25
1200.00	($468.75)	$5,025.00	$4,556.25
1250.00	$2,031.25	$5,025.00	$7,056.25
1300.00	$4,531.25	$5,025.00	$9,556.25
1350.00	$7,031.25	$5,025.00	$12,056.25
1400.00	$9,531.25	$5,025.00	$14,556.25
1450.00	$12,031.25	($2,475.00)	$9,556.25
1500.00	$14,531.25	($15,000.00)	($468.75)
1550.00	$17,031.25	($22,500.00)	($5,468.75)
1600.00	$19,531.25	($30,000.00)	($10,468.75)

Strike Price	Option Price	Dollar Amount	IV Level
Long 1 1120 Call	89 3/8 Cents	($4,468.75)	44.50%
Short 3 1400 Calls	33 1/2 Cents	$5,025.00	47%

Figure 11.10 Soybean Ratio Option Spread P&L Breakdown

market ends up at expiration right at the short strike level of 1400. This would give us a profit of more than $14,000.

We would start to lose money somewhere just below the 1500 level, which is a solid 460 points ($4.60 per bushel) higher than the current level of the July soybean futures of 1038.5. This is a great buffer and margin for directional error for us. A 460-point move ($4.60 per bushel) is an extremely large move for the soybeans to make in the five months before expiration, which is the amount of time when I wrote this in January 2009.

Contrast that 460-point buffer against our previous soybean ratio trade when the buffer was only about 250 points. That 210-point difference is a big deal and can really make a huge impact in the amount of profitability.

A few reasons for why the new ratio spread is more desirable:

1. The larger absolute levels of IV now compared to the previous example.
2. Soybean futures have just made a large 250-point move to the upside, which tends to increase IV levels.
3. Soybean futures were trending lower in the previous trade, which tends to decrease IV levels.

Looking back at the preceding P&L spreadsheet (Figure 11.10), we can see that with the larger spread between strikes now ($2.80 versus $1.40), our P&L configuration will give us a much larger profit potential with a much larger cushion for directional error. This is a much more attractive ratio option spread.

RISK MANAGEMENT

As with any option-selling technique, you need to have a contingency plan if the trade starts to go sour, especially ones that have open-ended risk. Even though we concentrate on shorter-dated OTM options that decay the fastest, we still have to be prepared for adverse movements. In a trade like this, you *must* have a stop-out point if the market reaches a certain threshold. That threshold is dependent on your risk tolerance and is based on a level you set ahead of time. You can either close out the trade if the soybeans reach a certain level (the breakeven point, for example) or if you've reached a maximum dollar drawdown in your account. Whichever you choose, make sure you stick to it.

Some traders will base their decision on a specific technical level being breached (50-day moving average for example) or if the trade has incurred a paper loss of $1,000. It's all up to what your comfort levels are. I used this trade successfully for years in the crude oil options market but with the **put option ratio spread** version. I never had to close out the trade early, but that doesn't mean it can't or won't happen in the future. Losses can add up extremely fast with a trade like this, so you must take an active role in its management. The worst-case scenario would be a gap open higher with an explosion in volatility levels. That would make it even harder and more expensive to buy back the short options. Even though the long option would be profitable, the speed of the movement in the soybean futures would cause the short options to overtake that profit and hand you a nasty loss. If you plan to do a trade like this, it's critical that you respect your stops.

ONE OF MY FAVORITE RATIO MARKETS

I want to show you another market that is a favorite of mine for the ratio option spread. It presents a reverse skew that never seems to go away. I'm talking about the stock indexes, of course. Ever since the market crash of 1987, the OTM put options in the Dow Jones Industrial Average, Standard & Poor's (S&P), and NASDAQ have all exhibited a large reverse skew, making the sale of far OTM put options offset by the purchase of not-so-far OTM put options a big winner.

I love executing this trade in the electronic Mini Dow and Mini S&P options. You can sell some really far OTM put options for a few points and buy closer ATM put options as the hedge and still have a credit on the trade. We're talking about selling the put options so far OTM that it would be almost unheard-of for the Dow or S&P to get down to that level to cause any danger to the position. Here are a few trading confirmations from my account at Interactivebrokers.com.

On March 16, 2006, I sold 56 contracts of the June 2006 Mini Dow 7000 strike put options for two points each. (See Figure 11.11.)

Options on Futures							
USD							
Symbol	Date Time	Exchange	Quantity	Price	Amount	Commission	
YM JUN06 7000 P	2006-03-16, 10:42:56	ECBOT	-14	2.0000	140.00	-29.82	
YM JUN06 7000 P	2006-03-16, 10:42:58	ECBOT	-14	2.0000	140.00	-29.82	
YM JUN06 7000 P	2006-03-16, 10:43:00	ECBOT	-14	2.0000	140.00	-29.82	
YM JUN06 7000 P	2006-03-16, 10:43:01	ECBOT	-14	2.0000	140.00	-29.82	

Figure 11.11   Mini Dow Options Brokerage Statement

Source: Courtesy Interactive Brokers LLC. All rights reserved.

The symbol for the Mini Dow is YM. Each point is worth $5, so I took in $560 on this trade alone ($10 × 56 = $560). Now, in order to appreciate the high probability of profit on this trade, you have to really look at the level of the strike price that I just sold. These options are based on the Dow futures contracts, which move in tandem with the Dow itself. So with the Dow at roughly the 11,000 mark in March 2006, I just sold some options that wouldn't see any danger unless the Dow broke down to the 7,000 level. That's 4,000 points lower than where the Dow is now! And it would have to make that move in 90 days' time! Do you think that would ever happen? That's 4,000 Dow points, people!

Never one to take on unlimited risk, though, even as far-fetched as the Dow dropping to the 7,000 level, I bought a smaller amount of not-so-far OTM June 10,400 put options to cover myself. (See Figure 11.12.) These were done just a few days before expiration. In this case, I didn't buy and sell the options at the same time. I opted to let time decay eat away at the 7,000 strike put options before buying the other options (which I bought for the same price). I spent just $30 on these options as the hedge against the short options. Even though it's a ratio of 3:56, the risk is extremely small. Take a look at the brokerage confirmation and the profit/loss (P/L) table in Figures 11.12 and 11.13, which shows the amount of money I could have made if the Dow had happened to drop down to 7,000 by option expiration in June 2006.

Look at the numbers. With the Dow still at the 11,000 mark in June 2006, I had such a large range for having a profitable trade. If the

Options on Futures							
USD							
Symbol	Date Time	Exchange	Quantity	Price	Amount	Commission
YM JUN06 10400 P	2006-06-14, 14:09:23	ECBOT	1	2.0000	–10.00	–2.13
YM JUN06 10400 P	2006-06-14, 14:09:23	ECBOT	1	2.0000	–10.00	–2.13
YM JUN06 10400 P	2006-06-14, 14:09:23	ECBOT	1	2.0000	–10.00	–2.13

Figure 11.12 Mini Dow Options Brokerage Statement

Dow did happen to move down to the 7,000 mark over the next few days before the June 2006 option expiration, I would have over $51,000 worth of profit built into the trade by the time I had to buy back my short options to cover myself. My only real risk, as I saw it in this case, was if the Dow gapped lower a sizable amount overnight due to some geopolitical event such as another terrorist attack. And by sizable, I mean at least a 1,000-point drop. As I finish off this chapter in August 2006, all options ended up expiring worthless, so I got to keep the $530 of total premium that was credited to my account from these two trades.

The thing that you have to remember, for whatever reason, is that people will buy OTM options because they think the stock or commodity might get to that level by expiration. But if someone

Dow Price	10400 Put Strike P/L	7000 Put Strike P/L	Total P/L
7000	$51,000.00	$560.00	$51,560.00
7500	$43,500.00	$560.00	$44,060.00
8000	$36,000.00	$560.00	$36,560.00
8500	$28,500.00	$560.00	$29,060.00
9000	$21,000.00	$560.00	$21,560.00
9500	$13,500.00	$560.00	$14,060.00
10000	$6,000.00	$560.00	$6,560.00
10500	($30.00)	$560.00	$530.00
11000	($30.00)	$560.00	$530.00
11500	($30.00)	$560.00	$530.00

Figure 11.13 Mini Dow Ratio Option Spread Profit/Loss

wants to buy options on a Dow move that is 4,000 points away, rest assured I'm going to sell them, especially when I can easily hedge them with more appropriate options. Do you really think the Dow will drop 4,000 points in 90 days? I don't, but others obviously do. It has taken years to move that same amount. (See Figure 11.14.) Believe me, if the Dow fell that much that quickly, there would be much more to worry about in terms of the whole financial community

Figure 11.14 Dow Monthly Chart

Source: eSignal.com.

than just my small options position. There would be blood in the streets without a doubt.

The same scenario exists in the E-mini S&P 500 options, where I can and will continue to sell far OTM put options in a larger quantity and buy a lesser amount of not-so-far OTM put options as protection. I've done so many of these that it would be too hard to list them all. And like the soybean options, the IV skew that exists in the Dow and S&P options is quite large, making those two products extremely ripe for the ratio option spread.

And just to prove a point, our probability calculator (Figure 11.15) gives a 0.1 percent chance of the Dow moving down to the 7,000 mark by option expiration in 90 days. I can't believe that it even gave

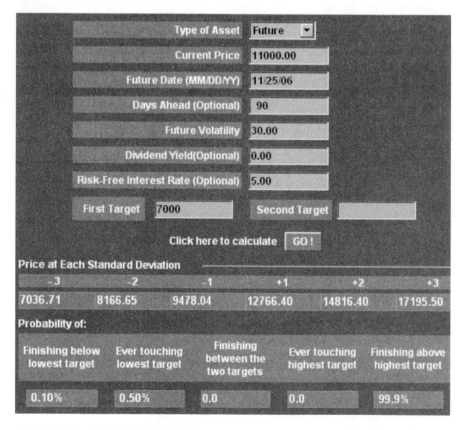

Figure 11.15 Probability Calculator

Source: © Copyright Optionvue Systems International, Inc.

Options on Futures				
USD				
Symbol	Security ID	Description	Quantity	Closing Price
P OYM OCT 05 6000	–	YM OCT05 6000 P	-83	1.0000
P OYM OCT 05 9300	–	YM OCT05 9300 P	5	1.0000
Total				

Figure 11.16 Monthly Brokerage Statement

Source: Courtesy Interactive Brokers LLC. All rights reserved.

it that much of a chance. That's why I buy options against the short side of the trade—just to cover myself in a worst-case scenario.

Oh, and I almost forgot. I just came across a few more trade confirmations in which I was able to sell the Mini Dow options at the 6,000 level! Insane, but people are buying these. See my monthly statement for September 2005 in Figure 11.16.

In this case, I was able to sell 83 contracts of the 6,000 strike put options and I bought 5 contracts of the 9,300 put options against them as a hedge. There was a credit received on the trade so if all options expired worthless (which they did), I would at least walk away with some money. That was a 3,300-point buffer, which would allow me to make at least $82,500 at expiration if the Dow happened to close for trading at the 6,000 level (3,300 points × $5 multiplier × 5 contracts = $82,500). Sweet! It doesn't get much better than that, but still remember the warning: *There is unlimited risk exposure, so make sure you stay sharp!* And don't even think about trying to steal my trade idea here. This is part of my bread and butter!

2009 RATIO OPTION UPDATE

Although I don't have another actual ratio option spread trade to present to you in the e-mini options, I can tell you that the availability of quality of trades is still there. In light of the current market meltdown, the IV reverse skews remain just as wide as ever, making far OTM put options great candidates to sell, while being able to purchase not-so-far OTM put options as protection.

When I scanned through the March 2009 Mini Dow YM options (on January 19, 2009), I could see that you could sell 50 of the 4000 strike put options for 10 points each, which would bring in $2,500 into your account. The Dow itself was at the 8300 level on January 19, 2009, meaning the 4000 strike put options were over 4,300 points OTM! That's a huge distance the Dow would have had to travel lower in the next 60 days at option expiration.

While selling those, you would have needed to purchase other options as a hedge, and that could be 5 of the 6250 strike put options, for 97 points. That would cost you $2,425, leaving you with a very small credit after commissions.

With a 2250-point cushion between the strike prices, you would have a profit of $56,250 (2250 points × $5 multiplier × 5 contracts) built up if the Dow itself moved down to the 4000 level mark at March 2009 expiration (which was two months into the future from my analysis)—another potential profitable trade.

Even though the idea of the Dow dropping over 4300 points in two months' time seems totally absurd, you still need to protect your bottom line and have a stop-out point. You can create your own spreadsheets and run through the numbers, giving yourself an idea of where you might want to set your limits. Use an option calculator to run what-if scenarios, because that could tell you how much each option might be worth at various levels of the Dow and various IV points. Use the tools, because these trades have unlimited risk and you always need to be prepared.

SUMMARY

The ratio option spread lets you take advantage of a directional bias without incurring an initial debit or having to speculate on low-probability OTM options. It allows you an extremely wide range of profitability under three different market scenarios. The trade is made more attractive by the implied volatility skew of the options involved. Try to make sure you receive a credit at the outset of the trade, including commissions, so that if all options expire worthless, at least you'll end up with some money in your pocket.

The ratio spread can get tricky if the market makes a large adverse move very quickly soon after putting on the trade. Try to keep the distance between the strike prices quite wide, as that offers you even more protection. Remember, this trade involves selling naked options, so if you are uncomfortable with that approach, then it might not be for you. Make sure you know all the risks before entering a ratio option spread trade.

PART THREE

GETTING READY
TO TRADE

CHAPTER 12

TOOLS
OF THE TRADE

Now that I've given you five incredible ways to profit in the option market, I'd like to discuss the tools that can help with the execution of those trades. Specifically, I want to talk about the free and paid services you can choose from to get your market data and the options-related software to help manage your positions.

Since I run my own trading business, I need to have all real-time and professional-quality products. At present, most of those products are fee-based, but I also use some free ones, which I will share with you. In order to take advantage of these products you must have a computer and a high-speed Internet connection. I can't believe I'm saying that you must have a computer. How strange is that? Who doesn't have a computer these days? High-speed Internet access is not as crucial for the casual investor, but if you are a full-time trader, how could you survive without it? A cable modem or telephone digital subscriber line (DSL) high-speed connection will suffice.

Right now I use eSignal.com as my data vendor for all of my stock, option, and commodity quotes. This requires a monthly fee for the service in addition to having to pay for real-time exchange fees. Exchange fees are a cost that you must pay to the stock and commodity exchanges if you want to get their data on a real-time basis.

And for whatever reason, the commodities exchanges in New York and Chicago charge a steep price to get that data in comparison to the stock exchanges. The most popular exchanges are: ICE futures U.S. (formerly the New York Board of Trade (NYBOT)). This is the home for trading in coffee, sugar, cocoa, orange juice, and cotton. The monthly fee is $60. Add this to the New York Mercantile Exchange (NYMEX), the Chicago Mercantile Exchange (CME), the Chicago Board of Trade (CBOT), and the New York Commodity Exchange (COMEX). All of which are $60/mo. You're talking upwards of $300/mo. for streaming real-time quotes. Compare that to the stock and stock option exchanges, which charge only a few dollars for their real-time data. I always wondered if the high price of commodity data is what keeps a lot of potential traders out of those markets.

I am quite happy using eSignal for my market data. They provide me with my stock, stock option, futures, and futures options data all in one package at a fairly competitive price. There are others, though, that offer a comprehensive data service, and although I don't use them, here's a short list:

www.tradestation.com
www.dtniq.com
www.cqg.com
www.equis.com
www.barchart.com

I know many of you are probably interested in the free products and web sites that I mentioned being available, and who wouldn't be? They're free! I spend a fair amount of time scouring the Web for good options-trading material because I like to see what's out there and compare it to what I already have. You can always pick up a nugget or two from somebody or somewhere about a service or product that you haven't seen before. So let me run down my list of the best free data, software, products, and web sites that I've come across to date. And I'm sure by the time you read this book, many of these sites might be obsolete, as that's how fast the Web changes these days. As a note, I'm not compensated in any way for recommending these websites and products.

If you are looking for a free quote and charting platform, I highly recommend a product from www.medved.net/quote tracker/. The software is called Quotetracker and it's an excellent platform for quotes, charts, and trading (if you use a supported broker). The platform itself is free but it doesn't give you the data feed. You have to pick one of the supported data feed partners from their list. The list includes just about every brokerage and other data feed vendor available today. If you trade through a broker such as optionsXpress, E★Trade.com, Schwab.com, Scottrade.com, TDAmeritrade.com, Fidelity.com, or Interactive brokers.com, you will be able to get your quotes through them using Quotetracker. Even if you already have a fee-based subscription to eSignal or IQFeed, you can still use Quotetracker as a backup platform.

Now that you have some data choices, let's run down my favorite trading-related web sites. Without a doubt, one of my top web sites for options information is IVolatility.com (www.ivolatility.com). I use this site extensively in my own option analysis and I've mentioned it quite a few times in the book. IVolatility.com is an amazing site for a wealth of information, most specifically the volatility data—both historical and implied. The volatility charts help me determine whether stocks have cheap or expensive options and the option calculator is top-notch. This site should be placed high on your list as one of your core options resources. Both free and paid services are available.

Without a doubt, my top free web site for futures data and news is www.futuresource.com. For clean and reliable commodity data, you can't beat Futuresource. I check this web site every single day for whatever information I might need at that time. It has recently been acquired by eSignal, but as of today, Futuresource still has its own products, both free and fee-based.

In terms of options software that can help track your positions, graph your positions, do what-if scenarios, and provide basic help with options in general, I recommend www.888options.com. This is the web site for the Options Industry Council (OIC). The OIC's job is to get the word out to investors that options are a viable and useful form of trading. The OIC does not charge fees and you can call toll-free with any option question you may have. That's sweet, and I've called OIC myself! The OIC also offers a free software package called the "Options Investigator" on CD-ROM—well worth your free money!

Here are some other sites that have free and fee-based services:

www.optionistics.com
www.snowgold.com/download/downopt.html
www.option-chart.com
www.mindxpansion.com/options/index.php
www.samoasky.com

And for you Microsoft Excel users:

www.hoadley.net/options/options.htm (A pretty intense and sophisticated options web site for users of Excel. Give it a look.)
www.optionstar.com
www.quotein.com
www.fintools.com (My current options software was created by
these guys.)

Don't forget the web sites for the options exchanges. Make sure you check the education sections of these web sites, as they have some fantastic and **free** archived online webinars that you can watch in the comfort of your own home.

www.cboe.com
www.ise.com
www.amex.com
www.phlx.com
www.nymex.com
www.cbot.com
www.cme.com
www.theice.com

If you need stock and option scanners to help you find trades, here are a few that I've tried in the past. All have their advantages:

www.poweropt.com
www.stockfetcher.com

www.tradestation.com
www.trade-ideas.com
www.marketscreen.com

Here are a few more random web sites that I like to frequent in no particular order:

www.elitetrader.com (A top pick.)
www.optionstrategist.com (Larry McMillan's site.)
www.optionetics.com (For commodity volatility charts like the ones in this book.)
www.optionvueresearch.com (For the probability calculator used in this book.)
www.stockcharts.com
www.bigcharts.com

You can also get free magazine subscriptions to:

www.sfomag.com
www.futuresmag.com
www.tradermonthly.com

There you have them—the web sites that I use most frequently in my own trading. By no means is this an exhaustive listing, as there are literally hundreds, if not thousands, more to choose from that I haven't mentioned. I hope you will at least find some of these web sites, products, and software worthy of your time, especially the free ones. I've spent a good deal of time researching them and wouldn't have put them in my book if I didn't think they had some useful features.

CHAPTER 13

BROKERS AND COMMISSIONS

Now that I've given you the strategies and the tools, you need to have a way to put those trades into action. The focus of this chapter will be on the subject of brokers, trading platforms, and commissions. The electronic marketplace is taking over and the open-outcry system is on the way out. I mentioned in the Introduction that I wanted to share with you the importance of getting ahead in the electronic age because that's the way it's all going to be. There's no turning back. Technological advancement is key to allowing us smaller retail players to stay on even ground with the rest of the marketplace. We've come a long way in terms of new technology and lower option commissions in just the past few years alone. I believe that stems from just two things:

1. The Internet.
2. The opening of the all-electronic International Securities Exchange (ISE).

It's all about the electronic marketplace, people. The Internet has allowed many traditional brokers to streamline their operations and to cut down on the costs associated with doing things manually. Also, with the introduction of the ISE, we have seen a major competition brewing among the other options exchanges with regard to trying to keep market share.

All in all, that has led to one thing—lower commissions for us retail market participants. I've personally gone from paying $19.95 per stock option contract just a few years ago to paying only $1 today per stock option contract. That's a sweet deal.

WHO ARE THE BROKERS?

Let's talk about the various types of options brokers so you can get an idea of what the playing field looks like. In my opinion, if you're paying more than $20 per option contract, then it might be time for you to either find a new broker or negotiate a new rate. I understand that some investors who have never before traded options will need some initial hand-holding from their brokers, and that's okay. You are going to be charged for that extra service. But even so, I still don't think that the commission should be more than $20. When you get to a point where you don't need the extra help, make sure the commissions reflect this new change.

There's a huge difference in the commission structure between stock options brokers and futures (commodities) options brokers, and I will address that issue.

STOCK OPTIONS BROKERS

First, let's hone in on stock options. There are two levels of commission rates that I'm aware of. The first one is the broker that will charge you a low rate per option contract, but will then add on an additional "minimum charge per order" fee. It looks something like this: $.75 per option contract with a minimum charge of $12.95 per order. This occurs at some of the mainstream, big-name brokers like options X-press, Schwab.com, E★Trade.com. Commissions are changing all the time, so consult the web sites for up-to-the-minute pricing.

There's absolutely, positively nothing wrong with these guys, and I have Schwab and optionsXpress accounts for myself (for other purposes), but they are mostly geared toward more hand-holding, which lends itself to charging a higher commission. If you are comfortable with your brokers and like how they operate, then by all means stick with them. I'm just here to tell you that there are cheaper commissions available and to be aware of all costs. I'm not here to bad-mouth anybody, and the last thing I would need is to be blackballed in the trading community.

I particularly like optionsXpress because of all the free tools it offers for options traders. I would highly recommend them if you're just starting out in the options game. With regard to the commissions, if you're not trading more than 20 contracts per order, the $.75 per option rate doesn't really come into play. From talking to many traders at option conferences, I believe most do not hit the 20-contract threshold to take advantage of that commission structure. Also, most of these brokers still operate on a browser-based trading platform (more cumbersome in my opinion), although some do offer a standalone version for those customers with a higher asset base.

The second type of stock options broker is one that offers "Direct-Access" trading. These are much higher-end brokers who cater to very active traders who don't need any help with their trading. The trading platform is very sophisticated and has a direct link to all the exchanges, which allows you to direct your trades to whichever exchange you want. These are truly the "point-and-click" type of trading platforms that require minimal keystrokes to enter a trade.

The main advantage to using direct-access brokers is that the reduced cost to them to run their business in turn lowers the commission for us. One such broker, and the one that I use for a majority of my stock, options, and electronic futures trades, is Interactivebrokers .com (www.interactivebrokers.com). It is one of the front-runners in this area and is used by a multitude of active traders. Interactive brokers charges $1 per option contract. No joke. That's $1 per option contract with no other fees attached whatsoever. It's a great deal, especially if you trade in small quantities. In order to protect your bottom line, you need to save on commissions. Be warned, though, the trading software does have a learning curve to it and you're pretty much at the mercy of the online tutorial to figure out how to use it. But like anything, once you've used it for a while, it's a snap. And you'll be amazed at how many things you can do with it.

My advice once you're comfortable with trading on your own and you don't require any more hand-holding is to step up to a direct-access broker and reap the rewards of lower commissions. In order not to play favorites and single out only Interactivebrokers, let me mention two other brokers that fit into the direct-access category. These also are highly regarded by the trading community and have a large following: www.tradestation.com and www.thinkorswim.com.

COMMODITIES BROKERS

Let's move on to the open-outcry/pit-traded commodities markets. Unfortunately, the futures options arena is still light-years behind the equities markets in terms of going all-electronic although that is quickly changing now. Most of the commodities exchanges still operate under the "human–interaction" model, thus keeping commissions sky-high. The markets that I'm referring to are such commodities as gold, silver, oil, corn, soybeans, coffee, sugar, cocoa, orange juice, cotton, pork bellies, and hogs. You can certainly trade these contracts online through your computer, but many of the orders are still handled by human pit traders for execution.

When opening an account to trade these commodities, you have to open a "commodities" account. It's different from a stock account. They both can be held at the same brokerage (if they handle both types) but they will be two separate and distinct accounts. Here's where the commissions get tricky, so listen up. When you initiate a commodity option trade, you can be hit with at least five different types of fees. They are:

1. *Commission fee.* This is the commission your broker will charge you.
2. *Clearing/processing fee.* This is the fee your broker will charge you to clear the trade through its system.
3. *Exchange fee.* This is the fee collected by the exchange where you make the trade.
4. *Floor brokerage fee.* This is the commission the floor broker will charge to execute your trade on the exchange. Some floor brokers work as "independent contractors" and may or may not be

employed by your regular brokerage firm. This is one fee that
will be eliminated if your trade is executed electronically.

5. *National Futures Association (NFA) fee.* This is the fee charged to
you by the NFA. Every trader gets hit by this one.

As you can see, everyone seems to have a hand in your trade and
you will pay for it, unless you know how to work the system. That's
what I'm here for. In addition to the previously mentioned fees, the
broker will charge you on a **round-turn basis.** This means that
the broker is charging you up front for the opening and closing transactions, regardless of whether you end up closing the transaction.
Specifically, I'm referring to options that expire worthless. When you
buy or sell an option, that option might be worthless at expiration.
Those options don't need to be offset because they'll just expire. But
the brokers still charge you up front for both sides of the transaction
whether it expires or not.

What you want to do before opening a commodity option
account is to ask your broker to charge you on a **half-turn basis.**
This means that you will be charged the appropriate fees only when
you make a trade. So, if you own an option that expires worthless, you
won't be charged for that side of the transaction. The round-turn
basis is very sneaky, and I'm sure many investors miss that on their
statements. I still don't know why the commodity industry operates
that way, but it does. Be smart and negotiate the half-turn basis if
you can. Some brokers may oblige, but that might depend on your
account size and how many trades you do. Don't be afraid to ask.
Also, try to negotiate on the five other fees I mentioned. Some brokers will be happy to waive the clearing/processing and floor broker
fees if you do enough business. And just in case you are wondering, I do a major part of my commodity trading business through
www.5perside.com. These guys are a division of MF Global and run
a great operation. I highly recommend them.

COMMODITY UPDATE 2009

When I updated this chapter in January 2009, there were some big
changes for the better in the commodity option arena, especially for the

off–floor, retail investor. I finished the first version of this book in August 2006, so I want to fill you in on what's transpired since then, as it mostly has to do with the technological advances of the exchanges.

Beginning back in June 2007, the NYMEX officially brought back the electronic version of their options to trade simultaneously side by side with the pit version of their options. The NYMEX offered this type of trading during the night-session back in the mid-1990s, but discontinued it in early 1998 for some reason. This included the COMEX division of the NYMEX, where metals options and futures are traded. The NYMEX had already begun trading their futures contracts electronically side by side with the pit in September 2006 (which essentially put the nail in the coffin for all the futures pit traders), but the options didn't come on board until almost a year later.

This was a big advancement for the NYMEX because it now allowed retail traders to bypass the pit altogether and place their own options orders directly into the electronic system. So not only could you still use your broker to call option orders into the pit if you wanted, but you could also enter the orders through your broker's trading platform into the electronic marketplace. This was great news.

Although the electronic options is a great way to trade, they haven't caught on yet, as most of the option volume is still traded in the option pits on the floor of the NYMEX. Even though it's very easy to trade single options electronically, the technology to implement option spreads has not been available yet. Right now, I still give the nod to the options pits as far as getting more volume done and being able to place multi-legged option spreads, but for the small trader who just wants to buy or sell straight up calls or puts, the electronic market is a great alternative. Over time, I believe the electronic options will take over as the most popular way to trade NYMEX options, but for now, having both the pit and electronic available to you is a great combination.

The ICE Futures Exchange—theice.com (formerly the New York Board of Trade—NYBOT) started trading their options contracts (coffee, sugar, cocoa, orange juice, and cotton) electronically in March 2008 side by side with the pit options on the floor.

The CME itself has offered electronic trading for many of its financial futures and options products for longer than any of the other commodities exchanges. They were the pioneers of getting the e-mini S&P 500 and e-mini Nasdaq futures going in 1997, which was a huge success right off the bat. They added the options on the e-minis soon after that. The CME, which has also bought out the CBOT (Chicago Board of Trade), has offered electronic trading of their flagship grains markets, too (corn, wheat, and soybeans). You can find all you want about these products by just going to the home pages of each exchange.

One of the great things about the electronic options market for the NYMEX, CME, CBOT, and ICE is that they are open for trading many hours longer than the pit options market. The NYMEX uses the CME Globex system, so both have options trading available 23¼ hours a day, while their pit options market still closes each day in the afternoon until the next trading day. The ICE's electronic options are open in a range of four to five hours longer (depending on which market you're considering) than the pit options market.

These are great advances and a testament that technology is on the move. On the downside, though, many floor traders are losing their jobs because the electronic trading of certain futures contracts has put them out of business. I know that when the NYMEX offered electronic futures trading in September 2006, it essentially ended the pit futures market almost instantaneously. And it is having the same effect on the other pit futures markets that were offered on the CME, CBOT, and ICE.

The best effect of these advancements for us is that we will continue to see lower rates on our commissions. Although you still need to go through your broker to trade these electronic options, cutting out the middleman (pit trader) will help reduce your costs. And on that note, let's go over some more specifics on the commodity brokerage account.

OPTION APPROVAL

The one other hitch to setting up a stock options account is the "approval levels." Believe it or not, the brokerages will approve you for certain types of option trading strategies based on the risk level of each trade. Almost everyone is approved right off the bat for straight buys of calls or puts and to execute covered calls. The second level puts you into the category of option spreads; the third level allows you to do naked put option sales (yay!); and the fourth level, which is the most risky, is to sell naked call options. This level is reserved for the most experienced and well-capitalized traders. Even though I am approved for all levels, I still will not sell naked call options.

Once you've filled out the application, your broker will tell you what level you've been approved for. If the level doesn't meet your trading needs, talk to your broker about it. He or she might be able to get you approved for the next level. Usually, the only things that might hold you back are the years of experience you have trading options and/or the dollar size of your account. Once again, try to negotiate these items, and if you have to, try a few different brokers until you get to the desired level of trading.

LAST WORDS

Bottom line, commissions factor into your net profits. You need to be aware of how much you're paying for each trade. Do some comparison shopping and look for the best deal. It's not unheard-of to have a few accounts running at the same time to see who treats you the best. I've done it and I know many other traders who do it as well. The brokerage landscape is changing very quickly, so you might find yourself switching brokers from time to time. It may seem troublesome to keep moving around but I believe you will eventually find a broker that you are comfortable with and whose commission structure is acceptable. Remember, your trading is a business, so treat it as such. Keeping costs low and profits high is vital to long-term success.

As an end note, here's a list of some popular brokers:

www.interactivebrokers.com
www.optionXpress.com
www.schwab.com
www.thinkorswim.com
www.5perside.com
www.mfglobal.com
www.rcgdirect.com

CONCLUSION

Whew! We covered quite a bit in this book. I'm very thankful that I had the opportunity to write it. I know that it might take some time to understand and grasp all the nuances of every trade that I've shown, but it's the same with everything—practice makes perfect. My goal was to outline and explain in detail the best options trading strategies that have allowed me the opportunity to succeed in this business and to provide you a blueprint for doing the same. My suggestion is to reread the book as many times as necessary. These strategies do work, and they can offer you better ways to increase your wealth and get rich with options.

If there's one thing that I want you to come away with after reading this book, it is the fact that you must be open to the idea of being an option seller as much as you would be an option buyer. I've shown you some incredible ways to generate steady income by using options from the sell side. Don't be under the impression that picking a market direction and being right on it is the only way to profit. Far from it. If you concentrate on selling out-of-the-money options, you will gain a much higher probability of profit from your trades. The reason for this is because even if the market moves against your initial directional call, the out-of-the-money options can still expire worthless, leaving you with a winner.

The **Deep-In-The-Money (DITM)** call strategy is the best way to artificially own a stock but with half as much money at risk. What other technique allows you to get all the same movement, while giving you a much higher return on your money? I don't know of any, so this is why I use the DITM trade. Stick with LEAPS options that will allow you to control the stock for up to three years into the future and use the money you save to invest in guaranteed income securities. Don't forget to take advantage of the delta factor by using options with at least a 90 percent delta.

The **Put-Sell** strategy not only gives you income from the buyer, but it also allows you the opportunity to buy a quality stock at a lower price. You will never again put in a limit-buy order on a regular stock purchase now that you know how to sell naked put options. Right? You'd better say "Right"!

The **Option Credit Spread** (my favorite) allows you to take your directional call and gain a huge margin for error. Even though the market might move against you, the probabilities will be on your side because the option strikes are out-of-the-money. These are singles and doubles that you're aiming for. There's no swinging for the fences here because those trades strike out too much.

The **Covered Call** is yet another excellent option-selling technique that offers you the opportunity to bring in cash flow income every few months of the year. Who would have thought that just because you own stock, someone will pay you money? It's a great concept if you know how to use it. Remember, stick to the out-of-the-money options to minimize your chances of assignment.

Finally, the **Ratio Option Spread** is one of my most risky, yet highly lucrative option trading tactics. Stay sharp and be on your toes with this one. It has unlimited risk potential, so you may want to have some serious thought before embarking on this trade. Although the risks are high, the profit potential can be very appealing. Make sure you use out-of-the-money options for both legs of the spread and that the distance between the strikes is fairly wide.

BROKERS AND SOFTWARE

Heed my tips on opening up trading accounts and don't be intimidated by either the process or the brokers. The brokers need you just as much as you need them. Talk to them and negotiate a deal. The landscape is changing all the time, so make sure you try to get the best for yourself. And use all the free web sites and software I mentioned. Before you plunk down $2,000 on a slick marketing seminar, do yourself a favor and read all the free stuff that's available on the Web. I've given you a good starting point, which should keep you busy for a long time.

Once again, I just want to address the critics of my book who had a problem with the title, *Get Rich with Options*. I don't think they understood how much money is out there for the taking when you sell options correctly.

Between selling OTM put options and OTM covered calls, you're increasing your account value with money that otherwise would not be yours.

Don't let your long stock positions sit idle—sell covered calls! If you want to buy a stock below the current market price—don't use limit buy orders, use a put-sell order!

Lastly, use the DITM strategy to save yourself 50 percent off the price of the stock and invest the savings in guaranteed income. This is how you *Get Rich wtih Options*.

That's it, folks. I hope you enjoyed my book and that it puts you on the path to becoming a successful options trader. Good luck and good trading!

INDEX

Special Offer for
Get Rich with Options Readers

Get a <u>**75% discount**</u> on a subscription to Lee Lowell's investment research service...

IN$TANT MONEY
——— TRADER ———

With this research service, you'll receive a weekly buy, sell or market update from Lee.

You will also get his free report: ***"Profitable Put Selling Made Easy."***

We normally offer this annual subscription at $795 (retails at $2,500) but we're extending an exclusive discounted rate to readers of *Get Rich with Options*. Your annual fee will be $595.

To place your order immediately, please call **888-570-9830 or 410-454-0498** and offer **Priority Code: IIMTK901**.